Mastering Investment
Banking Securities

Mastering Investment Banking Securities

A practical guide to structures, products, pricing and calculations

NATASHA KOZUL

**Financial Times
Prentice Hall
is an imprint of**

Harlow, England • London • New York • Boston • San Francisco • Toronto • Sydney • Singapore • Hong Kong
Tokyo • Seoul • Taipei • New Delhi • Cape Town • Madrid • Mexico City • Amsterdam • Munich • Paris • Milan

PEARSON EDUCATION LIMITED

Edinburgh Gate
Harlow CM20 2JE
Tel: +44 (0)1279 623623
Fax: +44 (0)1279 431059
Website: www.pearsoned.co.uk

First published in Great Britain in 2011

ISBN 978-0-273-74479-5

British Library Cataloguing-in-Publication Data
A catalogue record for this book is available from the British Library

Library of Congress Cataloging-in-Publication Data
A catalog record for this book is available from the Library of Congress

10 9 8 7 6 5 4 3 2 1
15 14 13 12 11

Typeset in 11.5pt Garamond by 30
Printed and bound in Great Britain by Ashford Colour Press Ltd, Gosport, Hampshire

To my family

Contents

Foreword

My name is Dr Natasha Kozul and I gained my MSc in Computing and PhD in Nuclear Biophysics at the University of London, United Kingdom. I subsequently worked in Investment Banking divisions of Barclays Capital and Royal Bank of Scotland in City of London for almost 10 years.

I still remember the first time I set foot in one of those banking giants for my job interview. Fresh from research work, spending days surrounded by X-ray generators and specimens, I was plunged into the world of marble and polished steel, of open-plan offices and trading floors full of young high-earning and ambitious people. It was an instant shock, but I easily adapted to it and loved it. It was not just the financial rewards that attracted me, or others, to this environment. It was the idea that we, 25- to 30-year-olds, were driving the world economy. That we, each in a different way – from a quantitative analyst who writes the product pricing models, to the programmer who codes the software – made a difference in the international business. That came with enormous amount of responsibility, but it gave us a huge 'buzz'. Even now, when I am no longer working in investment banking, I enjoy following the market moves, merger stories and reminiscing about the 'good old days'.

I have written this book in the hope that it will provide an interesting insight into this wonderful world, closed off from everyday people. It should arm its reader with a comprehensive overview of the workings of the investment banking industry. It covers a wide range of products and strategies, providing an excellent basis for further study or an entry position in any financial institution worldwide.

Even though most concepts covered in this book are extremely complex, I have tried to explain them in a way that would not put a non-mathematician to sleep. I hope that you will enjoy reading it and find it useful in your day-to-day work and future career.

Dr Natasha Kozul

The aim of the book

This book is a practical yet comprehensive guide on 'how to hit the ground running' in your financial markets career; covering major product classes, their trading motivation and strategies, pricing techniques and risk management. It is the answer to the age-old problem each new entrant to the financial markets is facing: how to get ahead of the fierce competition? The answer is simple: get to know 'the big picture', i.e. understand the investment banking structure, divisions and businesses and gain as much knowledge on the products, their risks and benefits, pricing methodologies and trading strategies. As bookshop shelves are filled with books on banking, investments, financial markets, derivative securities, pricing methodologies etc. one would assume that the above is an easy task. All you need to do is buy a book and spend some time studying. The only problem is, there isn't a single book that covers all of the above. Unless you are prepared to buy a dozen books and then sift through the myriad of information, you are destined for failure. This book is the solution. It is a comprehensive manual on the full range of issues encountered in daily jobs of workers in the financial industry. It provides enough information on all the topics, without overwhelming the readers with details that are needed by only a few specialists. It offers a well-structured and practical source you can come back to time and time again as you progress in your career.

Within these covers you will find all the knowledge that market practitioners need for a successful investment banking career in a single volume. It is a practical guide to the major product classes, their trading motivation and strategies, pricing techniques and risk management. Important fundamental concepts on statistics, yield curves and quantitative modelling are also covered.

This book should be an interesting and easy read (save for some more complex formulae) to many people interested in world economy and finance. However, it is primarily aimed at financial institutions employees, university staff and students and many others who will benefit from solid knowledge of the investment banking industry and financial products. Programmers, dealers, risk managers, company directors, investors and other market practitioners who were not overjoyed at the prospect of solving differential equations in school will find that this book provides an excellent grounding on all aspects of financial markets. It is an essential guide to financial markets for the new entrants to the industry. Graduates of all backgrounds starting their first job in investment banking often get a list of recommended books to read to prepare them for their new career. I should know, as I was one of them. After obtaining my PhD in Nuclear Biophysics I accepted a job in the City without much knowledge of investment banking and finance in general. I found the recommended reading quite complex, without providing that much-needed 'big picture' on what it was all about. So this book represents all the fact that I wish I could have read in a single book when I first started out.

All classes of investment products are covered, with a strong emphasis on those financial instruments mostly traded in the world markets. The fundamental pricing concepts are also included, without the need for the complex mathematics. This was done deliberately, as many readers would be discouraged rather than helped by too much detail, unnecessary for most investment banking jobs.

This book was conceived as a complete, stand-alone, financial markets manual. Those wishing to grasp the 'big picture' should feel well-equipped upon reading it. But it is also a very useful introduction to further study of specific topics.

Introduction

When we think of the financial markets, the first thing that comes to mind is a frenzy of young guys in multi-coloured jackets shouting and waving hands simultaneously on the Exchange floor. That is a typical working day of any Stock Exchange worldwide that is still open to 'Open Outcry' trading. But this is just the 'tip of an iceberg' and much more 'action' takes place daily behind closed doors, using computer screens and over the phone.

In the following chapters we will get the chance to enter this mystical world and see how it really operates and the driving forces behind it.

This book is structured in five distinctive sections:

Part 1 – Structures

Part 2 – Money markets and capital markets instruments

Part 3 – Financial derivatives

Part 4 – Pricing and valuation tools

Part 5 – Risk management

PART 1 – STRUCTURES

This section covers the investment bank structure and the various departments it requires for smooth business operation. It will aid understanding of how it all fits together and serve as an excellent guide for job selection and planning career progress.

PART 2 – MONEY MARKETS AND CAPITAL MARKETS INSTRUMENTS

Standard short- and long-term financial instruments used for lending and borrowing funds are the subject of this section. To ease us into the world of strangely named products and strategies, we will first get familiar with the main cog of this giant machinery – money and its time value. We will learn the concepts of present value (PV), calculate interest on investments, compare values of different cashflows and lots more. This will come in useful in the following chapters where we delve deeper into each class of investment products (also known as securities or instruments). This is followed by the simplest type of instrument – money market instruments – short-term loans and deposits, transacted and fixed at the time of trading. Capital markets instruments, used for longer term financing, are covered next.

PART 3 – FINANCIAL DERIVATIVES

The fairly safe products covered in the previous section will be followed by a range of speculative and therefore much riskier instruments – derivatives, covered in this section. A chapter will be devoted to a brief overview of different product classes currently in the market, from the most popular and most widely transacted interest rate derivatives, to commodity derivatives and various exotic and hybrid securities. Subsequent chapters deal with specifics of each product class in more detail. Financial futures – exchange traded contracts for purchase/sale of an underlying product at some future date, and forward rate agreements (FRAs) – over the counter (OTC) products with similar characteristics, will be introduced first.

Swaps – contracts for exchange of cashflows of different origins between two counterparties over a period of time – are discussed next. The reasons behind various 'flavours' of such transactions with the advantages provided to both sides of the deal are presented.

The very popular topic of foreign exchange (FX) will follow, enabling the reader to calculate spot and future exchange rates for various currency pairs and providing insight into the range of FX products available for trading.

Then we finally come to more speculative products – options, which offer to the buyer a certain downside protection and potential unlimited profit, but at a price; and for the seller a huge 'headache' if his/her view of the market moves is proven to be wrong. To price options, two approaches are taken: analytical (typically a variation of the famous Black–Scholes model), and numerical (using binomial trees). Both approaches will be covered, together with their advantages and disadvantages.

Bond and equity derivatives – speculative instruments typically used to borrow and land funds without the investment bank as an intermediary – are covered next. Commodity and credit derivatives will get their well-deserved mention in the chapter that follows. But as their portion of the derivatives market is so small compared to interest rate products, only a brief overview of the product ranges will be given without any calculations. As the investment banking world is coming up with an ever increasing number of financial instruments, this book would not be complete without exotic products and hybrid securities. These are truly innovative strategies tailored specifically to the client's requirements and transacted rarely, hence their pricing is extremely complex and uncertain.

PART 4 – PRICING AND VALUATION TOOLS

This section provides a selection of tools and techniques required for successful product valuation. Some basic concepts on probability are covered first, including types of distribution and binomial tree construction. To give the rationale for decisions on short- vs. long-term investment, the concept of yield curve – a current market view of how the economy and interest rates will evolve with time – will be introduced in the chapter that follows. Next, the role of the quantitative analytics department, mathematicians who write models used for pricing all financial instruments, is briefly addressed and the model classification with their brief overview is also given. This is followed by a summary of all pricing formulae and key points from the previous chapters.

PART 5 – RISK MANAGEMENT

This final section includes chapters on credit risk and market risk, aiding the understanding of the risks associated with trading derivatives, their identification, assessment, monitoring and management.

Finally, a graphical representation of various option strategies can be found in Appendix 1, whilst ISO (SWIFT) currency codes are listed in Appendix 2. A glossary of the terms used in the book and a list of references and sources are included at the end. Enjoy!

STRUCTURES

Part
1

Investment bank divisions

Mergers and acquisitions (M&A)

Capital markets (CM)

Securitisation

Sales and trading

INTRODUCTION

An investment bank is a financial institution that provides services to governments and corporations. Unlike commercial and retail banks, it does not transact with individuals or take deposits. It assists its clients in raising funds through underwriting or issuance of securities (debt obligations, equities, stocks or derivative instruments). It can offer assistance to companies in the process of mergers and acquisitions and further services in trading fixed income instruments, equity securities, foreign exchange, commodity and derivatives. Most investment banks are comprised of multiple divisions, including:

- Mergers and acquisitions
- Capital markets
- Securitisation
- Sales and trading.

MERGERS AND ACQUISITIONS (M&A)

The mergers and acquisitions division devises and executes innovative, customised solutions in domestic and international transactions including, but not limited to: acquisitions, divestitures, mergers, corporate restructurings and recapitalisations.

The terminology explained

Acquisition is a term used to describe a takeover of another company or institution. In the UK, this only applies to public companies; whilst in the USA both public and private companies can either be takeover targets or initiators. Takeover can be *friendly*, where the board of directors of the target company agrees to the acquisition and recommends it to the shareholders; or *hostile*, when the initiator uses various strategies to bypass the target company's management, unwilling to agree on the proposed terms. In either case, the acquisition involves the purchase of target company shares, requiring substantial funding. The required capital can be raised through bond issuance, or more commonly though a bank loan. Acquisitions financed through debt are known as *leveraged buyouts*. The role of the investment bank M&A department is the assistance in raising and structuring acquisition finance, management of the acquisition process (structuring of debt and repayment schedule) and advice on alternative financing strategies.

Divesture (or divestment) is a term opposite from investment or consolidation. It refers to the reduction in company size, typically through a sale of subsidiary or a part of the business. The motivation can be either financial (raising funds, creating increased company value through the break-up into component parts etc.) or strategic (achieving greater stability by eliminating a risky or loss-making part of the business or by reducing the diversity of services by concentrating on the core business). Whatever the reasons behind the divesture, investment banks act as advisors and agents in structuring, finance management and investment of acquired funds.

Merger is the term often used as a synonym for acquisition, even though it has a somewhat different meaning. Whilst acquisition (friendly or hostile) implies that the target company is acquired by the initiator, and thus legally ceases to exist, merger is typically seen as a partnership of equals choosing to become a single company for a mutual benefit. Mergers involve complex valuation of both businesses (their assets, historical and projected earnings etc.), thus investment banks offer valuable service in raising finance, debt structuring, business valuation and a wide range of ancillary issues associated with the merger process.

Corporate restructuring is the process of redesigning the company structure. The motivation is either strategic or financial. *Strategic restructuring* is typically initiated when the company outgrows its original size, such that its operational structure can no longer be effectively maintained. Restructuring provides the opportunity for greater profitability, a move in a new direction or simply more efficient management. *Financial restructuring* is typically driven by financial difficulties within the company, the sector, or the economy as a whole. It is done through reduction in personnel, product lines, merger of departments or other cost-cutting measures. Investment banks provide financial and strategic advice before, during and after the restructuring process, helping the corporation achieve its goals more efficiently and successfully.

Recapitalisation is the process of restructuring company's debt-to-equity ratio, motivated by the need for stabilising its capital structure and improving liquidity. It can also be implemented in order to minimise taxes or as a defence strategy against a hostile takeover. In essence, recapitalisation is the exchange of one type of financing for another, such as replacing bonds with company shares or vice versa. Investment banks act as advisors and agents in providing bond issuance, share valuation and other financial aspects of recapitalisation.

The role of the M&A division

The first stage in any M&A project is securing the actual client. There is fierce competition within the investment banking industry, offering the clients a choice of who to transact with. Hence, for any potential new project, the M&A team typically produces a 'pitch book' containing a list of all services the client can expect the bank to provide. The client will ultimately choose the bank with the best reputation, providing the highest level of service at the most competitive prices (in terms of fees and debt structuring).

Once the client is secured, the services that the M&A department provides are typically carried out in two main stages: proposal pitching, marketing and origination; and deal execution.

The first stage in any project is proposal pitching, client marketing and deal origination. Here the M&A team meets the client, suggests strategies, and performs industry overviews and competitor analysis in order to identify the issues affecting the company. Regardless of the type of deal involved, the bank acts on behalf of the client who is either on a *buy* or a *sell* side.

Mergers and acquisitions clearly involve two parties – the originator and the target. The banks can be approached by either, in two different scenarios: either the client has already identified the counterparty for the transaction, or the bank is expected to find a suitable counterparty.

If the client is on the *sell* side, i.e. wishes to merge or sell off its assets to another company, the role of the M&A team is finding a suitable company to acquire the client. Firstly, the initial research and analysis of the client company's assets is performed, resulting in objective valuation and, ultimately, the suggested price. All the relevant information is collated in a proposal (pitch) document that will be sent to a potential (or targeted) counterparty. Even if the counterparty is already known, typically several other potential contenders may be identified in order to make the sale more competitive. A similar approach is taken when the bank is entrusted with finding the suitable counterparty, but it is extended to a broader range of companies. This is followed by marketing the client, making the proposal attractive to the potential suitors. The client matching process can be very lengthy and require time and effort in producing documentation, analysis and answering queries. Once both parties are willing to transact, the deal origination can proceed. This involves drafting the initial documentation, performing more detailed analysis on both parties and proposing strategies for the deal execution.

A similar procedure is followed when the client is on the *buy* side of a merger or acquisition process. If the client is simply buying (acquiring) another company, the bank is either entrusted with finding a suitable target – according to specified criteria – or, if the target is already identified by the client, the role of the M&A team at this stage is ensuring that the target company is willing to participate in the deal. The pitching process is followed by the marketing, and finally the deal origination.

In the merger process – which typically assumes voluntary participation of two entities in a future partnership of equals – the client matching process also involves research and analysis of client company's assets, resulting in valuation. This is crucial in securing a suitable partner, as it will impact the financial aspects of the deal as well as the structure of the future joint company. Again, the pitching and marketing process are followed by the preliminary proposals, i.e. deal origination.

Other transactions (divestures, restructurings and recapitalisations), even though they are primarily concerned with only the client company, often involve selling parts of the existing business or acquisitions of new ventures. Hence the procedures described above would still be incorporated.

The second stage of a typical M&A project is the execution of the transaction itself. Essentially this is a major project in which the M&A division works closely with the legal and finance departments in order to negotiate the specifics of the deal. This includes, but is not limited to: structuring the new entity that results from the transaction, management of financial transactions on behalf of the client and providing the debt finance – if required. Debt structuring is often the key aspect of the transaction and typically involves other investment bank divisions.

In order to achieve the best possible outcome for the client, the M&A team works with a wide range of colleagues in different areas throughout the entire process.

CAPITAL MARKETS (CM)

The capital markets division offers services to clients wishing to raise capital through: initial public offerings (IPOs), debt structuring or leveraged buyouts. They originate, structure and execute public and private placement of a variety of securities: equities, investment-grade and non-investment-grade debt and related products. They offer market solutions that enable clients to mitigate strategic, operational, credit and market risks.

The terminology explained

Initial public offering (IPO), also known as 'flotation', refers to the issuance of company stock or shares for the first time. It is typically used by new companies as means for raising capital; however, it is not uncommon for old and successful privately owned companies, looking for additional funds or opportunity for public trading, to 'go public'. As the successful IPO depends on many factors, including timing of issuance, share price or type of shares (preferred vs. common), the assistance of an underwriter is of great value. Most investment banks provide *underwriting* services, meaning – in this context – that they provide detailed asset valuation in order to advise on the appropriate share price under the IPO. They also assist the 'floated' company in share issuance and provide a full range of related banking services.

Debt structuring is the process of customising debt to suit the borrower's needs. Its main purpose is lowering the debt burden, either by reducing the repayment amount or deferring the repayment. Structured debt can have many components, spanning across different financial instruments and/or markets. Hence it is the job of investment banks to provide advice and debt management services to their customers. The capital markets division is responsible for meeting client's bespoke requirements either through the existing product range or through innovative structures, often involving exotic and hybrid products.

Leveraged buyout occurs in acquisitions/takeovers (described earlier) funded mainly through borrowing (leverage). The capital markets division provides debt structuring services within the leveraging process.

The role of the capital markets division

In most investment banks the capital markets division is further subdivided into three main departments: equity capital markets, fixed income capital markets, and leveraged and acquisition finance. Their key roles and responsibilities are very different, with some areas that not only overlap within the division but also transcend into another part of the business.

The key responsibility of the *equity capital markets* department is raising finance on behalf of the client in the equity market, through IPOs or issuance of new shares of existing public company. The department is involved in each stage of the process, from deal origination to final execution of transactions. The key aspect of the origination is valuation of the company's assets and, using complex financial models, calculation of an accurate share price. The execution involves managing the equity issue process and all financial services related to, and resulting from, this transaction.

The *fixed income capital markets* department provides clients with strategies for raising capital in the fixed income market (typically through bond issuance). It provides the company valuation, thus suggesting the best financing options and terms the company can achieve. It further offers valuable updates on market news and trends and how these affect the client's access to the debt capital markets. Other responsibilities include weekly market updates, working with trading and syndication departments on interest rate forecasts, product management and assisting in deal execution.

The leveraged and acquisition finance department works closely with the M&A division in the final stages of deal execution, when debt financing is required. It provides clients with financing alternatives in the context of debt and/or loan financing, leveraged buyouts and acquisition financing. As a part of the service, it builds complex financial models – working closely with M&A specialists – to develop projections, valuation and merger analysis in relation to valuation of capital structure alternatives.

SECURITISATION

Securitisation is a process of aggregation of debt instruments in a pool and their reissuance in the form of a new security to be traded separately. Thus, the securitisation division provides services in structuring, underwriting and trading collateralised securities: asset-backed, residential mortgage-backed, commercial-backed and collateralised debt obligation securities.

The terminology explained

Asset-backed security is a security whose value and financial proceeds are derived from and are backed by a pool of underlying assets (mortgage payments, credit card loans, student loans etc.). These assets are typically illiquid and cannot be traded separately. Through *securitisation*, they are grouped and structured into products suitable for sale to general investors, diversifying the risk in the process. The securitisation division is responsible for aggregation of underlying assets, their structuring into new products and their successful issuance in the market.

Mortgage-backed security is a type of asset-backed security, where the underlying assets are residential mortgages. Due to the large number of home loans, the market in mortgage-backed securities is expanding. The job of the securitisation division is to create bespoke and innovative structures that can be successfully sold to investors.

Commercial-backed security, akin to the above, is an asset-backed security collateralised by a pool of commercial mortgage repayments. It is perceived to carry less risk to the investor, as commercial mortgages are often subject to lockout clauses that provide some protection against default. The role of the investment bank is very much the same as for other types of asset-backed securities.

Collateralised debt obligation (CDO) is a type of asset-backed security that derives value and income from a pool of fixed income underlying assets (bank loans, corporate bonds, insurance payments etc.). They are often split into seniority tranches, whereby the most senior class takes priority in coupon and principal repayment over others, thus carrying least default risk. The securitisation division is responsible for structuring CDOs, assessing tranche repayment schedules, associated default risks and evaluation of required risk premiums that investors would be willing to accept on lower-grade tranches.

The role of the securitisation division

The key role of the previously capitalised (securitisation) division is in structuring, underwriting and trading collateralised securities.

Structuring involves segmentation of cashflows and risks underpinning the collateralised transaction. Since the size of original investments (mortgages, bank loans, insurance payment etc.) involved in securitisation is either too large or too small, often involving complex risk components, they are structured into a form that is more desirable to the investors. This initially involves careful analysis of underlying cashflows, market and credit risks, followed by the creation of tranches and prepayment schedules. Each tranche thus carries a different level of risk and associated investment potential to an investor. The securitisation division works on behalf of the client, aiming to ensure the best possible outcome, whilst providing an investment-grade product that would be attractive to investors.

Underwriting involves assessment of the underlying securities' credit-worthiness, repayment ability and collateral valuation. Since collateralised securities are essentially packages of a large number of smaller underlying assets, this assessment is a very complex process. The securitisation department has to establish the likelihood of default on each asset class; and in the event of default, how much of the original value can be recovered. This involves complex mathematical models that predict – based on historical data, credit ratings, market trends and a host of other variables – the most likely payment schedule. Furthermore, in order for the repackaged securities to be transformed into an investment-grade product, the investment bank 'underwrites' the risks associated with the underlying securities, making them more attractive to investors.

Trading of collateralised instruments falls under the remit of the sales and trading division (described next). However, pricing and trading strategies are the responsibility of the securitisation department, as it has the necessary expertise in this product class. It is further entrusted with monitoring credit rating changes, regular evaluation of default probabilities, monitoring prepayment schedules etc.

SALES AND TRADING

Sales and trading on behalf of the bank and its clients is the primary function of a large investment bank. With an increasing number of OTC derivatives products, it is the fastest growing division. In market making, traders enter into transactions to maximise profits. Banks also undertake risk through proprietary trading. Typically the sales and trading division is split according to the product classes that are the subject of this book: money markets, capital markets, interest rate derivatives, credit derivatives, commodity derivatives etc.

The sales and trading division actively pursues clients and executes their orders. This can be done by offering an existing range of products or through tailor-made structures specifically created to meet a client's needs. More details on sales and trading are provided in the following chapter.

Investment bank organisational structure

Front office

Middle office

Back office

INTRODUCTION

Investment banks are broadly split into three sections: front office, middle office and back office. This division is necessitated partly by the operational needs, allowing the common functions to be grouped together, thus functioning more efficiently. However there is also a statutory requirement to separate investment-making divisions from the compliance, control and risk management departments. This ensures the impartiality and objectivity of all reporting lines.

There is a common perception that the most interesting jobs can be found in the front office, but each investment bank department plays a crucial part in the successful business operation, offering a broad range of varied, interesting and challenging roles.

FRONT OFFICE

Front office is the profit-making section of investment bank. It is typically organised according to the business lines, i.e. product ranges the bank is offering to its clients. Each department is further split into sales and trading desks.

Sales desks

Sales desks are in regular contact with clients, suggesting trading ideas and taking orders. Their role is essential in acquiring new clients and maintaining good relationships with existing ones. The sales force tends to comprise young, energetic and articulate individuals who work well under pressure and keep their composure in stressful situations. Attention to detail is also important, as they have to ensure that all details of the client order are accurately recorded and passed on to the trading desks.

The sales team is mostly focused on relationships with clients – analysing, exploring and marketing new financial offers that they believe will be attractive and profitable. The typical activities of a sales person include:

- Gathering information and analysing the market
- Identifying issues affecting clients
- Developing client relationships and presenting ideas to clients
- Securing deals with existing and new clients
- Keeping market-making traders informed of the relevant issues and requirements relating to their customers.

Trading desks

Trading desks price and execute trades, or structure new products that fit specific needs. They are constantly monitoring market information dissipated through market data providers (such as Bloomberg, Reuters and Telerate) to ensure that their decisions are timely and backed by the latest available information. Depending on the product type, they can either work on volume, as in money markets where market prices are readily available, volumes are high and there are virtually no valuation uncertainties; or they can trade tailor-made securities (such as exotic derivatives) that involve complex valuation, and hence take time to price and execute. Thus trading roles vary widely across different departments. Volume-driven trades require individuals who think and act fast, keep their composure under pressure and multitask well. In contrast, complex and exotic trades are usually executed by more analytical types with the ability to create innovative strategies and structure client's requirements into a suitable product, whilst being aware of the risk exposure.

The traders can be proprietary or market makers. *Market makers* buy and sell products in the financial markets on behalf of banks' clients. The product range varies and individual desks typically specialise in only one class of products. They make prices and execute trades, seeking to maximise profit or minimise financial risk. *Proprietary traders* trade on behalf of the bank itself. Their aim is to buy low and sell high. They do this by analysing economic data, performing technical analysis, exploiting cross-asset correlations and identifying undervalued and overvalued prices.

There are many similarities between the roles of market makers and proprietary traders. Their main focus is on executing trades at the right price. Markets can move rapidly and trading can be hectic. Their success relies on making instant decisions, informed by in-depth market reports provided by the investment researchers and analysts and by the sales desks, as well the constantly updated market news. Traders also use their own technical analysis.

The typical activities of a trader include:

- Market making in their relevant product range
- Executing trades electronically or by phone
- Liaising with sales desks on market movements and client requirements
- Anticipating market moves, buying and selling accordingly (this is particularly relevant to derivatives traders who are dealing with future values carrying implicit uncertainty).

Structuring

Structuring is a relatively recent concept necessitated by the increase in derivatives trading. It provides bespoke, often complex, products that meet specific client needs; including, but not limited to, payment schedules, required returns, exit clauses, credit and market risk exposure and/or mitigation. Structuring is provided by a specialised, highly educated team who take on client orders that trading desks are unable to structure, either due to their complexity or the time pressure. The typical duties of the structuring department include:

- Liaising with quantitative analysis, risk and finance teams to ensure suggested structures can be priced, risk managed and booked within the existing framework
- If that is not the case, providing joint solution for the innovative product, in terms of valuation, risk exposure quantification and capture, and setting the trading limits and reserving policy.

Quantitative analytics

Quantitative analysts are highly technical and numerate employees, creating mathematical models for complex structured products that typically offer much greater margins and returns than underlying cash securities. Quantitative analysts (also known as 'quants') tend to work in teams specialising in product classes, typically: interest rate derivatives, FX and equities, commodities and credit derivatives. Most 'quant' teams are further split into analytics and IT, whereby the former write the complex mathematical models and the latter 'translate them' into software further used within proprietary IT systems. These positions are highly sought after, as they are interesting and challenging. As there are only a few in each investment bank, competition is fierce and only the best succeed. Typical requirements are a PhD in maths, physics or a technical subject and excellent IT skills.

Typical duties within this department are:

- Development of innovative pricing and valuation methodologies for the existing product range
- Creating innovative trading and structuring strategies backed up by mathematical valuation methods
- Full understanding of strengths and weaknesses of their models and providing strategies for resulting risk exposure capture through hedging strategies and reserving policy
- Liaison with trading desks to keep abreast with the clients' requirements

- Collaboration with market risk and financial control departments in ensuring appropriate management of trading activities, through risk capture, setting trading limits and reserving policy
- Maintaining close links with relevant IT departments to ensure that the models are accurately incorporated into the IT systems.

Strategists

Strategists advise external as well as internal clients on the strategies that can be adopted in various markets. They specialise in market sectors, enhancing their expert value to the client. Their role involves diligent monitoring of market trends and developments, and creating innovative ideas that provide advantage both to the bank and to its clients.

Their duties typically involve:

- Producing strategies and analyses that lead to capital markets transactions with clients
- Using models to simulate and evaluate corporate income statements, balance sheets, funding and risk management strategies
- Performing capital structure optimisation and strategic risk management analysis for corporate and sovereign clients
- Taking an active role in the innovation and development of quantitative tools for corporate finance analysis.

Research

Responsibilities of the research department involve providing critical analytical support to investment banking, sales and trading activities. It incorporates economic research (interest rates, market trends), and individual company research (credit ratings, equity valuation). The research department is further responsible for providing written and verbal updates on market trends and company analysis to sales and traders, as well as analysing company and economic data and making forecasts.

Typical duties include:

- Closely monitoring and summarising business trends, competition and regulatory policies that might affect the bank and client performance, as well as recommending any potential business opportunities this may present
- Analysing markets, industries and clients to proactively identify revenue growth opportunities
- Delivering market research and data analysis focusing on key markets and sectors as well as existing and prospective clients, in an accurate and timely manner.

MIDDLE OFFICE

Middle office comprises control, analysis and management functions required for a successful business operation. It offers a wide variety of interesting and challenging roles, mainly to those with a background in finance, accounting or business.

Risk management

The risk management department analyses the market and credit risk of daily positions the traders are creating. It also sets the trading limits in each product class, depending on their potential to adversely affect the bank. Another key middle office role is to ensure that the risks are captured accurately, correctly and in a timely manner. Risk managers often work directly on the trading floor, to ease communication with the trading desks and facilitate a timely response to potentially high-risk exposures. Their background is typically in a numerical or technical subject, as the role requires the analytical processing of highly complex information.

The market risk team is typically responsible for:

- Market risk monitoring and ensuring compliance with market risk limits imposed by trading mandates
- Development of innovative and enhancement of existing risk metrics
- Working on market stress scenarios and analysis of their impact on P&L
- Liaising with the quantitative analytics team in order to understand weaknesses in valuation models and finding practical solutions/compensating controls to mitigate the weaknesses
- Working with financial controllers on P&L analysis.

Credit risk roles and responsibilities include:

- Surveillance and monitoring of the bank's investment portfolio
- Credit analysis of individual credit exposures
- Evaluation and reporting on current market conditions in terms of credit ratings and exposures
- Evaluation and active participation in management of large credit exposures
- Working with trading desks, finance and quantitative analytics to provide joint solution to credit exposure management.

Corporate treasury

The corporate treasury is responsible for funding, capital structure management and monitoring of liquidity. Its responsibility is to enable the smooth operation of trading departments, by providing finance and credit lines. It also monitors overall expenditure within the bank, including non-profit-making parts of the business. The roles within this department are most suited to those with a finance and accounting background. Most employees study for professional certification and are members of professional bodies.

The key aspects of corporate treasury roles are:

- Ensuring that the bank's cashflow is adequate for effective operation
- Forecasting future cashflow requirements and anticipating potential challenges arising from limited cashflow
- Undertaking risk management activities to protect and progress the bank's financial wellbeing and reputation
- Making decisions on funding of various sectors within the investment bank
- Evaluation of proposed new projects and investment strategies to ensure that they are beneficial to the bank.

Financial control

Financial control tracks and analyses the trading positions and capital flows of the bank and acts as the principal adviser to senior management on the profitability and structure of its various business units. It usually encompasses corporate strategy, risk and treasury. Product control function is a major part of the finance department and is most directly linked to the trading business. It is responsible for monitoring all daily positions, their independent pricing and the production of daily, weekly, monthly and annual P&L reports. Its structure is aligned with the trading units, enabling more efficient communication and control. The valuation (pricing) of all open positions is done independently from the front office book management to ensure impartiality in P&L reporting. Depending on the type of product, it is done either by using market prices, or, for less liquid and more exotic products, by analysing and pricing product components or factors that affect its market value. This can be a very complex process, thus product control staff tend to be very numerate and highly skilled individuals, typically with a maths, finance or accounting background and further professional qualifications.

Typical activities within the finance department include:

- Maintaining, tracking and improving the daily, weekly and monthly end-of-day processes
- Development and implementation of monthly and annual P&L reporting process
- Contribution to strategic business decision management
- Development and application of robust control processes
- Liaison with front office to ensure the work complies with regulatory standards
- Ensuring that issues and weaknesses are identified and dealt with in a timely manner
- Analysis of data to support the overall strategic objectives.

Compliance

The compliance department is responsible for the investment bank's compliance with external (government and trading authority) and internal regulations. It performs regular audits of all departments by monitoring business procedures and daily roles and responsibilities of teams and individual employees. Extensive knowledge of legal and regulatory mandates is essential; thus members of the compliance team are constantly updating their knowledge to keep in line with new developments. The compliance roles are not particularly technical, but as they require involvement with all aspects of investment bank operations, they are versatile and challenging.

Typical duties involve:

- Implementation and maintenance of compliance systems and controls
- Monitoring standards of compliance across the business
- Providing solutions to business managers, supporting the commercial objectives and balancing the bank's internal and external compliance obligations
- Raising staff awareness and understanding of compliance and risk management
- Promoting a positive culture toward compliance.

BACK OFFICE

Operations

The operations division is responsible for data checking trades that have been conducted and transacting the required transfers. The key aspects of daily operations department responsibilities are: input of all trade details, checking client information, credit lines, trading limits, ensuring that all the information is entered accurately and in a timely manner. It is a highly responsible job, requiring attention to detail, good organisation and time management, excellent verbal and written communication, numeracy, IT competence and diligence. Unfortunately it is perceived as the least attractive part of the investment bank, thus by most new entrants it is typically viewed as a starting point for further career progress.

Typical day-to-day duties involve:

- Dealing with client queries
- Clearing and settlement of daily transactions made in the front office
- Solving problems arising from incomplete documentation or trade data
- Interfacing with other divisions of the bank, finance in particular.

Technology (IT) department

The technology (IT) department provides technical support to all areas of the bank as well as writing the in-house software. Its role is becoming increasingly important, as most sales and trading desks are using electronic trading, whilst proprietary OTC products require bespoke software for trading and booking deals. Most investment banks employ several thousand IT staff in various roles, including:

- IT support
- Database administrators
- Network engineers
- Systems analysts
- Systems developers
- Application developers
- Web developers.

Their roles and responsibilities vary widely – from maintaining and upgrading the internal computer network, to creating complex trading platforms used by front office. Investment bank IT departments tend to be populated by young, energetic and highly technical individuals who thrive on pressure and tight deadlines. They have to be very innovative to produce fast and reliable IT solutions for the ever increasing complexity of the business they support.

The *IT support* team monitors and maintains the computer systems and networks within the bank. They are also on call outside business hours as the first line of support. Their further responsibilities include user account administration and security issues, as well as help with rolling out new systems or applications.

Database administrators are in charge of the performance, integrity and security of all databases within the bank. They are further responsible for strategic planning and development of new database solutions as well as troubleshooting during day-to-day operations. In addition, they control access permissions and privileges; develop, manage and test database back-up and recovery plans; and make sure that storage, archiving, back-up and recovery procedures are functioning correctly.

Network engineers are responsible for installing, maintaining and supporting computer communication networks within the bank. Their role includes:

- Monitoring network usage
- Installing, supporting and maintaining new server and network infrastructure
- Implementing, maintaining and monitoring network security, particularly internet access.

Systems analysts design new IT solutions to improve business efficiency and productivity. They examine existing business models and flows of data and design appropriate improved IT solutions, assessing them for both technical and business suitability and feasibility.

Systems developers solve computer internal hardware and software problems using existing systems or incorporating new technologies to meet particular needs. They test, diagnose and resolve system faults. As most investment banks purchase or lease all their IT equipment, there aren't many jobs in this category.

Application developers translate software requirements into concise and robust programming code. Most specialise in a specific development environment and have in-depth knowledge of relevant computer languages. Their role usually involves writing specifications and designing, building, testing, implementing and sometimes supporting applications using programming languages and development tools.

Web developers are responsible for both internal and external (client-facing) internet applications. They are in charge of the functionality, design and visual appearance of all web applications, as well as compliance with security issues. This is the fastest growing IT sector, with new technologies and programming languages emerging daily.

MONEY MARKETS AND CAPITAL MARKETS INSTRUMENTS

2

MONEY MARKETS AND CAPITAL MARKETS INSTRUMENTS

3 Money market products

4 Capital market instruments

Money market products

INTRODUCTION

The essence of a successful investment is profit enhancement and risk reduction. Whilst risks associated with unforeseeable events always remain, it is crucial to understand the products underlying a chosen investment strategy and be able to make comparisons with the alternatives. The concepts of compounding, reinvestment rates and future vs. present value of money are necessary tools for such comparisons. By using the virtually riskless loans and deposits as a benchmark, we can assess the suitability of more risky securities. This chapter introduces the fundamental concepts of financial investments and the simplest products – short-term lending and borrowing instruments. Their understanding will greatly enhance progress through the more complex topics that follow. Readers familiar with the pricing fundamentals can simply skip to the next section.

TIME VALUE OF MONEY

The reasoning behind even the most complex financial markets products can be reduced to two concepts:

> *'There is no such thing as a free lunch'* – in an efficient market it is generally not possible to achieve risk-free profit

It should not be possible to purchase an asset and immediately sell it for profit. If that were the case, the supply and demand for such an instrument would soon eliminate this opportunity. If we expect more profit, we have to accept a greater risk.

> *The time value of money* – in a positive interest rate environment any amount of money is worth more today than in the future

If we have money now, we can put it on deposit in a bank and earn interest, we can invest it in a business venture, purchase assets that would appreciate in value and much more. If have to wait for it, we expect to be compensated. That is why we expect to receive higher interest on longer term deposits than on our current bank account.

To help us understand these concepts and compare different investment strategies, the following sections will introduce interest and cashflow comparison methods.

Simple interest

The interest on short-term (less than one year) instruments is usually 'simple'. If we place £100 on a deposit at 6 per cent for 80 days, as the interest rate is usually quoted annually, we expect to receive the correct proportion, i.e.:

£0.06 × 80/365

which would bring our total to:

£100 (1 + 0.06 × 80/365)

In general:

> Total value of short-term investment
> $= \text{Deposit principal} \times \left(1 + \text{interest rate} \times \dfrac{\text{days}}{\text{year}}\right)$

Calculation Summary

Where the interest rate is quoted annually, the deposit principal is usually abbreviated only to 'principal' and days/year implies 'number of days in the period divided by number of days in the year'. The reason for the abbreviation is twofold: firstly it is, of course, easier to write in equations and secondly, and more importantly, it applies to all countries and markets where year conventions vary (365, 366 or 360).

Compound interest

If the above investment period is extended to two years, we would expect to receive £6 at the end of the first year and another £6 at the end of the second. Hence the total proceeds would be £112. But it is quite possible that the first £6 would be reinvested for the second period of one year together with the original £100. Thus, in the second year the interest would not only apply to the principal, but to the interest as well, bringing the total amount after two years to:

£100 (1 + 0.06) × (1 + 0.06) = £112.36

In general, for any principal amount invested for N years, the total proceeds are:

> Total long-term investment proceeds after N years
> $= \text{Principal} \times (1 + \text{interest rate})^N$

Calculation Summary

NOMINAL AND EFFECTIVE RATES

If we, as above, deposit £100 at 6 per cent for one year, but with interest payments made quarterly, payments of 1.5 per cent would be made every three months. Hence, instead of £6 at the end of the year, we would have on deposit (assuming that the quarterly interest payments were reinvested for the remainder of the deposit period):

After the first period:	£100 × (1 + 0.015)
After the second period:	£100 × (1 + 0.015)^2
After the third period:	£100 × (1 + 0.015)^3
After the fourth period:	£100 × (1 + 0.015)^4

Therefore our total investment proceeds would be £106.14.

This concept can be extended to any payment frequency, monthly, weekly or daily, so that in general:

Calculation Summary	Investment proceeds at rate i with n payments per year $= \text{Principal} \times (1 + i/n)^n$

Banks often quote rates for different tenors (monthly, daily etc.) and with various frequencies of compounding (how often the interest is credited to the account). Therefore it is essential to be able to convert the rate from one quote to another. The most useful quotation is the annual percentage rate (APR).

Let's assume that we invest £100 for one year at 10 per cent annual rate. With the interest paid at the end (annual compounding) we would receive:

$$£100 \times (1 + 0.1) = £110$$

However, if the interest was compounded semi-annually we would receive:

$$£100 \times (1 + 0.05) \times (1 + 0.05) = £110.25$$

Compounding quarterly, we would get:

$$£100 \times (1 + 0.025)^4 = £110.38$$

and so on. Clearly the amount increases with the frequency of compounding. The general formula is:

$$D_N = D_0 \left(1 + \frac{i}{n}\right)^n$$

where D is the deposit amount, i is the quoted annual rate and n is the compounding frequency.

Therefore to calculate the effective rate, we would calculate the equivalent annualised rate that would give us the same proceeds, i.e. we would equate:

$$\text{principal} \times (1 + \text{APR}) = \text{principal} \times \left(1 + \frac{i}{n}\right)^n$$

yielding:

$$\text{APR} = \left(1 + \frac{i}{n}\right)^n - 1$$

Generally the quoted (nominal) rate and the effective (APR) rate are linked by the following expressions:

> **Calculation Summary**
>
> $$\text{APR} = \left(1 + \frac{i}{n}\right)^n - 1 \qquad i = \left[(1 + \text{APR})^{\frac{1}{n}} - 1\right] \times n$$

Continuous compounding

If the above ideas are extended to ever increasing interest payment frequency down to a second, millisecond etc. we would reach the limit, called the *continuously compounded* interest rate. This, of course, has no bearing on real-life investments as no bank would credit an account continuously, but it is an important concept in financial instrument pricing.

It can be shown that the equivalent rate in the case of continuous compounding is ln(1+ nominal annual rate), where ln is the natural logarithm $\log_e$ (e $\approx$ 2.7183).

The continuously compounded rate is:

$$r = \frac{\text{year}}{\text{days}} \times \ln\left(1 + i \times \frac{\text{days}}{\text{year}}\right)$$

where i is the nominal interest rate.

For the annual effective rate (APR) the expression above simplifies to:

$$r = \ln(1 + \text{APR})$$

Reinvestment rates

The above ideas of reinvestment can be further extended to encompass the more realistic scenario where reinvestment rates for different periods are not the same. If we place £100 on deposit for a period of three years, it is likely that the interest rate will be reset at the prevailing market rate at the end of each year (or other pre-agreed period). Therefore the situation can be that for the first year we would receive 4 per cent, for the second 5 per cent and for the third 3 per cent, giving our total proceeds at maturity:

$$£100 \times (1 + 0.04) \times (1 + 0.05) \times (1 + 0.03)$$

In general, investment proceeds at maturity at different rates i_k for N years are:

Calculation Summary	Proceeds = Principal $\times (1 + i_1)(1 + i_2)(1 + i_3) \ldots (1 + i_N)$

Future value vs. present value of money

As could be seen above, it is essential that we can compare different investment scenarios that differ in investment periods, the absolute period to which the quoted interest rate applies and the frequency of interest payments. In order to do that, we introduce the concept of *present value* (PV), the key concept to pricing financial instruments.

Key Point	Present value (PV) is the value of future cashflows today

Short-term investments

If we put £100 on deposit for 90 days at 6 per cent annual rate we will receive at the end of investment period:

£100 $\times (1 + 0.06 \times 90/365) = $ £101.48

It can be said that the *present value* (PV) of our investment is £100 and the *future value* (FV) is £101.48.

In other words, at the prevailing annual interest rate of 6 per cent, we should be indifferent whether we accept £100 now, or £101.48 in 90 days' time.

Now another important question could be asked: if somebody offered us £104 in 120 days in exchange for £100 now, what rate of return (yield) did we achieve?

The above equation can be turned around to give:

Yield = (£104/£100 − 1) $\times 365/120 = 0.1216$ or 12.16%

In general, for short-term investments:

$$FV = PV \times \left(1 + i \times \frac{days}{year}\right) \quad PV = \frac{FV}{1 + i \times \frac{days}{year}} \quad i = \left(\frac{FV}{PV} - 1\right) \times \frac{year}{days}$$

$$\text{Effective (annual equivalent) rate APR} = \left(\frac{FV}{PV}\right)^{\frac{year}{days}} - 1$$

Calculation Summary

Long-term investments

For investment periods over one year, compounding has to be taken into account. As we have seen earlier, £100 now invested at 6 per cent for two yeas would give:

$$£100 \times (1 + 0.06) \times (1 + 0.06) = £100 \times (1 + 0.06)^2 = £112.36$$

Again, this means that the PV of £100 results in FV of £112.36 at 6 per cent annual rate. Or the yield on investment can be calculated as:

$$\text{Yield} = \left(\frac{£112.36}{£100}\right)^{\frac{1}{2}} - 1$$

Generally, for long-term investments we have:

$$FV = PV \times (1 + i)^N \quad PV = \frac{FV}{(1 + i)^N} \quad i = \left(\frac{FV}{PV}\right)^{\frac{1}{N}} - 1$$

Calculation Summary

Discount factors

As in financial calculations PVs and FVs are often calculated, the division by $\left(1 + i \times \dfrac{days}{year}\right)$ is so common that it is standard practice to introduce a new term, *discount factor* (DF), equivalent to its reciprocal value. Hence we have:

$$\text{Simple interest DF} = \frac{1}{1 + i \times \frac{days}{year}} \quad \text{Compound interest DF} = \frac{1}{(1 + i)^N}$$

Calculation Summary

CASHFLOW ANALYSIS

Net present value (NPV)

In the examples above we assumed that all our cashflows were positive, i.e. we simply put the money on deposit and didn't have any expenses. However, in reality, our cashflows would be both positive and negative. To calculate their present value, we simply discount them back to today at the prevailing interest rate to get *net present value* (NPV).

Internal rate of return (IRR)

When a client is deciding between several choices of investment, they are discounting future cashflows to today, and whichever one gives them greater PV would be the most beneficial choice. So from the previous example of APR, we could see that they would be indifferent between £100 now and £110 in one year's time providing that prevailing market rates are at 10 per cent compounding annually. However, if they could get the interest to compound more frequently, e.g. semi-annually, they would be better off (£110.25/1.1 = £100.23, which is more than £100 today). What the investor would like to know is the margin of error in their calculation, i.e. how far the interest rates can move before their choice of investment becomes unfavourable. The interest rate that allows the investor to break even is the *internal rate of return* (IRR).

Example

We have £100 and the choice of three investments:

A. Put the money in the bank at 10% for 3 years

B. Get £40 at the end of each year

C. Get £135 at the end of 3 years

We have to decide which one is the best under the prevailing interest rates of 10%.

A. Money in the bank will grow to $£100(1+ 0.1)^3 = £133.10$, which discounted back to today at 10% will give us £100 as expected

B. £40 each year will have the PV of:

$£40/1.1 + £40/1.1^2 + £40/1.1^3 = £99.47$

This is clearly less than investment A by £0.53

C. £135 discounted back to today gives us $£135/1.1^3 = £101.43$ which is better than both A and B

Hence we decide to go with the investment choice C.

All the above assumptions are based on 10 per cent rates. What would happen if the rates changed?

Below is the NPV of the investments B and C (compared to the bank deposit) based on different interest rates:

Rate %	Investment B £	Investment C £
7.5	4.21	8.67
10	(0.53)	1.43
12.5	(4.75)	(5.19)
15	(8.67)	(11.24)

In other words, in lower interest rate environments the investment C would actually be a better choice than B. But with an increasing interest rate, both investments become unfavourable compared to option A. From the table above it is clear that the rate that would make the NPV = 0 (IRR) is somewhere between 10 per cent and 12.5 per cent, as that is the point where NPV changes sign.

To calculate IRR we could simply interpolate between 10 per cent and 12.5 per cent, but that would be too crude. Ideally we would take an iterative approach, whereby we keep repeating linear interpolations and changing the boundaries until we have reached IRR.

Rate	NPV
10	1
12	–0.5

Linear interpolation will give us:

$$IRR = R_1 + \frac{NPV_1}{NPV_1 - NPV_2} \times (R_2 - R_1)$$

$$IRR = 10 + 1 \times (12 - 10)/(1 - (-0.5)) = 10 + 2/1.5 = 11.33$$

Let's assume that the NPV for the rate of 11.33 per cent is –0.1. As it is of the same sign as for 12 per cent, we will replace 12 per cent with 11.33 per cent and proceed with the linear interpolation:

$$IRR = 10 + 1 \times (11.33 - 10)/(1 - (-0.1)) = 11.21$$

We will then calculate the NPV for 11.21 per cent and proceed as above until we reach NPV ≈ 0.

In summary:

Internal rate of return (IRR) is the rate that discounts all the cashflows, including any cashflow now, to zero.

IRR discounts all the future cashflows to a given NPV.

OVERVIEW OF MONEY MARKET PRODUCTS

Money market products is the term that describes all short-term financial instruments based on the current interest rate. It is often called 'cash market', as there is virtually no risk involved. If we are investing today for a period under one year, there is no uncertainty in the interest rate, it is publicly known. One may wonder why banks and other institutions trade them. The answer is that the rate the investor can achieve depends on many factors, creditworthiness being the main one. Banks can borrow their funds more cheaply than individuals, hence they make profit by offering loans at a higher rate than they have achieved. There are also several types of money market products where their features affect the interest rate.

Time deposit – loan

This is the simplest form of financial instrument, familiar to all. It refers to a deposit placed in the bank, which typically cannot be withdrawn until maturity. It cannot be transferred to another party, i.e. it is not 'negotiable'. Typically the investment term is less than one year, with all interest paid at maturity. For longer periods, the interest payment frequency is agreed at the outset.

Certificate of deposit (CD)

A CD is similar to a time deposit, in that the funds are deposited at the bank, but the certificate (CD) is issued to the depositor, and can then be traded in a secondary market. It is typically not registered, i.e. any holder ('bearer') of a CD can withdraw the funds at maturity. It can be quoted in any currency.

Commercial paper (CP)

A CP is issued in the same way as a CD, but instead of banks, the issuers are companies with high credit rating (although some banks do issue

CPs). It typically pays no interest, hence it is issued at a discount. From the difference between the FV and PV, the yield on investment can be calculated. It is in 'bearer' form, allowing it to be traded in secondary markets. As companies typically have lower credit rating than banks, the yield on CP is expected to be higher, accounting for the credit risk that the investor is accepting. It can be quoted in any currency.

Treasury bill (T-bill)

Again, a T-bill is similar to the above instruments, but the issuer is the government. It is typically issued at a discount and can be traded in the secondary market. Unlike, CDs and CPs, in most countries T-bills are issued only in domestic currency.

Bill of exchange

All the instruments described above were deposits. If a client needs funds, instead of simply borrowing at the prevailing rates (higher than deposits, to allow for the bank's profit) they can enter into a contact called a *bill of exchange*. The client becomes the *drawer* of the bill and the bank the *acceptor* and the client is issued a *banker's acceptance* (BA). In this way the bank becomes the guarantor for the repayment at maturity. The BA is very valuable to the client as it passes the credit risk to the bank. It is used for trade purposes, where the client's creditworthiness may make their position unfavourable. Bills of exchange are typically issued at discount, i.e. the client receives less than he/she is required to repay instead of having to pay interest on the loan. The term is typically under six months.

Repurchase agreement (Repo)

Repo is another instrument used for borrowing funds. It is essentially a collateralised loan, as one party agrees to sell a security now to another party and repurchase it later at higher price. The collateral is usually a government bond, or another asset of high credit quality. Hence the interest rate implied by the repurchase price is generally lower than for an unsecured loan. A repo can also be used by an investor who accepts the collateral in exchange for funds now and receives repayment at maturity. From the investor's point of view, this is a *reverse repo*. The term is usually very short. A repo can be issued in any currency, but is not negotiable.

MONEY MARKET CALCULATIONS

As money market instruments are basically short-term loans and deposits, there is no complex maths involved in pricing them and analysing cash-flows. As all variables are known at the time of entering into an agreement, pricing money market instruments comes down to the fact that an investor is prepared to pay for an instrument today no more than the present value of all future cashflows, i.e. Price = PV.

Pricing a CD

A CD is issued at face value and pays interest (coupon) at maturity together with the principal amount. Hence, the price the investor is prepared to pay for it *in the secondary market* at any time until maturity depends on the prevailing interest rates in the market and the size of the coupon (which can be higher or lower).

Calculation Summary

$$P = \frac{F \times \left(1 + \text{Coupon} \times \dfrac{\text{days}}{\text{year}}\right)}{\left(1 + i \times \dfrac{d_{pm}}{\text{year}}\right)}$$

where F is the face value of CD and d_{pm} is the number of days from purchase to maturity.

If the CD is bought in the secondary market after the issue and sold before maturity, and hence no coupon was received, the yield achieved can be calculated as:

Calculation Summary

$$\text{Yield} = \left(\frac{P_{sale}}{P_{purchase}} - 1\right) \times \frac{\text{year}}{d_{ps}}$$

where d_{ps} is the number of days between the purchase and the sale.

Pricing discount instruments

Coupon bearing (interest paying) instruments repay more in the future compared to the face value today. In contrast, discount instruments repay face value in the future, compared to less now, to account for the lack of a coupon. But pricing formulae are essentially the same, as the price in the secondary market will always be the PV of the future cashflows (in this case, the face value of security).

$$P = \frac{F}{\left(1 + i \times \dfrac{d_{pm}}{year}\right)}$$

Calculation Summary

where F is the face value of the instrument and d_{pm} is the number of days from purchase to maturity.

4

Capital markets instruments

OVERVIEW OF CAPITAL MARKETS INSTRUMENTS

To raise capital for periods longer than one year, companies turn to *capital markets*. The lenders and borrowers tend to transact without the bank acting as an intermediary. The medium- and long-term securities that pay fixed coupon at regular intervals and repay the principal at maturity (redemption) are typically called bonds. There are many variations of this basic concept, some are discussed below.

Domestic, foreign and Eurobonds

The first distinction is made by the country of bond issue. A *domestic bond* is issued in the currency of the country of origin, whilst a *foreign bond* is issued in a different currency. *Eurobond* is somewhat confusing term that applies to an internationally issued bond, regardless of currency. Some bonds are registered, and if sold, the new owner has to be registered, in order to receive coupon payments and principal at maturity; whilst '*bearer*' *bonds* pay to whoever is holding the certificate and can be transacted anonymously.

Bonds can be issued by companies or governments. Government-issued bonds (in the UK called *Gilts*) tend to dominate domestic capital markets as they offer good liquidity and are considered risk-free. They tend to offer a lower yield than corporate-issued bonds on account of the absence of risk to the investors.

Fixed-coupon bonds

Fixed-coupon bonds offer a long-term investment with known cashflows until maturity. The principal amount is invested at the outset, and in return regular coupon payments are received until maturity when the bond is redeemed (principal returned). However, the risk associated with interest rates still remains. If the rates rise, the coupon may seem unfavourable, but it can be reinvested at the prevailing rates at the time, thus yielding more income and vice versa. Thus bond pricing calculations tend to be very complex.

Floating rate notes (FRNs)

FRNs are a variation of bond whereby the coupon is not fixed at the inception, but is reset at regular intervals to a level linked to (and typically above) a pre-agreed benchmark. In Eurobond markets, the benchmark rate is typically the six-month Libor (London Interbank Offered Rate – the interest rate at which a London bank of high creditworthiness offers funds to another London bank of the same credit standing). For an investor who believes the rates are on the rise, this can be a better choice of investment than a fixed-rate bond, as it provides potentially higher returns.

The above formula makes a crucial assumption that the bond yield is known at the outset. However, in practice, the investors are quoted bond prices and from the future cashflows they calculate the implied bond yield by iteration. By trial and error, they calculate the rate that would discount all outstanding cashflows back to the bond price. In that way they can compare different bonds in the market to see which one provides the greatest yield.

Bond pricing calculations also incorporate several important simplifications:

1. As bonds are typically issued for very long periods, even up to 50 years, and coupon payments (if there are any) are usually paid semi-annually, the coupon payments are assumed to be paid at exact intervals, without taking into account the actual number of days in those periods. For example, a bond with a 10 per cent annual coupon would be paying 5 per cent twice a year, even if the time periods do not match exactly.

2. When coupon payment are discounted back to present value, they are assumed to be paid at regular and equal intervals, not taking into account weekends, public holidays, leap years etc.

3. As bonds can be transacted at any time, the purchaser may acquire the security with the first outstanding coupon period shorter than the standard one. Even though technically this first coupon should be priced (discounted to the present time) using the money market convention of simple interest, compound interest is used instead. The reason for this discrepancy is to make bond pricing techniques more uniform.

Accrued coupon

When the bond is purchased/sold in the secondary market (at some point after the issue) it is likely that the time of transaction would not exactly match the coupon payment date. As neither party is willing to give up their rightful profit, the seller of the bond should be compensated for the loss of the portion of the coupon accumulated from the last payment date to the time of the sale. This is called *accrued interest* or *accrued coupon*. The original investor has earned it by holding the bond until the transaction date, but in fact when the next coupon is due the new owner will receive the full amount even though his/her holding period will be shorter than the standard coupon period. Accrued coupon is calculated using the expression below:

Calculation Summary

$$\text{Accrued coupon} = 100 \times C \times \frac{d_{cs}}{\text{year}}$$

where d_{cs} is the time period between the last coupon date and the sale of the bond.

In market terminology the bond calculation formula provides a so-called 'dirty price'. Once it is adjusted for the accrued coupon, it is called the 'clean price', which is typically quoted in the market. To take into account the accrued coupon payments, the bond valuation formula (based on units of 100) expands to:

Calculation Summary

$$P = \frac{100}{\left(1+\frac{i}{n}\right)^f}\left[\frac{C}{n} \times \frac{1-\dfrac{1}{\left(1+\frac{i}{n}\right)^N}}{1-\dfrac{1}{\left(1+\frac{i}{n}\right)}} + \frac{1}{\left(1+\frac{i}{n}\right)^{N-1}}\right]$$

where:

C is the annual coupon rate

N is the number of outstanding coupons

i is the annual bond yield, based on the payment frequency

n is the number of coupons per year

f is the ratio between the number of days until the next coupon and the full period.

Coupon dates

As mentioned previously, when calculating bond price, the coupon periods are assumed to be equal, depending on the payment frequency. The market conventions vary regarding when the payments are actually made. For example, for a bond with a 10 per cent coupon paid semi-annually that is issued on 15 March 2000, the assumed coupon dates would be 15 September 2000, 15 March 2001 and so on. Should any of those dates fall on a non-working day, the payments would be made either the day before or the day after, depending on market conventions. Also some markets make payments at the end of the month, regardless of the fact that it can be 28 February, 30 April or 31 August, whilst some pay on the exact day. The pricing formulae do not take account these discrepancies and the valuation is virtually unaffected.

Ex-dividend

Another issue related to the secondary bond market valuation is the change of bond ownership. If a bond is a bearer bond, i.e. not registered, this does not apply, but in the majority of cases the administrative procedure may take some time to complete. If the bond is sold before the coupon date but the ownership is transferred some days after, the bond becomes *ex-dividend* or *ex-coupon*. The original owner receives the full coupon, whilst he/she has only earned a portion of it, i.e. the rightful new owner did not receive his/her fraction. The ex-dividend coupon is calculated similarly to the accrued interest, but the payment is due to the buyer, rather than seller.

$$\text{Accrued coupon} = -100 \times C \times \frac{d_{pc}}{\text{year}}$$

where d_{pc} is the time period between the bond purchase and the next coupon.

Calculation Summary

Bond yield

As mentioned earlier, the bond pricing calculations are based on the assumption that the bond yield is known. In reality, the reverse is true and the yield is calculated from other known parameters. There are many yield measures, each with their own advantages and disadvantages. The simplest yield measure is the *flat yield* or *current yield*. It ignores the time value of money, as it does not take into account the timing of coupon payments and gain/loss on the redemption amount compared to the purchase price. It simply gives the value of the coupon as a fraction of the price paid. It is a crude measure of the bond yield and only provides a 'quick glance' idea of its value.

$$\text{Flat yield} = (\text{coupon rate}/\text{clean price}) \times 100$$

Calculation Summary

A better measure of bond yield is the simple yield to maturity, also known as Japanese gross redemption yield (JGRY). It does take into account capital gain/loss arising from the difference between the price and the redemption amount, but not the timing of the payments.

$$\text{Simple yield to maturity (JGRY)} = \frac{\text{coupon rate} + \left(\dfrac{\text{redemption amount} - \text{clean price}}{\text{years to maturity}} \right)}{\text{clean price} \big/ 100}$$

Calculation Summary

In practice, the bond yield is calculated by iteration, using more complex formulae, where timing of payments, capital gain/loss and time value of money is taken into account. Market practitioners would typically use the formulae below, entering various yields i into the valuation formula until the market price is reached. This measure of yield is known as *redemption yield*, *yield to maturity* or *gross redemption yield* (GRY).

Assuming the yield applies to the coupon period and that all the periods are equal:

Calculation Summary

$$\text{Price} = \sum_{t=1}^{n} \frac{C_t}{(1+i)^t} + \frac{R}{(1+i)^n}$$

Taking into account the irregular first coupon payment period:

Calculation Summary

$$P = \frac{100}{\left(1+\frac{i}{n}\right)^f} \left[\frac{C}{n} \times \frac{1 - \dfrac{1}{\left(1+\frac{i}{n}\right)^N}}{1 - \dfrac{1}{\left(1+\frac{i}{n}\right)}} + \frac{1}{\left(1+\frac{i}{n}\right)^{N-1}} \right]$$

where:

C is the annual coupon rate

N is the number of outstanding coupons

i is the annual bond yield, based on the payment frequency

n is the number of coupons per year

f is the ratio between the number of days until the next coupon and the full coupon period.

Whilst the flat yield underestimates the actual bond yield, as it takes no account of the capital gains, the JGRY overestimates it (it spreads the capital gains evenly until redemption). Hence the correct yield is somewhere in between. It is useful to calculate the flat yield and the JGRY, as they will bound the true yield from either side, and proceed with iteration using those boundaries.

Portfolio duration

Convexity

The relationship between bond prices and their yields is non-linear. Let's assume that we have three bonds B_1, B_2 and B_3 with the prices equally spaced out, i.e. $B_2 - B_1 = B_3 - B_2$. We can calculate their respective yields to be Y_1, Y_2 and Y_3. Even though the bond prices are equidistant, the same cannot be said about their yields, i.e. $Y_2 \neq (Y_1 + Y_3)/2$. The expected yield will exceed the actual bond yield. This difference is known as *convexity adjustment*. The calculation of convexity adjustment is not a simple process and is the subject of extensive research, but is not within the scope of this book.

Duration

Most financial products (particularly exchange-traded ones) are easy to compare when it comes to the income they provide. That is normally not the case with bonds, as there are so many different varieties (different coupons, payment frequencies, maturities etc.).

One useful measure of risk/return often used for bond comparison is *duration* or *Macauley's duration*. Duration is a composite measure of bond risk/return expressed in years. It is a weighted average length of time to the receipt of half of the bond benefits (both the notional and the coupons) where the weights are the PVs of the cashflows.

Mathematically the above can be expressed by the following formula:

Calculation Summary

$$\text{Duration} = \frac{\sum_{t=1}^{n} t \times PV_t}{\sum_{t=1}^{n} PV_t}$$

where:

PV_t is the present value of the cashflow at time t (discounting is done using the redemption yield)

n is the number of periods.

Example

A 10% annual coupon bond with 5 years to maturity with gross redemption yield of 10.5% will have duration calculated as follows:

Time	1	2	3	4	5
Cash	10	10	10	10	110
PV	9.05	8.19	7.41	6.71	66.77

Using the above formula, we calculate duration as:

$$\frac{9.05 \times 1 + 8.19 \times 2 + 7.41 \times 3 + 6.71 \times 4 + 66.77 \times 5}{9.05 + 8.19 + 7.41 + 6.71 + 66.77}$$

Duration = 4.16 years

This means that it will be over 4 years until we recoup half of the bond investment.

Properties of duration

- *Lower coupon* bonds will have longer durations. This intuitively makes sense, as the biggest proportion of cashflows (redemption amount) will be received at the end of a bond's lifetime. Ultimately, the zero-coupon bond will have duration = maturity, since there are no cashflows until redemption.
- *Longer dated bonds* will have longer duration. Again, we will have to wait longer for the largest proportion of the cashflows.
- *Lower yield bonds* will have longer duration. This is because the PV of the cashflows far in the future (which are weighted the most) will rise and will tip the balance.

Modified duration

Modified duration is developed as a means of measuring the impact of yield change on price. The basic proposition is that the product of yield and its sensitivity will give the proportionate change in price:

Calculation Summary

$$\Delta Y \times \text{Modified duration} = \frac{\Delta P}{P}$$

Modified duration is linked to Macaulay duration by:

Calculation Summary

$$\text{Modified duration} = \frac{\text{Macaulay duration}}{1 + \text{GRY}}$$

The properties of modified duration are the same as for duration, i.e. modified duration is higher for:

- Longer dated bonds
- Lower coupon bonds
- Lower yield bonds.

PV01

We have seen from the above that modified duration (MD) relates the bond price sensitivity to the change in yield. For example, a bond with MD = 6.5 will change price by 0.065 per cent for every basis point (bp − 100th of 1 per cent) change in yield. The change in the market price is then simply the product of this sensitivity and the current market price. It is useful to calculate a present value of the basis point (PVBP) or PV01, which is a measure of the absolute change in price of £100 nominal bond for a 1bp (0.01 per cent).

This is done using the following calculation:

PV01 = Modified duration × Dirty bond price × 0.0001

Calculation Summary

Due to the curvature of the yield curve, the change in yield will not correspond to the linear change in price due to convexity (see above). Moreover, as we move in time, the change in yield is the result of both passage of time (horizontal shift) and actual upward/downward shift in rates (vertical shift).

The two can be separated out by moving one day at a time without changing the rates (for horizontal shift) and shifting the rate up/down on the same day (vertical shift).

OTHER BOND MARKETS

So far we have discussed bonds as capital markets instruments. This market is very large and active, but bonds play a crucial role in other, more speculative markets, the most prominent being the derivatives market. Here, the most common instruments are bond futures (an agreement to purchase/sell a bond at some future date at the price agreed today) and Repos (repurchase agreements, whereby the bond is bought/sold today and sold/bought back at an agreed price at some future date), which will be covered in Chapter 10. Furthermore, many structured financial products incorporate bonds (e.g. convertible, callable or puttable bonds), with the examples given in Chapter 12. They are of further interest in the wide range of credit derivatives, whereby protection against a bond downgrade or default can be bought or sold. Some examples of credit derivative products are covered in Chapter 11.

Part 3

FINANCIAL DERIVATIVES

5

Speculative financial instruments – derivatives

OVERVIEW OF DERIVATIVES MARKETS

So far we have discussed the financial instruments used mainly for borrowing and investment of principal both short term (money market) and long term (capital market). Those securities appear on clients' and banks' balance sheets and can 'block up' the credit lines. Most market participants have exposure limits in each product sector and once those are exhausted no further funds can be utilised. To overcome this problem they can trade 'off-balance sheet' instruments that do not involve exchange of principal, more commonly known as *derivative securities*. These financial instruments derive their value from the underlying asset, hence the term *derivative*. There is a wide range of products available for trading, both at listed exchanges and OTC. The exchange-traded products provide protection against counterparty default, but trading is only open to the exchange members. Furthermore, the contract specifications are exact and the product range is limited. There are over 40 recognised derivatives exchanges worldwide, the most popular ones are listed in Table 5.1. Some exchanges are physical, where transactions are executed openly on the exchange floor, whilst still providing electronic trading after hours. On the other hand, some exchanges are purely electronic, such as LIFFE and NASDAQ, providing a virtual derivatives market.

Table 5.1	Most popular worldwide derivatives exchanges		
Region	**Country**	**Exchange**	**Full name**
USA	USA	CBOT	Chicago Board of Trade
	USA	CME	Chicago Mercantile Exchange
	USA	CBOE	Chicago Board of Options Exchange
	USA	NYMEX	New York Mercantile Exchange
	USA	ASE	American Stock Exchange
Europe	UK	LIFFE	London International Financial Futures and Options Exchange
	UK	LME	London Metal Exchange
	UK	IPE	International Petroleum Exchange
	France	MATIF	France Futures and Options Exchange
	Germany	DTB	Deutsche Terminbörse
	Netherlands	ASE	Amsterdam Stock Exchange
	EU	EUREX	European Derivatives exchange
Asia/Pacific	Japan	TGE	Tokyo Grain Exchange
	Japan	Tiffe	Tokyo International Financial Futures Exch.
	Singapore	SIMEX	Singapore International Monetary Exch.
	Hong Kong	HKFE	Hong Kong Futures Exchange

The product range offered by each exchange varies, and some of the most common are listed in Table 5.2, together with their OTC counterparts.

Most popular exchange-traded and OTC securities

Table 5.2

Category	Derivative	Underlying	Market
Interest rate (IR) derivatives	IR futures	Forward interest rate	Exchange
	IR FRAs	Forward interest rate	OTC
	IR swaps	Government bonds	OTC
	FX options	Foreign exchange	Exchange/OTC
	FX swaps	FX/bonds	Exchange/OTC
	Bond futures	Bonds	Exchange/OTC
	Bond options	Bonds	Exchange/OTC
	IR swaptions	Government bonds	Exchange/OTC
	IR caps/floors	Forward interest rate	OTC
	IR collars	Forward interest rate	OTC
Equity derivatives	FTSE 100 futures	FTSE 100 index	Exchange
	FTSE Eurobloc futures	FTSE Eurobloc index	Exchange
	FTSE 100 options	FTSE 100 index	Exchange
	Dow Jones options	DJ index	Exchange
	Single stock options	Stock price	Exchange
	Equity index swaps	Equity Index	OTC
Commodity derivatives	Energy futures	e.g. Oil price	Exchange
	Energy options	e.g. Oil price	Exchange
	Energy caps	e.g. Oil price	OTC
	Energy collars	e.g. Oil price	OTC
Credit derivatives	Credit default swap	Asset (e.g. bond)	OTC
	Total return swap	Asset (e.g. bond)	OTC
	Credit spread swap	Two assets (debt vs. bond)	OTC
	Credit spread option	Two assets (debt vs. bond)	OTC

Due to the limitations imposed by exchanges (product range, strict specifications, market participation), the OTC market is growing rapidly. The investment banks are devising new product structures and investment strategies daily to meet exact client specifications. However, each buyer and seller must take on the credit risk of their counterparty.

The main characteristics of exchange-traded vs. OTC derivatives are listed in Table 5.3. Both exchange-traded and OTC derivative instruments can be split by settlement into two categories: single vs. multiple settlement. Some examples are listed in Table 5.4. They can also be split by premium requirements. Instruments which are obligations to enter into a contract at some future date cannot be abandoned, and hence require no premium. On the other hand, the securities that give a client the right but not the obligation to take action in the future will require the premium to be paid up-front. Hence, it can be summarised that the optionality has to be paid for, as it provides a worst-case scenario to the buyer; whilst the obligation does not incur such a cost.

Table 5.3   **The main characteristics of exchange-traded vs. OTC derivatives**

	exchange-traded	OTC
Quality	Specified by the contract	Specific to each client
Quantity	Contract size determined by the exchange	Specific to each client
Expiry/delivery	Dates fixed by the exchange	Specific to each client
Counterparty risk	None	Depends on credit rating
Margin	Normally required	Normally none
Liquidity	Good, varies with product	May be limited
Regulation	Significant	Less stringent

Table 5.4   **Examples of single and multiple settlement derivatives securities**

Single settlement	Multiple settlements
Interest rate options	Interest rate swaps
Currency options	Currency swaps
Financial futures/FRAs	Energy swaps
Stock options	Interest rate caps/floors/collars

Whether exchange-traded or OTC, derivatives offer greater exposure to the fluctuations of the underlying security compared to owning it outright. If a client purchases an option to buy a stock with the strike of £100 and pays £10 in premium; if the price increases to £120, he has made a profit of £10, 100 per cent of the original investment. If he owned the stock, he would only earn 20 per cent of his original investment. However, should the price fall to £90, the option holder will lose 100 per cent of his premium, whilst the stock holder will lose only 10 per cent of the original value. This loss is called 'gearing' and is the driver behind derivatives trades. Most market participants enter into transactions with the intention of earning a profit. Whilst derivatives offer greater potential, they can also incur significant losses when the market moves adversely. Therefore, derivative instruments should be traded prudently. The different motivations behind the trades are discussed in the following section.

USERS OF DERIVATIVES

There are different types of derivatives users:

Traders make a market in derivatives by creating various products and selling them to their clients.

Hedgers wish to protect themselves against exposure to adverse market movements.

Speculators take positions in derivatives based on their view of a particular market.

Arbitrageurs try to spot price discrepancies and profit from them.

The derivatives market is mainly populated by:

- Supranationals
- Governments and their agencies
- Investment banks
- Financial institutions
- Corporates
- Private clients.

Their motivation for using derivatives is varied, some examples are:

- Protecting a portfolio of stocks against devaluation
- Profit from increase of oil price
- Protection against interest rate increase on a loan
- Securing an FX rate on a future transaction
- Enhancing a yield of a portfolio
- Protection against payment default.

Each of the above requires a different type of derivative instrument. They are briefly covered below and further discussed in the following chapters.

INTEREST RATE DERIVATIVES

Interest rate derivatives derive their value from the movements in the underlying interest rate. As there is no principal involved, the difference between the market rate and that implied by the contract is settled between the counterparties. Hence they can be used to fix the borrowing rate for some future transaction (by buying a futures contract, or a call option), change payments from floating rate to fixed (by entering into a 'vanilla' swap), change frequency and reference rate of payments (basis swap), secure FX rate for a foreign business contract (currency option or future) etc.

There is a wide range of interest rate derivatives, some are exchange-traded, but the largest volume and variety exists in the OTC market. They can be classified in variety of ways:

- By maturity
- By settlement
- By complexity.

Derivative securities maturities range from overnight to over 30 years. Table 5.5 shows the terminology used when referring to derivatives of different types.

Table 5.5	Types of interest rate derivative securities by maturity

Maturity (years)	Instrument type
0–1	Money (cash) market
1–2	Short-term instruments
2–5	Medium-term instruments
5–10	Long-term instruments
10+	Very long-term instruments

Further division of derivative securities can be done by the type of settlement. Whilst some have only a single settlement date (and consequently one exchange of cashflows), some derivatives have multiple fixings (comparisons against the pre-agreed benchmark). In general, the number of fixings (and hence payments) is related to the maturity of the instrument – longer-dated securities typically having multiple settlement dates. Table 5.6 shows some examples of single- and multiple-fixing types of derivative securities:

Types of interest rate derivative securities by settlement type　　　　Table 5.6

Settlement	
Single	Multiple
Financial futures	Interest rate swaps
Forward rate agreements (FRAs)	Interest rate caps
Interest rate swap options	Interest rate floors
Interest rate options	Interest rate collars

The choice of derivative security the investor will make depends on many factors:

■ Risk aversity

■ Understanding of derivatives risks and exposures etc.

■ Size of investment

■ Market accessibility

■ Period of exposure

■ Type of exposure.

Clients with substantial knowledge on derivatives products, their valuation principles, market and credit risk are typically more willing to accept greater risks as they feel that they have better understanding of those risks and can manage them better.

Market accessibility and the size of investment are also crucial drivers in the derivatives investment choice. For example, exchange trading is open only to its members and the trading is allowed only in whole numbers of contracts of fixed size and tenor.

Period and type of exposure are still the main factors influencing the investment decisions. Most derivative securities offer only a limited range of maturities, or better liquidity for certain tenors. Furthermore, the underlying exposure limits the number of instruments suitable for investment. In other words, long-term borrowing cannot be suitably hedged by buying a strip of futures or FRAs; equally, overnight borrowing cannot be fixed by entering into a swap.

Table 5.7 offers an indication of the type of instruments the investors typically use, depending on the exposure period. A full range of interest rate derivatives is covered in Chapters 6, 7 and 9, with further coverage of OTC exotic derivatives in Chapter 12.

| Table 5.7 | **Interest rate derivative products by exposure periods** |

Maturity (years)	Instrument type
0–1	Futures, FRAs, options, caps, floors, collars
1–2	Futures, FRAs, options, caps, floors, collars, swaps, swaptions
2–5	Caps, floors, collars, swaps, swaptions
5–10	Caps, floors, collars, swaps
10+	Swaps

EQUITY DERIVATIVES

Value of equity derivatives is based on, or derived from, the value of the underlying equity, equity index or a basket of stocks. A client who finds it prohibitively expensive or impractical to buy stocks can enter into an equity swap, whereby he/she receives return on an equity index and pays a variable interest rate. Or a portfolio manager who would like some protection against a fall in stock prices would buy an equity put option. Holders of individual stocks can also transact in options, depending on their view of price movements, in order to realise potential profit without having to sell the stocks at the outset.

It can be seen from the above that the main motivations for trading equity derivatives are as follows:

- Equity market speculation
- Enhancement or hedging of the equity portfolio returns
- Gaining access to equity market.

Speculators often take only a very short-term view, aiming to realise profit by reversing the original transaction well before the maturity date. Hence their choice of product will mainly be driven by their view of the short-term market trends.

On the other hand, portfolio managers base their decisions on several factors, including:

- Portfolio structure
- Portfolio size
- Risk aversity
- Period of cover.

The manager of a relatively static portfolio would greatly benefit from short- to medium-term derivative securities with single, more volatile stocks as the underlying. However, pension and fund managers often aim to track and outperform the equity index, hence they are more risk-averse and require long-term exposure.

Finally, investors without direct exposure to equity markets will base their instrument choice on:

- Type of desired exposure
- Type of underlying exposure in a different market
- Size of investment
- Risk aversity
- Understanding of the equity derivatives market and associated risks and exposures.

They typically aim to swap existing exposure in one market (e.g. interest rate) to equity returns. Hence their product choice is driven by their risk aversion (typically linked to their understanding of the equities market), underlying exposure (single vs. multiple settlement) and exposure period. Examples of equity derivative products classified by the exposure period (maturity) are given in Table 5.8. Equity derivatives are covered in Chapter 10.

Examples of equity derivative products classified by the maturity   Table 5.8

Maturity (years)	Instrument type
0–2	Equity index futures, equity index options, single stock options
2–5	Equity index swaps, equity index swaptions
5+	Equity index swaps

COMMODITY DERIVATIVES

As there are many commodities traded in the world markets, so are many derivatives products. But the most commonly traded ones are energy derivatives, as the price of energy impacts on so many sectors. A manufacturer that uses large quantities of oil, instead of buying it now to secure the price and having to pay for storage, can enter into a call option contract or a futures contract and achieve the same effect more efficiently. An energy company that fears the fall in prices would enter into an opposite transaction.

The types of available trading strategies are a clear indication of how the market participation in commodities sector has changed over the years. At present there are three types of energy markets:

- The spot or physical market
- The forward market
- The energy futures market.

The spot market is used for direct delivery of cargo, hence its participants are typically large corporations with extensive energy consumption.

The forward market is an informal, short-term market mainly populated by speculators, with contract volumes far exceeding the actual production, and contracts changing hands several times before the actual delivery. Thus only a small percentage of participants are the actual energy users and producers.

Finally, the official energy futures markets typically offer a limited number of a short-term contracts and are mainly populated by the investors, rather than actual energy users or producers.

For more exotic products and longer-term exposure, the investors have to turn to the OTC equity market. The most popular OTC equity derivatives are swaps, but the range of products can be extended to meet exact client specifications. Commodity derivatives are covered in Chapter 11.

CREDIT DERIVATIVES

Credit derivatives are currently traded in OTC markets only (even though some credit derivative features can be imbedded into money markets products). They are contracts that allow one counterparty to accept – in exchange for a premium – a reference asset credit risk from another counterparty (who does not have to own the asset). The counterparties are respectively referred to as credit protection seller and credit protection buyer. The use of credit derivatives is widespread, as there are many types of reference assets (e.g. bond, loan or equity) as well as types of credit risk (credit rating downgrade, bankruptcy, failure to pay etc.).

The contracts can be bilateral, whereby the two counterparties swap all or a part of reference credit exposure for mutual benefit. This is typically done to diversify market exposure without actually investing in a range of assets.

But more commonly, credit derivatives are traded as separate securities, by stripping the credit risks on the underlying asset from the asset itself.

Similar to other derivatives markets, the users of credit derivatives are broadly split into hedgers and speculators:

Hedgers typically become protection buyers when they own the reference asset and wish to eliminate risks associated with adverse credit events.

Speculators can be both protection buyers and sellers, depending on their view of the market.

As the credit derivatives market is OTC, each trade is tailor-made to fit the exact client needs. Therefore the classification by market accessibility, contract size, maturity etc. does not apply. Furthermore, the payments are contingent on credit events, the timing of which is impossible to predict. Credit derivatives are covered in Chapter 11.

Financial futures and forward rate agreements (FRAs)

INTRODUCTION

Futures and FRAs are derivative instruments based on a short-term forward interest rate. They enable investors and borrowers to fix the interest rate today for a period that starts in the future. There is no exchange of principal amount, only the difference between the futures/FRA rate and the underlying cash (spot) market rate is settled. Futures are exchange-traded securities and implicitly offer liquidity, credit default protection and price transparency. The contract range and specification is fixed, hence the clients who need more flexibility would trade FRAs in the OTC market. The main purpose of both instruments is the same, with some differences that will be highlighted in the following sections where they are discussed in more detail.

FINANCIAL FUTURES

Futures market

Futures are instruments that have existed in various forms for over 100 years. They became exchange-traded instruments in 1970s and since then their popularity has grown. There are many international exchanges offering variety of futures contracts, the oldest ones being:

- CBOT (Chicago Board of Trade)
- CME (Chicago Mercantile Exchange).

These, together with

- LIFFE (London International Financial Futures and Options Exchange)

trade the largest volumes of futures contracts.

Some futures contracts are available globally, whilst some exchanges cater for their own domestic market. The main users of futures are investment banks and large corporations; smaller investors may find trading them expensive, as they have to transact through an exchange member, incurring additional, often prohibitive, costs.

Futures contract specification and trading

Futures contracts are clearly specified by the exchange. For example, a LIFFE three-month sterling contract is specified as shown in Table 6.1.

LIFFE three-month interest rate future contract specification

Table 6.1

LIFFE three-month-interest rate future contract specification	
Unit of trading	£500,000
Delivery months	March, June, September, December
Delivery day	First business day after the last trading day
Last trading day	11:00 a.m., 3rd Wednesday of the delivery month
Quotation	100 minus interest rate
Minimum price movement	0.01% (or 'tick')
Tick value	£12.50
Trading hours	8:00 a.m.–9:00 p.m.

Each futures contract will have a similar specification. Based on the contract specification, a trader can buy or sell a whole number of futures contracts, each based on a notional amount of £500,000, as no actual borrowing/lending takes place. The contract is the obligation between the counterparties to settle on delivery day the difference between the futures price and Libor (fixed at 11:00 a.m., third Wednesday of the delivery month). The delivery months, and thus available futures contracts, run in the cycle March–June–September–December for several years in the future. As one contract expires, a new one is added, keeping the number of available contracts constant. The futures price is quoted as 100 – rate, which can be counterintuitive, as to protect himself against the interest rate increase the client needs to sell the future. The 'tick' value of £12.50 is derived from the fact that futures contracts are three months long, whilst the implied rate is annual; hence only a quarter applies to the futures period.

Most exchanges worldwide require margin payment. This enables the exchange to take the role of counterparty to each side of transaction, thus accepting the credit risk. There are two types of margin:

Initial margin is payable at the inception of a contract. The amount required for each contract is based on the estimate of potential daily loss for that type of security. At contract expiry the initial margin is paid back to the client with interest.

Variation margin is calculated and paid daily, based on the profit/loss on the contract compared to the official settlement price. This is called 'marking to market'. If the variation margin is not settled by the close of the business day, the exchange closes out the position, minimising the exposure. Hence the futures contract at expiry already has all but the last day's profit/loss incorporated into the margin.

Futures valuation

Valuation refers to the pricing of futures contracts available for trading. Futures prices depend on several factors including the cash market (spot market) values, market expectations of interest rate movements, supply and demand, the economic and political situation and many others. The relationship between cash and futures prices is called simple basis:

> Simple basis = Cash price − Futures price

Typically, futures prices are expected to be higher than spot prices, due to the risk associated with uncertainty. Such market is said to be in *contango (premium)*. The term for the opposite situation is *backwardation (discount)*.

Another measure of the futures price is theoretical basis:

> Theoretical basis = Cash price − Fair value

and value basis:

> Value basis = Fair value − Futures price

The *fair value* is the futures price that would make the investor indifferent to whether they buy an underlying now or in the future. As in the case of interest rate futures the underlying is the three-month interest rate, this means that the futures buyer should achieve the same rate if he borrows money in the cash market now for the entire period and deposits it until the start of the futures contract as if he simply buys the future now and then borrows the funds at the prevailing market rates when needed.

For example, it is 21 March and a client requires funds for the period covered by June futures (three months). He can either:

- Borrow money now for six months at six-month Libor and immediately invest it in a three-month Libid until 21 June (start of the June futures period), or
- Buy June futures now.

The two transactions should achieve the same net result. In practice any discrepancies in the futures prices would soon be eliminated from the market, due to supply and demand, hence it can be assumed that the futures price and fair value are one and the same. However, such price would only be theoretical, as the traders will build in the spread to allow for their profit. Naturally they would sell (offer) contracts at a higher price than buy (bid), creating a bid/offer spread around the theoretical price.

Futures settlement price

Calculating the futures settlement price is relatively simple. Whether the contract is held until expiry, or closed out by entering into an opposite transaction (if we bought a future, we would need to sell it), the settlement price can be calculated as:

Futures settlement price

Calculation Summary

$$\text{Profit/Loss} = \text{Notional} \times \frac{\text{Sale price} - \text{Purchase price}}{100} \times \frac{1}{4}$$

Or, expressed in terms of 'ticks':

Profit/Loss = Tick movement × Tick size × Number of contracts

Buying a futures contract for a single delivery month will only provide an interest rate guarantee for a period of three months. If a longer period needs to be covered, there are two possible strategies:

Futures strips consist of trading the appropriate number of futures contracts that span the entire period of exposure, whilst

Futures stacks require purchase of the required number of contracts in the nearest month and then rolling over to the next delivery month and so on.

Whilst the first option is clearly more desirable, as it provides certainty in the cost of funds, it may not be practical due to the lack of liquidity in the far-dated contracts. The second option overcomes this problem, but leaves the client exposed to uncertainty in the interest rate movements.

The futures strip rate can be calculated from the individual futures implied rates as follows:

Futures strip rate

Calculation Summary

$$\left(1 + f_1 \times t_1\right)\left(1 + f_2 \times t_2\right) \cdots \left(1 + f_n \times t_n\right) = \left(1 + f_s \times t_s\right)$$

where:

f_i are individual futures implied rates

t_i are time periods (fractions of a year) covered by the respective contracts (three months)

f_s is the achieved strip rate

t_s is the total time period covered.

FORWARD RATE AGREEMENTS (FRAs)

Introduction

Forward rate agreements (FRAs) are an OTC alternative to futures contracts. They are based on the same underlying instruments (short-term forward interest rates), but the contract specifications are tailored to individual customer needs. In contrast to *forward–forward borrowing/lending,* where a cash borrowing or deposit starts on one forward date and ends in another, there is no principal exchange involved. The FRA contract only pays the difference between the agreed rate and the prevailing spot interest rate (Libor) at settlement. It is assumed that the principal (if needed) is transacted elsewhere. Unlike futures, FRAs can have flexible start and end dates, as long they are both in the future. Hence the futures stack and strip strategies can be simplified by entering into longer-period FRAs. Another FRA characteristic is that FRAs are settled at the start of the contract period, whilst futures are margined (marked to market) daily during the lifetime of the contract. Hence their pricing methods vary slightly. The FRA market is very liquid with contracts available in different currencies, for many periods, start dates and underlying forward interest rates (typically three-month and one-month Libor).

FRA valuation

FRA valuation is based on the forward–forward borrowing of a notional amount. Just as in the example of futures fair price, if a principal amount is borrowed for six months and immediately deposited for the first three, the net result in the initial period is zero, thus creating a forward–forward three-month borrowing that starts in three months from now. The forward–forward three-month rate should reflect this, i.e.:

Calculation Summary

$$\text{Forward–forward rate} = \left[\frac{1 + i_L \times \dfrac{d_L}{\text{year}}}{1 + i_S \times \dfrac{d_S}{\text{year}}} - 1 \right] \times \frac{\text{year}}{d_L - d_S}$$

where:

i_L and i_S are the interest rates for the longer and shorter periods

d_L and d_S are the number of days in the longer/shorter periods

year is the number of days in the year.

In forward–forward borrowing two rates would come into play, the longer period Libor and the shorter period Libid. As FRAs always settle against Libor, their valuation would be exactly as above, but with either Libor used for both long- and short-term rates or with a spread added to the theoretical price.

FRA settlement price

The settlement price for FRAs is the difference between the rate under FRA and the Libor prevailing at the start of the FRA period, discounted at Libor. Discounting is done because the FRA contract is settled at the beginning of the period and the borrowing interest rate (which the FRA contract fixes) is repaid at the end of the FRA period. If there was no discounting, the investor would simply deposit the excess amount to realise risk-free profit. Thus:

Calculation Summary

$$\text{FRA settlement price} = \text{Notional principal} \times \left[\frac{(f - \text{Libor}) \times \dfrac{d_f}{\text{year}}}{1 + \text{Libor} \times \dfrac{d_f}{\text{year}}} \right]$$

where:

  f is the FRA interest rate

  d_f is the number of days in the FRA period

  year is the number of days in the year.

Just as with futures contracts, FRA strips and stacks can be purchased to create a fixed rate for a desired period. FRAs are particularly useful for covering periods outside the futures delivery cycle, e.g. 2v5 month FRA, or 7v10 month FRA.

FUTURES VS. FRAs

An important practical difference between futures and FRAs is their settlement. FRAs are settled at the beginning of the period they cover (and discounted at the prevailing market rate), whilst futures are margined daily. This creates price discrepancy between otherwise identical contracts. A FRA is sensitive to two rates (the forward rate underlying the contract and the spot rate used for discounting), whilst the future is only sensitive to the forward rate due to daily marking-to-market. Thus, the relationship between future payoff and forward rate is linear, whereas it is convex for FRAs.

Another important point is that futures prices are quoted as *100 − interest rate*, whilst FRAs are quoted as *interest rate*. Hence they move in opposite directions: if the borrower believes that the interest rates will rise, he/she will *buy* a FRA but *sell* futures and vice versa. Similarly, for hedging purposes one should either buy FRA and future or sell both contracts.

It can be shown that a short futures position is more profitable than purchase of a FRA, as it will respond quicker to the interest rate increase. The futures profits are marked to market daily and can be reinvested at the higher rate, increasing the profit even further. In contrast, FRAs settle up-front and cannot further benefit from the increase in interest rates. Hence, the implied futures rate is higher than the equivalent FRA rate. This difference is often called *convexity*. It will be referred to later in Chapter 14 on yield curve construction.

7

Swaps

INTRODUCTION

As mentioned in the introduction, derivatives products can be split into single settlement and multiple settlement products. FRAs, covered in the previous chapter, are single settlement securities that provide protection against fluctuations in an underlying interest rate for a short period of time. If a longer period needs to be covered, a FRA strip can be purchased, but liquidity of far-dated contracts might make this strategy impractical. An alternative is an interest rate swap.

BASIC SWAP CONCEPTS AND APPLICATIONS

Swaps are OTC products, specifically tailored to customer needs, but typical periods they cover range from 2 to 30 years. They are effectively a series of cashflow (coupon) exchanges over a period of time. The principal amount may be exchanged at inception and maturity, or alternatively only coupons based on a notional amount are exchanged at regular intervals (typically every six months). The two sides of the swap are commonly referred to as 'legs'. In practice, swaps where both legs are in the same currency do not involve principal exchange, as the net effect would be zero. The exchange of coupons is also 'netted', i.e. only the difference between the two legs is paid/received to minimise credit risk exposure. The market is liquid, particularly for shorter contracts. As in other derivatives products, the market participants can be split into three main categories: speculators, hedgers and arbitrageurs.

Speculators take risky swap positions independent of any underlying instruments, hence they can take a view on any type of swap. However, if a coupon swap (fixed vs. floating) is used, the receiver of the *fixed leg* takes the position with the view that interest rates are on the decline, thus benefiting by locking in the higher rate, whereas the receiver of the *floating leg* takes the opposite view. Since there is no principal exchange and no payments at the outset in terms of fees and premiums, it is very cost-effective to speculate in either a short- or a long-term interest rate derivatives market.

Hedgers enter into swaps to fix their borrowing cost. If they believe that the interest rates will rise, they can protect their floating rate borrowing (typically spread over Libor) by entering into a swap, whereby they pay fixed rate and receive Libor. The net cost of their borrowing thus becomes fixed rate + spread, as the Libor payment under the swap and the loan repayment cancel out. In this respect swap hedge works in a similar way to hedging futures and FRAs, as they aim to establish an equal and opposite position.

A client has invested in a fixed rate bond, thus receiving a fixed coupon semi-annually. However, his liabilities arise from floating rate borrowing, whereby he is exposed the risk of floating rate fluctuations. To mitigate the position unfavourably affected by the interest rate rise, a coupon swap can be used as a hedge. The arrangement is illustrated in Figure 7.1.

Matching asset and liability exposure using coupon swap

Figure 7.1

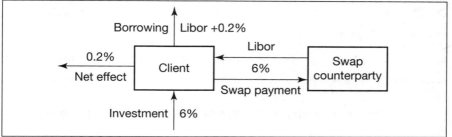

Arbitrageurs use swaps to exploit the discrepancies in the different funding methods. If two counterparties have access to both fixed and floating markets, but one counterparty has a relative advantage in one market over the other, they can enter into a swap and both achieve borrowing at reduced cost. This is best shown in an example.

Example

A company X requires floating rate borrowing and has access to funds at either 6% fixed rate, or Libor + 0.2%.

A company Y requires fixed rate borrowing and has access to funds at either 7% fixed rate, or Libor + 0.8%.

They can both transact in their preferred markets, or enter into a mutually beneficial swap. Company X clearly has better credit rating, reflected in more favourable rates in both markets. Hence, to understand the motivation for such a transaction the rates are summarised in Table 7.1.

Comparative borrowing rate advantage in fixed and floating markets

Table 7.1

Company	Fixed rate	Floating rate
Company X	6%	Libor + 0.2%
Company Y	7%	Libor + 0.8%
Comparative advantage	1%	0.6%

Clearly company X has a bigger advantage in the fixed market than in the floating market. The absolute advantage is the difference between comparative values in both markets, i.e. $1\% - 0.6\% = 0.4\%$. This is the rate difference available for sharing between the two counterparties.

Even though company X requires floating rate funding, it will borrow in the market where it has most advantage, i.e. at 6% fixed rate, while company Y will borrow at Libor + 0.8%. If the absolute advantage is to be split equally, they enter into a swap, whereby company X pays Libor and receives 6%, whilst company Y pays 6% and receives Libor. The net effect, as shown in Figure 7.2, is:

- Company X pays Libor (0.2% improvement on the original rate)
- Company Y pays 6.8% (0.2% improvement on the original rate).

Figure 7.2 **Exploiting comparative borrowing rate advantage using coupon swap**

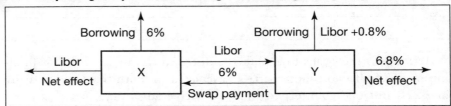

In practice the rate advantage may not be split equally due to the difference in credit rating. Furthermore, an investment bank would typically act as an intermediary, taking a cut of the profit and then passing on the difference to the counterparties.

The above swap involving the exchange of fixed coupon vs. floating rate is the simplest and the most common one. Other varieties are discussed below.

TYPES OF SWAPS

Asset swap

The swap in the example above was initiated due to the discrepancy between the funding costs in different markets. However, clients often wish to be net payers of fixed rate (to protect the borrowing costs) and would enter into a swap whereby they pay a fixed rate and receive a floating rate. This type of swap is also known as a 'vanilla' swap, as it is the most basic type of this security. The two legs typically have the same payment frequency (e.g. six months) and the underlying floating rate is equal to the payment period (e.g. the floating swap leg is fixed semi-annually against spot six-month Libor). This may not always be the case, as swaps are tailored to meet clients' needs, but any modifications need to be priced into the swap. Alternatively, if the rates are on the rise, a client receiving a fixed rate income could enter into a swap to benefit from this increase, without changing the investment strategy, as shown in Figure 7.3.

Graphical representation of asset swap

Figure 7.3

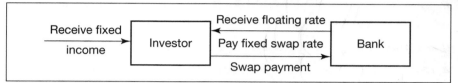

Basis swap

Counterparties with payment obligations based on one floating interest rate but receiving funds in the same currency based on another rate may enter into a *basis swap* to neutralise their basis exposure. For example, a high-street bank that receives mortgage payments on a monthly basis, but has outstanding debts incurring payments based on the three-month Libor, would benefit from bringing its assets and liabilities under the same denominator (basis). Just as in the earlier asset swap example, there is potential comparative advantage between floating rate funding costs that can be exploited by two counterparties. For example, if a company has a mortgage payment income based on the one-month Libor + 0.5 per cent and an outstanding loan based on the three-month Libor, it may be possible (subject to credit rating) to enter into a swap under which the client receives the three-month Libor and pays the one-month Libor + 0.3 per cent, thus not only converting assets and liabilities into the same rate, but achieving an improvement of 0.2 per cent. In practice, the opposite is more likely to be true. Basis swaps are highly sought after by the clients, thus the bank would charge spread over the leg that the client pays, as shown in Figure 7.4.

Graphical representation of basis swap

Figure 7.4

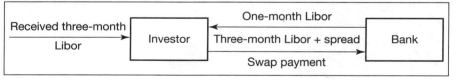

Currency swap

A currency swap, much like an interest rate swap, refers to an exchange of payments between two counterparties at regular intervals over a period of time. However, these cashflows are in different currencies and are subject to interest rate fluctuations in different countries. There is also the exchange rate exposure. Hence currency swaps typically involve exchange of principals where the initial amounts are fixed at the spot FX rate and the amounts at maturity are fixed to the forward FX rate, whilst the actual rate at delivery may be substantially different. The different types of currency swaps are:

- *Fixed-fixed*, where both interest rates are fixed
- *Fixed-floating*, where one leg is based on a fixed rate and another on a floating rate
- *Floating-floating*, where both interest rates are floating.

Amortising swap

An amortising swap attracts clients whose borrowing principal amount is repaid over time (amortised), such as mortgage obligations. Hence the required amount of interest rate protection reduces over time. If they entered into a 'vanilla' swap, receiving a floating rate and paying a fixed rate, their obligations under the swap would become increasingly mismatched to the underlying borrowing amount. Alternatively, if they estimate amortisation (e.g. at 25 per cent every six months) and enter into a 'stack' of four swaps, each based on 25 per cent of principal but with decreasing maturities, they would not only achieve an uneven payment schedule but also enter into too many transactions. The amortising swap is then the 'all-in' solution. The above example assumed fixed-floating swap, but basis or currency swaps can also be amortising in order to meet client requirements.

Forward-start swap

A forward starting swap is akin to a strip of FRAs, as the contract starts at some point in the future. Any type of swap described above can be tailored to start forward.

SWAP PRICING FUNDAMENTALS

Short-term interest rate swaps

Valuation at contract inception

Swap pricing is based on FRA rates, as the fundamental idea behind both these products is to fix the cost of funds. Since it is possible to purchase a series of FRAs to cover periods of 3v6 months, 6v9 months, 9v12 months and so on, it is possible to calculate an equivalent rate for an entire period that would achieve the same net result, the *swap rate*. A client should be indifferent to whether they borrow on a rolling quarterly basis at a three-month Libor and simultaneously entering into a swap (quarterly paying fixed and receiving a three-month Libor) or they borrow on a rolling quarterly basis at the three-month Libor and fix the cost of that borrowing by purchasing corresponding FRA contracts. Since the Libor transactions in both scenarios are the same, it is implicit that the swap and the FRA strip must be of equal value. This concept is the basis for swap pricing. The all-in swap rate calculated using discount factors (DFs) based on FRAs can be calculated from the equation below:

Short-term swap valuation at inception

$$1 = DF_N + \sum_{k=1}^{N} r_s \times \frac{days_k}{year} \times DF_k$$

where:

r_S is the annual swap rate, or coupon

$days_k$ is the number of days covered by the kth FRA contract

DF_k is the discount factor derived from the kth FRA rate f_k using:

$$DF_k = \frac{1}{1 + f_k \times \frac{days_k}{year}}$$

Swap valuation in the secondary market

Clearly at the inception it is implicit that both swap legs are of equal value. However, at any point in the future, as interest rates change, they move away from the equilibrium resulting in the payment from one counterparty to another. The later valuation follows the same principle of discounting future cashflows of both legs. Two approaches can be taken:

1. Valuation of the original swap using prevailing swap rates

In this scenario, the two legs are valued separately. Regardless of the change in the interest rates, the floating leg is still valued at par, as the rates used for discounting are the same as those for projecting the cash-flows, i.e. any changes cancel out.

The fixed leg, however is affected by the change, as the discount factors used for the valuation have moved away from the original calculation. Hence, its valuation can be summarised as:

Calculation Summary

Later valuation of short-term swap fixed leg

$$P = \left[DF_N + \sum_{k=1}^{N} r_s \times \frac{days_k}{year} \times DF_k \right] \times 100$$

where:

P is the value of the fixed leg at a later date

r_S is the swap rate, fixed at inception

$days_k$ is the number of days covered by the kth FRA contract

DF_k is the discount factor derived from the kth FRA rate f_k using:

$$DF_k = \frac{1}{1 + f_k \times \frac{days_k}{year}}$$

As the swap valuation at inception was based on a notional amount of 100, clearly the difference between the calculated fixed leg and the 100 is paid/received, depending on the prevailing interest rates. The receiver of the fixed benefits from rising interest rates, and vice versa.

An alternative approach to swap valuation follows.

2. Valuation of fixed swap leg using new swap rate

An alternative is to calculate a new swap rate that would price the swap at par. This is done using the original swap valuation formula, resulting in a new swap rate r_S^*.

This new swap rate is used to discount all future fixed leg cashflows, as follows:

Later valuation of short-term swap fixed leg using new equilibrium swap rate **Calculation Summary**

$$P = \left[DF_N + \sum_{k=1}^{N} r_s \times DF_k \right] \times 100$$

where:

P is the value of the fixed leg at a later date

r_s is the original swap rate, fixed at inception

$days_k$ is the number of days covered by the kth FRA contract

DF_k is the discount factor derived from newly calculated equilibrium swap rate applicable to the kth period:

$$DF_k = \frac{1}{\left(1 + r_s^*\right)^k}$$

It is worth noting that even though they are practically interchangeable, the two methods may produce slight discrepancies between the two values, due to the fact that the first method uses exact daycounts, whilst the second applies fixed periods for all future swap legs.

Long-term interest rate swaps

The above valuation is possible for swaps of relatively short maturity, so that their entire period is covered by futures and FRA contracts. If that is not the case, there isn't sufficient market information for arbitrage-free valuation. The long-term swap prices are normally linked to capital markets products, such as bonds. As with any other product, the supply and demand will ultimately dictate their price. Liquidity of long-term swaps is also an issue, as there are fewer market prices that can be used as references.

The typical approach to pricing long-term swaps is to evaluate each leg separately, using bond valuation principles. As the floating leg is directly liked to the long-term interest rate forward market, its value is always at par, whether it is priced at inception or at some future date. However, the fixed leg at inception also has to be valued at par; hence its rate needs to be iteratively adjusted until the convergence criteria are reached.

At any future date the two legs are simply valued separately and the net sum is paid/received depending on the prevailing interest rates.

PRICING CURRENCY SWAPS

Even though this chapter has so far dealt with interest rate swaps – by far the most popular type of swap – currency swaps are also included, as they are closely linked to the interest rate market. Foreign exchange (FX) and related financial instruments are covered in the following chapter. For more details on FX terminology and products see Chapter 8.

Currency swap is a contract between two counterparties to exchange cashflows in different currencies, thus exposing them to both the exchange rate risk and the interest rates linked to the currencies in question. Even though there are many 'flavours' of currency swaps (as there are for any other type), the main distinction is in the swap type:

Short-term swaps are typically structured so that only the principal is exchanged at inception and reversed at maturity, thus incorporating the interest rate and FX exposure through the uncertainty of the final cashflow market value.

Long-term swaps are structured similarly to other swap types, i.e. the contract commits the two parties to the exchange of regular payments (in their respective currencies), with the final exchange of principals at the exchange rate agreed at inception. The initial principal exchange may or may not be a part of the contract.

Short-term currency swap valuation

As in all other foreign exchange contracts, one of the two currencies is defined as a primary currency and most deals are structured so that the nominal value of the primary currency leg is equal at both inception and maturity. The secondary currency in the swap deal determines the notional amount of the second leg, as a function of the spot and forward exchange rates. In other words, at inception the notional amount of secondary currency is calculated as the product of the primary currency notional and the spot exchange rate. The principal amounts to be exchanged at maturity are fixed at the inception and calculated as the product of the primary currency notional and the forward exchange rate. Clearly, just like interest rate swaps, currency swaps are used for speculation, hedging and arbitrage.

Their valuation conforms to the same principles as described above, i.e. at inception the two swap legs are of equal value (based on the spot FX rate). The valuation at any point in the future, including maturity, is done in relation to the secondary currency (the primary leg being fixed); whereby the profit/loss on the secondary leg is calculated in relation to the prevailing FX rates for the corresponding tenor.

Long-term currency swap valuation

As explained above, the long-term currency swap involves both the regular cashflow exchanges throughout the contract and the exchange of principals at maturity (and sometimes at inception). Akin to other swap types, several variations may exist, the most common ones being:

■ *Cross-currency coupon swaps* in which fixed rate in one currency is exchanged for a floating rate in another, or

■ *Cross-currency basis swaps*, where floating legs in both currencies are exchanged.

Graphically, the structure can be represented as shown in Figure 7.5.

Graphical representation of cross-currency swap

Figure 7.5

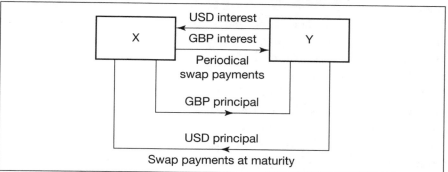

Valuation of the long-term currency swap, once again, conforms to the standard calculation of present value of cashflows implicit in the two legs. At inception this value is equal. At any other time the valuation implies the calculation of the present value of the the two legs, using (as in interest rate swaps) bond calculation principles. As here the two legs (i.e. bonds) are denominated in different currencies, the following steps are taken:

1. Each leg (bond) is valued in its own currency, based on the outstanding cashflows and relevant spot rates.

2. The two legs are converted to the same currency (base currency) using the prevailing spot rate for the tenor equal to the outstanding contract period.

3. The swap value is calculated as the difference between the two legs.

EQUITY SWAP VALUATION

Equity derivatives are covered in more detail in Chapter 10, whilst equity swaps are covered here as they are closely related to interest swaps and their valuation.

Akin to interest rate swaps, equity swaps are contracts between two counterparties to exchange a series of cashflows (typically semi-annually), without the exchange of principals at either inception or maturity. However, whilst one swap leg is typically linked to an interest rate corresponding to the payment frequency (e.g. six-month Libor), the other leg is linked to the performance of an equity investment (capital gains and dividends). Most commonly, the equity leg is based on the performance of an equity index (further discussed in Chapter 10). An important difference between the interest rate swaps and equity swaps is that the payments under different legs cannot be netted, as they are linked to different underlying variables. Thus, one counterparty always pays Libor, whilst the other pays total return on the equity investment. The important implication is that should the equity market fall, the payer of the Libor leg is responsible for both the floating leg payments and the equity capital depreciation.

As with all other swaps, the value of the two legs at inception is equal. It might seem improbable that the two legs are equal at inception, as in all previous cases one leg was adjusted in order to price the swap at zero. In contrast, in this case one leg is linked to Libor, and the other to an equity index performance, thus no adjustments can be made. However, using the principles of fair value, it is clear that the Libor leg will always be equal to par, as the rates used for discounting the cashflows are also used for projecting them. On the other hand, the equity performance is linked to the interest rate market, such that if there are any discrepancies between the returns in the two markets, an arbitrage opportunity would arise, quickly eliminating the discrepancy. Hence at inception an investor should be indifferent to which market he/she invests in, providing that all the products are priced fairly and disregarding transaction costs, market accessibility and volume limits.

At any other time the two legs are valued separately and the net value is paid/received depending on the equity performance. Three calculations are required:

1. Capital performance of the equity index.

2. Dividend income under the equity contract.

3. Floating rate payment.

Capital performance is calculated as the product of the notional amount and the ratio of the initial index value to its value at the time of valuation. It is important to note that, as stated earlier, in the event of a decline in the equity market, the receiver of the equity return is responsible for both the floating payment and the equity depreciation compensation.

Dividend income is calculated as the percentage of the notional amount, having clearly specified in the swap contract to which period the dividend payment relates.

Finally, the *floating leg* is calculated in the same way as for all other swaps, i.e. as a percentage of the notional amount accounting for the number of days in the relevant period. Thus, the value of the equity swap is equal to:

Valuation of the equity index swap

Equity swap valuation = Equity index capital gains
+ Equity index dividends – Floating leg payments

For more information on equities and equity derivatives, please refer to Chapter 10.

8

Foreign exchange

INTRODUCTION

Foreign exchange refers to the exchange of one currency for another. It is written in the form CCY_1/CCY_2. The two currencies are referred to as 'base currency' on the left and 'variable currency' on the right. Its value refers to how much variable currency is paid/received for one unit of base currency. In domestic markets the base currency is the domestic currency, whilst in international markets it is typically USD. More and more frequently, various currencies are quoted against EUR. In financial markets trades involving virtually any combination of currencies are executed and the exchange rate tables (FX tables) are used. Table 8.1 gives an example.

Table 8.1		Example of foreign exchange tables				

	USD	GBP	CAD	EUR	AUD
USD	1	1.491	0.978	1.335	0.911
GBP	0.671	1	0.656	0.895	0.611
CAD	1.024	1.523	1	1.365	0.931
EUR	0.749	1.118	0.732	1	0.682
AUD	1.099	1.638	1.074	1.465	1

The currencies in the column headings are 'base currencies', i.e. on the left of the CCY_1/CCY_2, whilst the currencies in the row headings are 'variable currencies' on the right.

SPOT EXCHANGE RATES

Spot exchange rates apply to trades executed now. In financial markets the delivery is typically two working days from the trade date to allow for necessary bank transfers and paperwork. The adjustments for holidays in both countries have to be made. As stated above, any currency pairs can be traded. However, most currencies are quoted either against EUR (interbank spot market), or USD (futures market), referred to as the *direct rate*.

Other currency combinations have to be calculated from two rates against USD or EUR and are called *cross-rates*. For example, to obtain the CHF/CAD exchange rate, the amount of USD received on sale of CHF would be calculated first, and then the amount of CAD purchased by USD would imply the CHF/CAD rate. The important aspect of cross-rates is that they involve both sale and purchase. As traders make profits from buying/bidding 'low' and selling/offering 'high', each exchange rate has two sides, creating bid/offer spread. Supply and demand influence the width of the spread. Typically for major currencies it is very tight; whilst for currencies quoted as cross-rates it is wider, accounting for lower liquidity and the implied intermediate sale/purchase of base currency.

DIRECT AND CROSS-RATES

Direct rates, regardless of the choice of the 'base' and 'variable' currency, are two-way bid/offer quotations, where *bid* indicates how much variable currency is received on the sale of one unit of base currency and *offer* gives the amount of variable currency needed to purchase one unit of base currency. For example, the USD/GBP rate would be 1.490/1.492.

Cross-rates involve a currency pair that does not have a direct exchange rate quotation in the market. Thus it requires two calculations, each against the base currency. As there is no market convention for non-standard currency pairs, the trader decides which is the 'base' currency in the final quotation.

Example

For example, to calculate the CHF/NOK exchange rate we would use two quotations:

Same base currency

Spot USD/CHF: 1.069/1.072

Spot USD/NOK: 6.055/6.061

To purchase NOK, we first have to sell CHF for USD (using the bid rate 1.069 on the left) and then with the received USD buy NOK (using the offer rate on the right 6.061).

This gives the value of $6.061 \div 1.069 = 5.670$.

Alternatively, to sell NOK for CHF, we first have to sell NOK for USD (using the bid rate 6.055 on the left) and then with the received USD buy CHF (using the offer rate on the right 1.072).

This gives the value of $6.055 \div 1.072 = 6.110$

Thus the two-way CHF/NOK exchange rate is 5.670/6.110.

We can see that the spread is wider than for quotations against the base currency, as two transactions are implicit in its calculation. If we accepted NOK as the 'base' currency, similar calculations would be performed. The bid side would be worked out as the amount of CHF received on sale for USD and then converted to NOK, i.e. $1.072 \div 6.055 = 0.164$. The offer would be calculated by working out the rate at which NOK would be exchanged for USD and then converted to CHF, i.e. $1.069 \div 6.061 = 0.176$. This creates the NOK/CHF exchange rate 0.164/0.176.

The above could have been done more simply, by taking reciprocals of the CHF/NOK and reversing the sides. To avoid confusion, it is important to remember the following:

- Traders always 'buy low and sell high', hence the lower number is always on the left.

- Cross-currency spreads are always wider, and thus combine quotations from the opposite sides of direct rates.

Example

It is possible that the required exchange rate would involve two currencies that have market quotations against the same variable currency. For example, if we required the EUR/GBP rate, but only the EUR/USD and GBP/USD rates were available, the calculation would proceed as:

Same variable currency

EUR/USD = 1.334/1.336

GBP/USD = 1.490/1.492

Calculate the number of USD obtained from sale of EUR as 1.334, then purchase GBP using the offer side of the quotation (1.492), deriving the EUR/GBP bid rate as 1.334 ÷ 1.492 = 0.894. Similarly, the offer side of EUR/GBP would be calculated as 1.336 ÷ 1.490 = 0.897. The two-way EUR/GBP quotation is 0.894/0.897.

Finally, in the case of two currencies, where one is quoted as base currency and one as variable currency, the calculation would be as follows:

Common currency is base currency in one quotation, but variable in another

EUR/USD = 1.334/1.336

USD/AUD = 1.096/1.102

First calculate the number of USD obtained from sale of EUR as 1.334 (bid side), then sell USD to obtain 1.096 for each unit (again the bid side!), deriving the EUR/AUD bid rate as 1.334 × 1.096 = 1.462. The offer rate would be calculated by multiplying the two offer sides, i.e. 1.336 × 1.102 = 1.472.

The above scenarios can be summarised as:

■ The exchange rates are always calculated to create the worst possible outcome, i.e. the lowest number for the bid, and the highest for the offer.

■ From two rates with the same *base* currency, opposite sides are divided. In the cross-currency quotation the numerator in the division becomes the *variable* currency, whilst the denominator is the *base* currency.

■ From two rates with the same *variable* currency, opposite sides are also divided. But in the cross-currency quotation the numerator in the division becomes the *base* currency, whilst the denominator is the *variable* currency.

■ From two rates where the common currency is the base currency in one quotation, but the variable in another, multiply the same sides. This creates a cross-currency quotation where the base currency in the original quotation remains the base currency, and vice versa.

This can be expressed more simply using mathematical notation:

Given exchange rates X/Y and X/Z, the cross-rates are:

$(Y/Z)_{bid} = (X/Z)_{bid} \div (X/Y)_{offer}$

$(Y/Z)_{offer} = (X/Z)_{offer} \div (X/Y)_{bid}$

and

$(Z/Y)_{bid} = 1/(Y/Z)_{offer}$

$(Z/Y)_{offer} = 1/(Y/Z)_{bid}$

Given exchange rates Y/X and Z/X, the cross-rates are:

$(Y/Z)_{bid} = (Y/X)_{bid} \div (Z/X)_{offer}$

$(Y/Z)_{offer} = (Y/X)_{offer} \div (Z/X)_{bid}$

and

$(Z/Y)_{bid} = 1/(Y/Z)_{offer}$

$(Z/Y)_{offer} = 1/(Y/Z)_{bid}$

Given exchange rates Y/X and X/Z, the cross-rates are:

$(Y/Z)_{bid} = (Y/X)_{bid} \times (X/Z)_{bid}$

$(Y/Z)_{offer} = (Y/X)_{offer} \times (X/Z)_{offer}$

and

$(Z/Y)_{bid} = 1/(Y/Z)_{offer}$

$(Z/Y)_{offer} = 1/(Y/Z)_{bid}$

FORWARD EXCHANGE RATES

The spot rates from the previous sections refer to transactions settled two working days from today. Even though the settlement is in the future, these transactions are not considered to be 'futures' or 'forwards', as the additional two working days have to be added to all cross-currency trades regardless of the security involved. The 'true' forward trades settle at some future date different from the spot settlement date.

Forward outrights

Forward outright contracts involve the outright purchase or sale of one currency in exchange for another currency for settlement in the future. The same rules of exchange rate calculations apply, i.e. there is a two-way price where the sale is made using a bid quotation and the purchase uses an offer quotation. In major currency pairs the two cashflows are exchanged at maturity, whilst in some less liquid contracts only the difference between the agreed rate and the prevailing market exchange rate is settled. The pricing of the forward outright is the same in both cases. Whilst the motivation behind trading forward outrights is the same as for FRAs, i.e fixing the rate for a time period in the future, the contracts are influenced by different underlying variables. FRAs are only exposed to the interest rate risk in the currency they are denominated in, whilst forward outrights are affected not only by the fluctuations in the exchange rate between the two currencies, but also by the interest rates in their domicile countries. This is reflected in their pricing. The forward outright is calculated as the ratio of variable and base currencies that would be available on the future date if they were both placed on deposit at their respective interest rates.

Calculation Summary

Forward outright exchange rate

$$FX_f = FX_s \times \frac{1 + r_v \times \frac{days}{year}}{1 + r_b \times \frac{days}{year}}$$

where:

FX_f and FX_s are the forward and spot exchange rates

r_v and r_b are the variable and base currency interest rates.

Forward swaps

From the formula above it can be seen that by entering into a forward outright transaction the counterparties are essentially taking a view on interest rates in the two currencies involved in the exchange, without actually participating in the interest rate market. An alternative is to actually buy/sell one currency now (at spot rate) and reverse the transaction by selling/buying back the same currency at a forward rate. This is known as a *forward swap* (briefly described in the previous chapter). As this involves selling low and buying high, if actual bid/offer spreads were taken into account, the swap would become prohibitively expensive. Thus mid quotes are typically used. As the initial swap is transacted at spot and reversed at maturity at the forward exchange rate, to avoid arbitrage the swap must be valued as the difference between the two rates:

Forward swap = forward outright – spot

$$FS = FX_f - FX_s = FX_s \times \frac{r_v \times \frac{days}{year} - r_b \times \frac{days}{year}}{1 + r_b \times \frac{days}{year}}$$

where:

FS is the forward swap price

FX_f and FX_s are the forward and spot exchange rates

r_v and r_b are the variable and base currency interest rate.

From the equation above it is clear that the forward swap enables traders to exploit interest rate differentials between the two currencies. If they expect the gap to narrow (either the base currency interest rate rises or the variable currency interest rate falls) they will speculate by buying the base currency now and selling it forward. The net effect of this transaction is borrowing in the base currency and depositing in the variable currency.

Discounts and premiums

From the equation above it follows that if the variable currency interest rates are higher than for the base currency, the forward exchange rate will be higher than the spot, and vice versa. The logic behind this pricing is that if we exchange higher-interest variable currency into lower-interest base currency at spot and place the amount on deposit, we would earn lower interest. However, if we buy the base currency forward, we are left with the original variable currency that can be invested at the higher interest rate until settlement. To make the investor indifferent as to which path to take, the forward rates have to be higher to compensate for the low interest rate. In this case the base currency is said to be 'at premium'. If the variable currency interest rates are lower than the base currency rates, the opposite is true. The base currency is then 'at discount' and the forward rate is lower than the spot.

Cross-rate forwards

Calculation of cross-rate forward follows the same rules as for spot cross-rate quotations:

Given forward exchange rates X/Y and X/Z, the forward cross-rates are:

$$(Y/Z)_{bid} = (X/Z)_{bid} \div (X/Y)_{offer}$$
$$(Y/Z)_{offer} = (X/Z)_{offer} \div (X/Y)_{bid}$$

and

$$(Z/Y)_{bid} = 1/(Y/Z)_{offer}$$
$$(Z/Y)_{offer} = 1/(Y/Z)_{bid}$$

Given forward exchange rates Y/X and Z/X, the forward cross-rates are:

$$(Y/Z)_{bid} = (Y/X)_{bid} \div (Z/X)_{offer}$$
$$(Y/Z)_{offer} = (Y/X)_{offer} \div (Z/X)_{bid}$$

and

$$(Z/Y)_{bid} = 1/(Y/Z)_{offer}$$
$$(Z/Y)_{offer} = 1/(Y/Z)_{bid}$$

Given forward exchange rates Y/X and X/Z, the forward cross-rates are:

$$(Y/Z)_{bid} = (Y/X)_{bid} \times (X/Z)_{bid}$$
$$(Y/Z)_{offer} = (Y/X)_{offer} \times (X/Z)_{offer}$$

and

$$(Z/Y)_{bid} = 1/(Y/Z)_{offer}$$
$$(Z/Y)_{offer} = 1/(Y/Z)_{bid}$$

Cross-rate forward swaps

The forward swap price is the difference between the forward outright and the spot exchange rate. When the currencies involved in the swap do not have a direct market exchange rate quotation, the cross-currency spot rate, as well as forward outright rates, have to be calculated using a common currency. Thus the cross-rate forward swap price calculation requires five steps:

1. Calculate spot cross-rate as previously described.
2. Calculate forward outright for one currency against the common currency.
3. Calculate forward outright for second currency against the common currency.
4. Calculate forward outright cross-rate.
5. Calculate cross-rate forward swap price as the difference between the forward outright rate and the spot rate.

Given spot exchange rates X_s/Y_s and X_s/Z_s and forward exchange rates X_f/Y_f and X_f/Z_f, the forward cross-rate swap prices are:

$$(Y/Z)_{bid} = (X_f/Z_f)_{bid} \div (X_f/Y_f)_{offer} - (X_s/Z_s)_{bid} \div (X_s/Y_s)_{offer}$$
$$(Y/Z)_{offer} = (X_f/Z_f)_{offer} \div (X_f/Y_f)_{bid} - (X_s/Z_s)_{offer} \div (X_s/Y_s)_{bid}$$

Given exchange rates Y/X and Z/X, the forward cross-rates are:

$$(Y/Z)_{bid} = (Y_f/X_f)_{bid} \div (Z_f/X_f)_{offer} - (Y_s/X_s)_{bid} \div (Z_s/X_s)_{offer}$$
$$(Y/Z)_{offer} = (Y_f/X_f)_{offer} \div (Z_f/X_f)_{bid} - (Y_s/X_s)_{offer} \div (Z_s/X_s)_{bid}$$

Given exchange rates Y/X and X/Z, the forward cross-rates are:

$$(Y/Z)_{bid} = (Y_f/X_f)_{bid} \times (X_f/Z_f)_{bid} - (Y_s/X_s)_{bid} \times (X_s/Z_s)_{bid}$$
$$(Y/Z)_{offer} = (Y_f/X_f)_{offer} \times (X_f/Z_f)_{offer} - (Y_s/X_s)_{offer} \times (X_s/Z_s)_{offer}$$

9

Options

MOTIVATION BEHIND OPTION TRADING

An option gives the buyer the right but not the obligation to enter at a future date into a transaction specified today. The buyer will obviously use it to his advantage and only exercise the option if it is beneficial compared to the prevailing market conditions at expiry. In the event of exercise the option seller must fulfil his obligation at loss. To accept this risk he charges a premium payable up-front. Clearly all the buyer can lose is the cost of the premium if the option expires unexercised, whilst the seller has an unlimited exposure. Hence his view of the market must be opposite.

Options are derivative instruments, i.e. their price is derived from the value of an underlying security. They are valuable tools used for hedging and speculation.

Hedgers use options as a form of insurance. If they believe that the price of an asset they will require in the future will increase they buy an option that allows them to fix the purchase price today. If their expectations prove to be correct, they will exercise the option. However, if they can transact more cheaply in the market, they will simply abandon the option. Similarly, an option to sell an asset in the future at a price agreed today protects the option buyer against the price decrease. Should the prices rise, the option would be abandoned and the asset sold more profitably in the market.

Speculators take their positions purely to make a profit from expected market moves. They neither require, nor own an underlying security and aim to close out their position by reversing the option contract prior to expiry. Alternatively, they can sell options with the view that they will not be exercised, expecting to keep the premium.

OPTION CONTRACT SPECIFICATIONS

The option contract gives the buyer or *holder* the right but not the obligation to transact with the option seller or *writer* in the future. At the inception, the following is agreed:

- *Expiry date* is the date when the option can be exercised. There are two types of options: *American option*, which can be exercised at any point until expiry; or *European option*, which can be exercised only at the expiry date.
- *Option type* specifies whether the option is the right to buy (*call option*) or the right to sell (*put option*). These can be viewed from the holder's or writer's point of view.

  Long call gives the right to buy an underlying.

  Long put gives the right to sell an underlying.

  Short call is an obligation to buy an underlying (if the option is exercised).

  Short put is an obligation to sell an underlying (if the option is exercised).

- *Underlying* is an asset (interest rate, equity, commodity etc.) from which the option derives value.

- *Strike price* or *strike rate* is chosen by the option buyer as the price at which the future transaction can take place. Its value is not derived from the forward market and depends on the amount of protection/speculation the buyer is willing to undertake.

  At-the-money (ATM) option has a strike price equal to the forward price.

  In-the-money (ITM) option has a strike price that is more favourable than the forward price.

  Out-of-the-money (OTM) option has a strike price that is less advantageous than the forward price.

- *Intrinsic value* of an option is the difference between the strike price and the current market price of an ITM option. For an OTM option it is zero rather than negative, as an option without value would simply lapse, rather than incur costs to the holder.

- *Time value* is the built in cost of the premium that allows for uncertainty of exercise. It is greater for longer-dated options and reduces to zero at expiry.

- *Option premium* is the cost of the option contract. It is based on its intrinsic value and time value.

TYPES OF OPTION CONTRACTS

Options can be traded at both recognised exchanges and OTC. The pros and cons of both markets are the same as for other financial securities. The exchange-traded options are limited in the range of underlying securities, whilst more 'exotic' products, tailor-made to specific client requirements, are traded OTC. Some examples of exchange-traded options are:

Interest rate options where the underlying is an interest rate. They are used as protection against adverse movements in interest rates, but unlike futures and FRAs they also allow for potential profit if rates move in the buyer's favour. On exercise only the difference between the interest rates is settled, based on the specified notional amount.

Cross-currency options have an exchange rate as an underlying. However, they implicitly derive their value from the interest rates in the two exchanged currencies. As above, on exercise only the difference between the rates is settled, based on the specified notional amount.

Stock options derive their value from the price of a single stock. On exercise, depending on exchange specifications, the stock can be bought/sold or the difference in price settled.

Equity index options are based on a specific equity index. They are always settled on price difference.

Commodity options have an actual commodity as an underlying (wheat, coffee, crude oil etc.), thus the delivery is usually expected, or implied in pricing (includes cost of storage, shipment etc.).

Some more exotic options traded OTC are:

Swap options or *swaptions* allow the holder to enter into a swap on exercise. They derive their value from the implicit swap underlying.

Binary option pays a fixed amount if the option is in the money at expiry. The underlying can be any security.

Spread option pays the difference between a pair of underlying asset prices.

Option types

As mentioned above, there are four possible option positions:

Long call is the right to buy an underlying at a specific price. For example, a long call option with the strike price 100 and premium 5 would be exercised if the market price at expiry is equal or greater than 100. The price achieved will have to incorporate the premium paid, thus the position will only turn into profit above 105. The payout profile would resemble that shown in Figure 9.1.

| Figure 9.1 | **Long call option payout profile** |

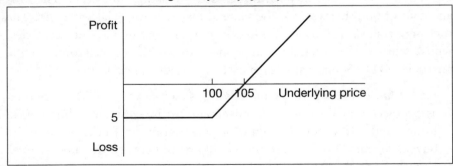

Short call is the above scenario from the point of view of the option seller. He receives the premium of 5 up-front. If the underlying price is below 100 at expiry, the option will be abandoned and the full premium will be realised as profit. As the price rises, the position crosses over into loss, as shown in Figure 9.2.

Short call option payout profile

Figure 9.2

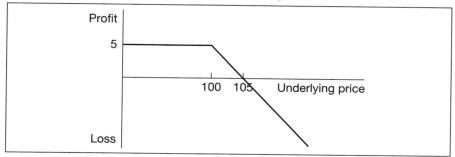

Long put is the right to sell an underlying at a specific price. For example, a long put option with the strike price 100 and premium 5 would be exercised if the market price at expiry is equal to or lower than 100. The price achieved will have to incorporate the premium paid, thus the position will only turn into profit below 95. The payout profile would resemble that shown in Figure 9.3.

Long put option payout profile

Figure 9.3

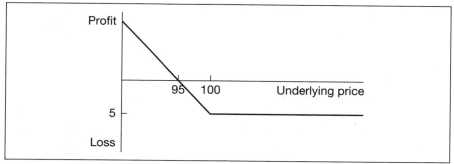

Short put is the above scenario from the point of view of the option seller. He receives the premium of 5 up-front. If the underlying price is above 100 at expiry, the option will be abandoned and the full premium will be realised as profit. As the price falls, the position crosses over into a loss, as shown in Figure 9.4.

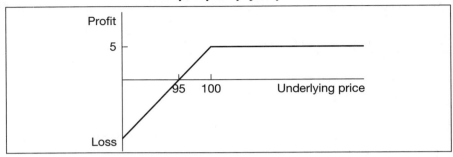

Figure 9.4

Short put option payout profile

There are many option strategies that can be based on the above four basic trades. They are graphically presented in Appendix 1.

OPTION CONTRACT RISKS AND BENEFITS

As the only cashflow at inception of the option contract is the premium, it is an 'off-balance sheet' instrument, which makes it an attractive instrument for those with limited credit lines. More importantly, the potential profit/loss can be multifold of the premium (a concept called 'gearing'), making options one of the riskiest derivative securities. For example, if a long call with strike 100 and premium 5 is exercised when the underlying is 120, it realises 15 in premium, which is 300 per cent of the funds required for the trade. If we owned the underlying, the same price increase would realise only 20 per cent of the initial value. The opposite is also true; if the underlying at expiry was worth 80, the option holder would lose 100 per cent of the premium, whilst the asset holder would lose only 20 per cent.

From the diagrams above we can also see that all the option buyer can lose is the cost of the premium. However, the seller of the call has unlimited exposure. In the case of the short put position the loss is limited to *strike – premium*, as the asset price can never fall below zero. This one-sided exposure implies that the option writers have very strong views on the future market movements, otherwise they would not enter into the transaction.

IDEAS BEHIND OPTION PRICING

The amount of premium the option seller requires is based on the probability that the option will be exercised and the expected loss this would incur. It is akin to travel insurance, whereby the premium is lower for a two-day city break than for two weeks of paragliding, as the latter has a much higher probability of resulting in a serious accident. Hence the option pricing takes into account:

The strike price – a more favourable strike price to the buyer implies a higher premium, as the option will have a greater intrinsic value. The *time value* will depend on the time to expiry. This relationship is not linear; at inception the option loses very little time value with each passing day, but as the expiry approaches the decay increases dramatically.

Volatility – the underlying price fluctuation. The more volatile the underlying the more time value the option will have and consequently the higher the premium will be. This is because more volatile assets have a greater chance to expire ITM. As the options writer is pricing options on an asset to be bought/sold in the future, the volatility relevant to the valuation is *future volatility*, something that cannot possibly be known.

Hence it is estimated assuming certain behaviour of an asset, using a *probability distribution*. This is the range of possible values the underlying can take with the probability of each outcome assigned. For example, an asset that has a current value of 100 cannot be worth less than zero and cannot reach infinity. It is also more likely to remain in the 80–120 range than to be priced at 50 or 200 and so on. In practice, traders assume that percentage changes in asset prices are *normally distributed*, whilst asset prices are *log-normally distributed*. Types of distributions and other aspects of probability and statistics relevant to option pricing are covered in Chapter 13.

Since future volatility can only be estimated, the alternatives are:

Historic volatility, taken from the analysis of historic market data.

Implied volatility, calculated from current option prices by working 'backwards' to see which value of volatility would result in the market price.

Neither measure actually predicts the future volatility, as historic data may be completely irrelevant to the events that will influence price fluctuations in the future, whilst implied volatility is simply other market practitioners' view of the future.

Option maturity – the more time the underlying price has to fluctuate, the more likely it is that the option will be exercised; hence the premium increases with maturity.

Interest rates – the relationship between interest rates and premiums is not unique, it depends on the type of the option and the underlying.

For *physically settled options* call premiums rise (as the option seller has to finance the purchase of the underlying at higher rates) and put premiums fall (it is the option buyer who incurs the cost and expects to be compensated by a reduced premium).

For *options on futures* with up-front premiums call and put premiums fall, as the option writer can invest the profit at higher rates.

For *options on futures* that are margined call and put premiums are unaffected, as the rate fluctuation will be incorporated into daily margins.

For *bond options*, *swaptions* and other options with interest rate derivatives as underlying, and exotic options in particular, the relationship between the premium and interest rate is more complex.

The above variables are incorporated into the option pricing methodology. There are two main approaches, analytical and numerical, which are described later.

PUT–CALL PARITY

Put–call parity describes the relationship between the prices of a put option, call option and an underlying asset. If one counterparty purchases a future at 100, their payout profile would be as presented in Figure 9.5. If another counterparty buys a call with strike 100 and premium of 10 and simultaneously sells a put with the identical strike and premium, their payout profiles at exercise would be as given in Figure 9.6.

Figure 9.5

Long futures payout profile

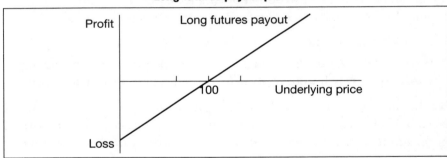

Figure 9.6

Synthetic long futures combined payout profile

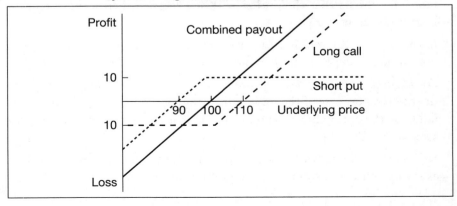

It can be seen that the combination of a long call and short put generates the same payout profile as a long futures position. This, in fact, is a common trading strategy known as *synthetic long futures*. It follows that if we know the futures and call prices, the put premium can be derived from the formula:

Put–call parity

$C - P = S - K$

where:

C and P are the call and put premiums

S is the futures price

K is the exercise price/option strike.

This concept has very important implications for option pricing. As will be seen in the following sections, the analytical model for option pricing gives the value of a call option; hence using the above expression, the value of the corresponding put option can be calculated. Alternatively, it can be used for hedging purposes to generate a zero net position. If a counterparty is long futures, to hedge they would sell a call and buy a put. For short futures positions a reverse hedge would be constructed.

This basic put–call parity formula can be extended to various types of futures contracts:

Put–call parity

Physically settled options:

$C - P = S - Ke^{-rt}$

where:

r is the continuously compounded interest rate

t is time to expiry expressed as $\dfrac{\text{days}}{\text{year}}$.

Options on dividend-paying stocks:

$C - P = S - Ke^{-rt} - D$

where D is the present value of expected dividend.

Options on stock index (dividend yield continuous):

$C - P = Se^{-dt} - Ke^{-rt}$

where d is the continuously compounded dividend yield.

Cross-currency options:

$C - P = Se^{-ft} - Ke^{-rt}$

Calculation
Summary

where:

f is the continuously compounded foreign currency interest rate

S is the spot exchange rate.

Options on futures with up-front premiums:

$C - P = S - K$

Options on futures with margined premiums:

$C - P = Se^{-rt} - Ke^{-rt}$

OPTION VALUE SENSITIVITIES – 'OPTION GREEKS'

As stated earlier, the option premium is the function of five parameters:

- Price of underlying
- Strike/exercise price
- Volatility of underlying price
- Time to expiry
- Interest rates.

The sensitivity of the *theoretical option value* to each factor is given a Greek letter, hence the commonly used term 'Option Greeks', summarised in Table 9.1.

Table 9.1

Option price sensitivities – 'Greeks'

Options sensitivity to	Named as
Underlying	Delta
Changes in delta	Gamma
Volatility	Vega or kappa
Time decay	Theta
Interest rates	Rho

Delta

Delta is the option sensitivity to the value of the underlying. Its value represents by how much the option price changes for 1 unit change in the price of underlying. However, it can be interpreted in other, more practical ways:

- Delta is the rate of change of the option value with respect to underlying security. In other words, delta of 0.25 implies that for a price change of 1, the option value would change by 0.25.

- Delta is the theoretical number of futures required to hedge the option position. If delta is 0.25, a trader would need four futures to replicate the option's exposure.

- Delta is also a probability exercise. The option with 0.25 delta theoretically has a 25 per cent chance of expiring ITM.

The relationship between option contract and the underlying determines the sign of delta.

The holder of a long call benefits from a rise in the underlying value, i.e. the value of the call increases with the price, implying positive delta. The position of the call writer is the reverse.

The holder of a long put is adversely affected by the increase in the underlying price, as the value of put (and the probability of exercise) decreases, hence delta is negative. The opposite is true for the short put. This can be summarised as shown in Table 9.2.

Sign of option delta depending on the position type   Table 9.2

Option type	Sign of delta
Long call	+
Short call	–
Long put	–
Short put	+

The delta changes with the price of underlying as well as time decay. Deep ITM options approaching expiry have deltas approaching 1, as it is almost certain that they would be exercised. Conversely, delta for deep OTM options is close to 0. ATM options have delta around 0.5, as there is a 50 per cent chance of exercise.

Gamma

Gamma is the rate of delta change, i.e. by how much the delta changes for 1 unit change in the value of the underlying. To put this into real-life perspective, if option was akin to distance travelled, delta would be velocity and gamma acceleration.

Mathematically, delta is the first derivative of option value with respect to the underlying and gamma is the second derivative. Gamma is very important for hedging strategies. If a trader's position was delta neutral, but the option had high gamma, that would imply potential rapid change in delta, making the hedge only temporarily effective. The re-hedging would have to be done so frequently that it would become impractical and prohibitively expensive. To derive a new delta value when the underlying price increases, gamma is always added whether the long position is a call or a put, as the call becomes more ITM and the put more OTM and vice versa.

In summary:

Key Point
Long calls and puts have positive gamma.

Short calls and puts have negative gamma.

As discussed previously, deltas change most rapidly for ATM options close to expiry, as there is a 50–50 chance that the option will be exercised and even the slightest movement tips the balance from ITM to OTM position. That implies the highest gamma. Equally, deep ITM and OTM options are almost certain to remain that way; hence gamma is close to zero.

Vega

Vega (kappa or zeta) is the change in option price for a 1 per cent change in the market-implied volatility. Intuitively ATM options have the highest vega, but as the volatility increases their vegas are relatively unaffected. This is because the ATM option has a 50–50 chance of being exercised, regardless by how much the underlying moves one way or the other. However, the ITM and OTM positions have lower vegas, but as volatility increases, so does the vega. This is because the higher volatility could move even the deep ITM or OTM option in the opposite direction.

Key Point
Long calls and puts have positive vega.

Short calls and puts have negative vega.

Theta

Theta is the measure of change in option price for a time decay of one day. It is taken as absolute value, thus the value of theta is added or subtracted from the option premium, depending on the option type.

Key Point
Long calls and puts have negative theta.

Short calls and puts have positive theta.

Rho

Rho is the measure of option premium sensitivity to a 1 per cent change in interest rates. As the interest rates affect option values differently, depending on the option type (as seen earlier), a short summary of rho can only be reduced to:

Options whose value increases with interest rates have positive rho.

Options whose value decreases with interest rates have negative rho.

Key Point

In summary, the different contract types will have option sensitivities to all factors (see Table 9.3).

Option sensitivities depending on the contract type

Table 9.3

Position	Delta	Gamma	Vega	Theta
Long future	+	0	0	0
Short future	–	0	0	0
Long call	+	+	+	–
Short call	–	–	–	+
Long put	–	+	+	–
Short put	+	–	–	+

OPTION PRICING: PRACTICAL IMPLEMENTATION

Binomial trees vs. Black–Scholes

When pricing options two approaches can be taken: numerical (using binomial trees) and analytical (using the Black–Scholes equation). The Black–Scholes model revolutionised derivatives trading when the two scientists Fischer Black and Myron Scholes introduced it in their 1973 paper, 'The pricing of options and corporate liabilities'. It simplified the pricing process as the options premiums could be calculated instantly, compared to the numerical methods which could be time-consuming. It was originally intended for pricing stock options. However, its use has since been extended to encompass many other types of options, introducing many assumptions and approximations. Since both numerical and analytical methods have their pros and cons, both are included in this chapter.

Option pricing using binomial trees

Binomial trees are a numerical method used to price options. The technique is useful as it is easy to understand and to follow the pricing steps. The main characteristics of the trees are:

General principles

- Typically used to price options on an underlying variable (e.g. stock).
- Assume that the stock price movements consist of very small binary steps in very short time intervals. The time to maturity is divided into small intervals and at each interval the stock price can only go up or down by a predetermined amount. The probability of up and down movements is assigned.
- Since payoff at maturity is known, it can be calculated at each branch of the tree. We then work backwards to find the price of the option today.

Pros and cons

- Useful for pricing products where decisions can be made at each step (e.g. American options).
- Useful for pricing dividend paying stocks.
- Can price options on indices, currencies and futures contracts.
- Can vary variables (interest rates, volatility) between the tree nodes.
- Can be used in conjunction with *control variate* techniques. For example, we can calculate the European option price using the Black–Scholes formula and compare it with the price obtained from the binomial tree. Assuming that this is the error that tree introduces into pricing, we can then adjust the price of an American style option (obtained using the tree) by this amount.
- Can be easily extended to non-recombining trees, trees with more than up/down movements (e.g. trinomial trees have a mid-path as well).
- Time-consuming, computationally extensive.
- Not suitable for derivatives dependent on past history.

Pricing European options using binomial trees

Constructing the tree

Binomial trees are used to model the evolution of the stock price over time. The timeline until expiry is divided into a number of steps. At each step the price can either go up or down (hence the name binomial). The up and down moves have a probability assigned to them and at each move a certain price change is allowed. As we increase the number of time steps, we can reduce the size of the price movements.

For example, from today until one year later it is quite realistic that the stock price can move from 100 to 120 or 80. If we divide the year into monthly intervals, then we can say that each month the price should not rise/fall by more than 2. Reducing the steps even further to one day or one hour, we will build a quite realistic picture of the price movements, but by now we will have too many steps to cope with. For illustration purposes, we will have only two steps in our tree. The terminology is the same as in Chapter 13 on probability and statistics:

- p is the probability of an upward move
- 1 − p is the probability of downward move
- u is the amount by which the price moves up
- d is the amount by which the price moves down.

The above quantities can be calculated using the current market conditions: volatility of the stock price and the forward stock price. This is to ensure that we are pricing the option fairly, i.e. in the risk-neutral way.

The probability weighted forward price that we are calculating must be equal to the current market forward price:

Probability-weighted stock price   **Calculation Summary**

$$S \times u \times p + S \times d \times (1 - p) = fwd(S)$$

As fwd(S) is equal to $S \times e^{rt}$ where r is the risk-free interest rate, we have:

$$u \times p + d \times (1 - p) = e^{rt} = R$$

hence

$$p = (R - d)/(u - d)$$

From the market volatility we can calculate the up and down price movements as:

$$u = e^{\sigma \sqrt{t}} \text{ and } d = 1/u$$

The above equations are sufficient for calculation of u, d and p. Knowing them, we can begin the tree construction.

Example

In this example the price of the long call position is calculated. As it is easier to use round figures (which does not happen often using market values) we will assume the following:

p = 0.6	u = 1.1	d = 0.9
S = 100	r = 10%	X = 110

The stock price tree is as follows:

Period	today	6 mth	1 year	Option payout
Fwd	100	105	110	
			D 121	11
		B 110		
	A 100		E 99	0
		C 90		
			F 81	0

The probability of reaching D is the probability of moving up and then up again, i.e. $0.6 \times 0.6 = 0.36$. For E we can go up and down or down and up, hence $0.6 \times 0.4 = 0.24$ and so on.

The probability tree will look like:

		D 0.36
	B 0.6	
A 1		E 0.24 (× 2)
	C 0.4	
		F 0.16
1	1	1

(all probabilities must add up to 1!)

Below are three different methods of calculating the option price.

Method 1

As the option can only be exercised at expiry, we are only interested in its value at the end of one year.

The intrinsic value of the option at each node will be calculated as the option payout multiplied by the probability of reaching that node. For a call option, its payout is equal to $\max(S - X, 0)$, or for the three nodes D, E and F:

Point	Payout	× Probability	= Option Value
D	11	0.36	3.96
E	0	0.48	0
F	0	0.16	0
Total:			3.96
PV:			3.6

Therefore today's price of the one-year call option with strike £100 is £3.6.

Method 2

This method is used most often when option prices are calculated. It works backwards from the expiry node by node until we reach today. The payout profile and the probability tree are the same as above.

We already know the value of the option at expiry (D, E and F). Moving backwards, we will calculate values at B and C and then from those values, the final (today's) option price at node A.

Node B

From B we can either go up to D or down to E, hence the option value at B must be equal to the probability-weighted average of the values at D and E discounted back:

B = (0.6 × 11 + 0.4 × 0)/1.05 = 6.286

Similarly for C we have:

C = (0.6 × 0 + 0.4 × 0)/1.05 = 0

Using the above, for A we have:

A = (0.6 × 6.286 + 0.4 × 0)/1.05 = 3.59

So the option price today is £3.59. The small difference between the two results is in the fact that we used a 10 per cent annual rate in the first one, and in the second 5 per cent for each six-month period, which when compounded adds up to 10.25 per cent. This was done for the simplicity of the illustration.

Method 3

This method is known as the hedge ratio method, as it calculates the ratio of the change in the option price vs. stock price. The hedge ratio has to be calculated at every step of the tree. This means that it has to be calculated for nodes B, C and A. Just for the illustration of the method we will ignore the intermediate steps and assume that we go from today to expiry in a single step. We can see that the maximum difference in share price is 40, whilst for option payout it is 11. Therefore to cancel out gains and losses we would need 11/40 shares for every option sold. This is a *hedge ratio* and can be written as:

Option pricing hedge ratio

Calculation Summary

$$h = \frac{C_u - C_d}{S_u - S_d}$$

where C_u, C_d, S_u and S_d are the call payout if the price goes up or down, and the stock value for the price up and down respectively.

To see if our hedge works, we buy 11 shares and sell 40 call options:

	Today	At expiry	
	S = 100	S = 121	S = 81
	C = ?	C = 11	C = 0
Write 40 calls	40C	– 440	0
Buy 11 shares	–1100	1331	891
		891	891

This means that we have 891 no matter how the market moves, i.e. what we own today (11 shares + 40 calls) has to be equal to the PV of £891. This method is also referred to as *risk-neutral pricing*, as we are neutral to the movements in the underlying. Hence, given that our stock is valued at 1100 and we have purchased 40 calls, to retain the risk-neutral position we can calculate the price of call as:

1100 – 40C = 891/1.1; C = 4.75

We can see that the price does not quite agree with the previous methods. This is partly due to the removal of the intermediate steps, but also because we did not use the *probability of up and down moves*. In the original examples, upward moves had a higher probability, whilst this method implicitly assumes a 50–50 chance of any move, hence the difference in valuation.

The above equations can be written mathematically as:

Calculation Summary

Pricing options using hedge ratio

$$(hS - C)e^{rt} = hS_u - C_u = hS_d - C_d$$

where hedge ratio is calculated as:

$$h = \frac{C_u - C_d}{S_u - S_d}$$

Pricing American style options

The difference between American and European style options is that the former can be exercised at any time, whilst for the latter we have to wait until expiry. It can be shown that it is rarely optimal to exercise options early, i.e. only if the value of the option is less than the price realised on early exercise. Hence the pricing approach is the same as above, using any of the three methods, whereby at each node, *the higher of the two calculated prices* (market value and option intrinsic value) is used in the lattice.

Valuing other options

Valuation of other types of options (dividend paying stock options, cross-currency options etc.) is done in a similar way to that just described. The tree is built in the same way, but the probabilities and hedge ratios have to be slightly adjusted.

Dividend paying stock options

$$p = \frac{e^{rt-yt} - d}{u - d}$$

Alternatively, if we use the hedge ratio, the mathematical formula becomes:

$$(hS - C)\, e^{rt} = hS_u - C_u + hS_u\,(e^{yt} - 1) = hS_u\,e^{yt} - C_u$$

Cross-currency options

$$p = \frac{e^{r_d t - r_i t} - d}{u - d}$$

Similarly, in the hedge ratio formula, yield will be replaced by the foreign currency interest rate r_f.

Black–Scholes model

The Black–Scholes (B–S) model and its variants have become very popular, as with only one formula we can replicate the very time-consuming construction of a binomial tree. The most basic B–S formula relates to pricing European options on non-dividend-paying stocks. As such, it has little practical use in pricing interest rate derivatives. However, many interest-rate-based products can be priced using a slight modification of B–S (Black model, briefly described below), because the model does not allow early exercise, and if that is the case interest rates are assumed to behave as tradable assets.

The B–S model is expressed by the following formula:

Black–Scholes model   **Calculation Summary**

$$c = SN(d_1) - Xe^{-rt}N(d_2)$$

where:

$$d_1 = \frac{\ln(S/X) + \left(r + 0.5\sigma^2\right)t}{\sigma\sqrt{t}}$$

$$d_2 = d_1 - \sigma\sqrt{t}$$

where:

S = underlying stock/share price

X = exercise price

r = annual continuously compounded risk-free rate

t = time (in years)

σ = annual stock price volatility

N(d) = cumulative probabilities that the deviations less than d will occur in an normal distribution with a mean of 0 and standard deviation of 1

$N(d_1)$ = probability of the stock price rising to a certain level

$N(d_2)$ = probability of the stock price rising above the strike (but it is irrelevant by how much).

These are the main assumptions that restrict the usage of the B–S model:

1. The underlying asset does not pay dividends or accrue interest.
2. The option is European style (no early exercise).
3. The risk-free interest rate is constant over the life of the option.
4. Spot movements on different dates are independent.
5. The volatility of the asset price is constant over the life of the option.
6. There is very low probability of large spot movements.
7. The underlying asset price is log-normally distributed.
8. There are no costs/taxes and trading is continuous.
9. Short selling of securities (selling securities that are not owned at inception) is permitted.

The above assumptions are discussed in more detail below:

1. The underlying asset does not pay dividends or accrue interest

This is easily overcome by reducing the stock price by the present value of dividends. Alternatively, dividends can be converted into a yield on stock, and the stock price discounted using this yield.

2. The option is European style (no early exercise)

This is generally not a restriction, as it is rarely optimal to exercise early. However, early exercise on dividend-paying stock entitles the holder to dividends, thus their value may exceed the time value of the option. Early exercise may also be optimal in cross-currency options, where lower yielding currency is converted into a higher-yielding one, as higher yield may compensate for the loss of optionality.

3. The risk-free interest rate is constant over the life of the option

The assumption of constant rates has a twofold effect on the option value; it affects the option premium and some underlying assets such as currencies and bonds.

As discussed earlier, the interest rate effect on the option premium (*rho*) depends on the type of option:

Options on physicals (e.g. stocks)

CALL	Rho +
PUT	Rho −

Options on futures (premiums paid up-front)

CALL	Rho −
PUT	Rho −

Options on futures (premiums margined)

CALL	Rho = 0
PUT	Rho = 0

Options on physicals (e.g. stocks)
A seller of a call will typically hedge the position by buying stock. In the increasing interest rate environment, the cost of financing the purchase will rise, increasing the call premiums. A seller of a put would short sell some stock as a hedge strategy. Due to the increased interest rates the money received can be reinvested at higher rate, reducing the put premiums. The dividend payments until expiry are captured by reducing the stock price by the present value of dividends. This is reflected in the Black–Scholes formula:

Black–Scholes for options on physicals **Calculation Summary**

$$C = SN(d_1) - Xe^{-rt}N(d_2)$$

Options on futures (premiums paid up-front)
Options on futures are exchange-traded products, hence the rules of the exchange specify if the option premiums are to be paid up-front or margined daily. As options on futures are cash-settled, there is no delivery or cost of carry. If the premium is paid in advance, the increase in interest rates will result in reduced PV of the option premium. Therefore for both calls and puts the option price declines with the rise in interest rates. The Black–Scholes formula is modified to:

Calculation Summary

Black–Scholes for options on futures (premiums paid up-front)

$$C = Fe^{-rt}N(d_1) - Xe^{-rt}N(d_2)$$

Options on futures (premiums margined)

If the exchange rules specify that the option positions are to be margined, the interest rate fluctuations do not affect the option position. The daily margins paid/received directly reflect interest rate movements; hence both call and put premiums are unaffected. The Black–Scholes formula is modified to:

Calculation Summary

Black–Scholes for options on futures (premiums margined)

$$C = FN(d_1) - XN(d_2)$$

Currency options

In currency options, the foreign currency is treated similarly to dividends in stock options; any increase in its value reduces the value of calls and increases the values of puts. The effect of domestic currency is always the opposite. The Black–Scholes formula is modified to:

Calculation Summary

Black–Scholes for currency options

$$C = Se^{-r_f t}N(d_1) - Xe^{-r_d t}N(d_2)$$

The interest rate effect on the value of the underlying asset is an asset valuation issue, rather than an option pricing issue. However, the value of the interest rate derivatives (e.g. swaptions) is affected by both the option and the asset valuation. Here rates are typically taken to be stochastic for the purpose of asset valuation, whilst for discounting purposes they are taken to be deterministic. Even though this is incorrect, in practice discounting is done at a financing rate for the purpose of P&L calculation. Since the cost of funds is typically fixed, the use of deterministic yields is not entirely wrong.

4. Spot movements on different dates are independent

It is likely that there is a relationship between the moves in stock prices from one day to the next. However, in the efficient markets, any trends are quickly eliminated, hence this assumption is deemed insignificant.

5. The volatility of the asset price is constant over the life of the option

This is an unrealistic simplification, as most stocks have periods of high and low activity (ultimately when markets are closed the volatility is zero). Thus constant volatility assumption results in options being under- or overvalued at some points over the option lifetime. However, if constant volatility is assumed to be equal to the weighted average of the volatilities over the lifetime of the stock, it will yield correct option valuation.

6. There is very low probability of large spot movements

The probability distribution function implicit in the B–S formula does not assign enough probability to large price movements. Hence implied volatility is not consistent across the option strikes; it increases for ITM and OTM options, creating a smile effect. This anomaly is well known in the market and various skew/smile adjustments exist to counteract this problem.

7. The underlying asset price is log-normally distributed

The log-normal distribution is very intuitive way to model asset prices, as it does not allow negative prices and it places equal probability on the price halving as for it doubling. However, log-normal distribution does not allow for bond pull-to-par (bond prices approach the redemption value as the redemption date gets nearer). Furthermore, it does not allow for mean reversion in interest rate derivatives products (interest rates will eventually converge to a long-term mean). This cannot be overcome by the B–S itself, but various modifications (such as pre-processing the input parameters to introduce the mean reversion variable) are typically done.

8. There are no costs/taxes and trading is continuous

The effect of costs and taxes can be easily overcome by modifying the stock price (as those costs will be known). This only becomes an issue in high gamma scenarios when costs of frequent re-hedging can be prohibitively large.

Continuous trading/hedging is impossible; hence the response to any large market movements can take time. Hedging is also done only periodically in order to save on transaction costs. Those assumptions cannot easily be dealt with and the best way is to have a prudent reserve in place that would account for potential closeout losses.

9. Short selling of securities is permitted

Short selling (selling 'naked options' without holding the underlying) is not available to all market participants. Hence this assumption does not take into account the cost of carry (transaction costs and expenses related to holding a position in the underlying). This may be accounted for through bid/offer spreads or additional reserves.

Black model

The Black model was developed for pricing interest rate derivatives. It is a slight modification of the original B–S model, thus all the assumptions and limitations of B–S still apply. Interest rates are not tradable assets. However, if the options are carried until maturity they can be valued in the same way as stock options.

By analogy with the B-S formula, the value of a call option is given by:

<table>
<tr><td>Calculation Summary</td><td>Black model for interest rate derivatives</td></tr>
</table>

$$c = FN(d_1) - R_x N(d_2)$$

where:

$$d_1 = \frac{\ln(F/R_x) + \sigma^2(t)/2}{\sigma\sqrt{t}}$$

$$d_2 = d_1 - \sigma\sqrt{t}$$

where F is the current market forward swap rate, and R_x is the underlying swap rate (option strike). All other variables have the same meaning as before.

The above formula is used to price vanilla caps and floors (calls and puts on the underlying interest rate), described in Chapter 12.

Bond and equity derivatives

INTRODUCTION TO BOND DERIVATIVES

In Chapter 4 on capital markets instruments, we covered bonds as a primary source of long-term funding. However, they also play a very important role in interest rate derivatives markets. They are traded both on recognised exchanges and OTC. Typical exchange-traded bond derivatives are bond futures and bond options. Various types of options and repos (repurchase agreements) are traded OTC.

Pricing bond futures

A bond futures contract is an obligation to buy/deliver a specific amount of precisely defined bond at a future date at a price agreed today. The contract can be taken to delivery, or closed out before maturity, just like other interest rate futures positions. However, the buyer can insist on bond delivery, which hugely complicates the bond futures pricing.

In practice, if a particular market-traded bond was specified for delivery, as various contracts expire, it would be possible that there wouldn't be enough of that bond to fulfil all obligations. Hence, a *notional bond* paying fixed coupon and of medium maturity is typically used. The exact particulars of each notional bond are specific to each futures contract and the exchange it is traded on.

As the seller cannot deliver a fictional bond, he must choose from a range of bonds allowed for delivery under the futures contract. These bonds are called *deliverable bonds*. The range of deliverable bonds will include contracts of different coupons and maturities; hence some common comparison criteria are required. Each exchange thus provides a list of deliverable bonds with their respective *conversion factors* that make their yields equal to the notional bond coupon.

> **Key Point**
>
> Conversion factor = Deliverable bond clean unit price at which its yield is equal to the notional bond coupon

At futures expiry, the futures price will be equal to EDSP (exchange delivery settlement price), hence the amount of bond to be delivered is:

> **Calculation Summary**
>
> Deliverable bond
>
> $$= \text{Face value} \times \left(\frac{\text{EDSP}}{100} \times \text{Conversion factor} + \text{Accrued coupon} \right)$$

Even though the Exchange aims to bring all the deliverable bonds to the common basis, it only publishes conversion factors periodically. Hence, at the time of delivery, it may be more favourable to deliver one bond over another, a concept known as 'cheapest to deliver' or CTD. The CTD bond changes with yield; when yields fall the bonds with lower duration (time until the receipt of half of the bond cashflows) become cheaper to deliver, as their prices rise less and vice versa.

Bond futures are priced using the no-arbitrage concept. Assuming that the bond will be delivered at maturity, the futures seller needs to hedge his position by buying a particular deliverable bond now. He needs to fund this purchase (cash bond price + the accrued coupon) at current prevailing interest rates. The further coupons received until maturity can be invested. Any profit/loss on the futures position is captured through the variation margin. Thus all the cashflows arising from holding the bond until delivery must be equal to the futures bond price, otherwise there would be potential for arbitrage. This can be summarised as:

$$\text{Bond futures price} = \frac{(\text{Bond price } + \text{ Accrued coupon now}) \times \left(1 + i \times \frac{\text{days}}{\text{year}}\right)}{\text{Conversion factor}}$$

$$- \frac{(\text{Accrued coupon at delivery } + \text{ Intervening coupon reinvested})}{\text{Conversion factor}}$$

Calculation Summary

The first part of the above equation refers to the funding of the initial bond purchase, whilst the second relates to the coupon cashflows. Since the futures buyer does not receive any paid and accrued coupons until delivery, this is deducted from the theoretical price.

The above formula is used by traders to calculate CTD bond.

Forward bond prices are calculated in the same way as the futures prices. However, forward contracts are obligations to deliver a particular, rather than a notional bond; hence there is no conversion factor.

$$\text{Forward bond price} = (\text{Bond price } + \text{ Accrued coupon now}) \times \left(1 + i \times \frac{\text{days}}{\text{year}}\right)$$

$$- (\text{Accrued coupon at delivery } + \text{ Intervening coupon reinvested})$$

Calculation Summary

Pricing repos

Repos are transactions where a transaction undertaken now is reversed in the future. In the bond market, they involve purchase/sale of a bond now and sale/purchase at a future date.

The nominal amount of the bond is the same at inception and maturity, whilst the payment at maturity incorporates interest incurred on the loan. The motivation behind this trade is either the need to borrow funds or to acquire a specific security. This is similar to a capital market loan, but as the bond is used as collateral, better rates are achieved.

The terminology used in repo transactions is opposite to that of the cash market, the *repo lender* is the seller of the security (borrower of cash), whilst the *repo borrower* is the investor, acquiring the security in exchange for cash. The standard repo transacton at inception and maturity is graphically represented in Figure 10.1, where the bank has the role of repo lender.

| Figure 10.1 | **Graphical representation of bond repo cashflows** |

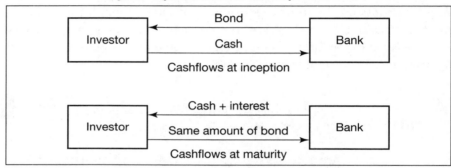

Repos are valued in two parts: the initial exchange (leg) is calculated using the prevailing bond price plus accrued interest, and the reverse transaction is based on the initial leg value increased by the repo rate. This can be summarised as:

Calculation Summary

Initial repo price = Nominal bond amount × (Clean price + Accrued coupon)/100

$$\text{Repo price at maturity} = \text{Initial repo price} \times \left(1 + r \times \frac{\text{days}}{\text{year}}\right)$$

where r is the repo rate and days refer to number of days until maturity.

Pricing bond options

A bond option gives the buyer the right but not the obligation to acquire/deliver a bond at a future date for a price agreed today. The underlying security is a nominal bond with specific coupon and maturity. Pricing of various option types was discussed in the previous chapter. However, the Black–Scholes model cannot be applied directly to bond securities because of the pull-to-par effect (the bond price converges to its redemption amount at maturity). As the maturity date approaches, the factors impacting on the bond price become known with increasing certainty, thereby decreasing its volatility. This is not incorporated into the Black–Scholes model. The Black model (described in Chapter 9) addresses this problem.

Using the Black formula, the value of a bond call option is given by:

Black model for bond options Calculation Summary

$$c = BN(d_1) - B_x N(d_2)$$

where:

$$d_1 = \frac{\ln(B/B_x) + \sigma^2(t)/2}{\sigma\sqrt{t}}$$

$$d_2 = d_1 - \sigma\sqrt{t}$$

where B is the forward bond price and B_x is the underlying bond price (option strike); all other variables have the same meaning as before.

Using the put–call parity principle, the value of the put option can be derived from the value of the bond call option and the bond future price.

In most major exchanges there are option contracts on bond futures. They are priced using the Black model. The put–call parity formula is given by:

Put-call parity for bond options Calculation Summary

$$C - P = Fe^{-rt} N(d_1) - Ke^{-rt} N(d_2)$$

where:

F is the futures price

K is the exercise price/option strike

r is the continuously compounded interest rate.

BACKGROUND ON EQUITY MARKETS

Equities are commonly thought of as *stocks* (American term) and *shares* (European term) in large corporations. A private corporation that requires funding may transact in cash or capital markets; whilst a public company, listed on an exchange, can sell shares in the *stock market*, also known as the *equity market*. This provides funding, but at a price. Shareholders become owners of the company and participate in company policy decisions and

Board of Directors elections. They also share profits/losses proportionate to the number of shares they hold. For an investor shares may seem an attractive prospect, but they do not guarantee returns. Returns on shares, known as *dividends*, are only payable if a company is in profit. If the investment proves unprofitable, the shares have to be sold in the secondary market, as there is no redemption or maturity date. The secondary market for single-company shares is illiquid and the price achieved may not be favourable. Small investor transactions also incur brokerage fees (as exchanges are open only to their members), reducing the profits even further.

Equity indices vs. single stocks

Shares are transacted in the equity market that comprises many different sectors, each with many listed companies. An investment in shares in a single company is affected by the performance of that company alone; i.e. even if the market overall is on the rise, the company may be performing badly and no dividends are paid. Hence larger investors tend to manage diversified portfolios of shares in different sectors, hoping that by spreading the risk they will make an overall profit. They will measure the performance of the portfolio, rather than be concerned about individual shares. This concept can be extended further to measure the performance of the equity market as a whole.

    The equity index or *stock index* mirrors the price movements of a hypothetical equity portfolio. The equities participating in the index are chosen and weighted by their market capitalisation. Thus typically only the biggest market performers are included in the index and the weighting ensures that their share price movements influence the index value proportionately. There are many equity indices in the world, each tracking the performance of the equity market in a particular country or industry sector. The main ones are listed in Table 10.1.

Stock baskets

As all the major indices are based on hypothetical portfolios with many underlying equities, they are used as a measure of overall market performance. Individual investors wishing to take a view on the equity market would find it impractical and expensive to transact in all shares comprising an index. An alternative approach is to construct a 'basket' of shares that would replicate the index performance with a minimum number of shares. Such portfolios are called 'index trackers'. It can be shown that holding 20 uncorrelated shares in the basket tracks the index with a 10 per cent error margin. This number can be further reduced by careful share selection. Investment banks leave that job to quantitative analysts who develop 'equity basket' mathematical models. Thus an individual investor stands very little chance of making an optimal selection.

Major equity indices

Table 10.1

Country	Index	Underlying equity
UK	FT-SE 100	Financial Times–Stock Exchange 100 Index: includes top 100 companies by market capitalisation
	FT 30	Financial Times Ordinary Share: includes top 30 companies by market capitalisation
USA	DJIA	Dow Jones Industrial Average: includes top 30 blue-chip companies by market capitalisation listed on the New York Stock Exchange
	NYSE	New York Stock Exchange Composite Index: includes shares in all companies listed on the New York Stock Exchange
	S&P 500	Standard & Poor's 500 Index: includes top 500 companies by market capitalisation
France	CAC 40	Compagne des Agents de Change 40 Index: includes 40 of the top 100 companies by market capitalisation listed on the 'forward' section of Paris Bourse
Germany	DAX	Deutsche Akten Index: includes top 30 blue-chip companies by market capitalisation
Japan	Nikkei 225	Includes top 225 blue-chip Japanese companies by market capitalisation listed on Tokyo Stock Exchange
Hong Kong	Hang Seng	Includes top 33 companies by market capitalisation

Note: All indices apart from Nikkei are based on equity prices weighted by market capitalisation.

Baskets can be constructed to mirror index behaviour, or to speculate with the intention to outperform the market. Speculative portfolios would typically involve several high-volatility stocks that would allow for larger exposure compared to the index.

Trading in equity markets can be prohibitively expensive, or simply unsuitable for an investor's needs. As with all other securities markets, an alternative is to trade equity derivatives. Those are off-balance sheet instruments that provide exposure to equity markets without actually owning the shares. The most commonly traded instruments are equity futures, equity options and swaps. As all other futures contracts, equity futures are exchange-traded only and are subject to same restrictions and regulations. Equity options can be traded OTC, but the market is very limited, whilst equity swaps are traded OTC only.

Stock index futures

A stock index future is a contract between two counterparties to compensate each other for the movement in the underlying equity index between the futures trade date and the settlement date. As the index is just a number, not a monetary value, in order to have practical implementations each index is assigned a monetary amount for each point of movement. This is known as an *index multiplier*. Hence, unlike other types of futures, equity futures contracts do not have specific contract sizes, as the value of the contract varies daily with index level and is calculated as:

Calculation Summary	Equity index futures contract size = Index level × Index multiplier

Whether a futures contract is bought or sold depends on the view of the equity market; if the investor believes that the index value will rise, he will buy the future and vice versa. Most contracts are closed out before maturity by reversing the position. Even if the future is taken to expiry, no actual shares are delivered. The difference between the futures value and the EDSP is settled. Like all other exchange-traded products, equity futures are margined, thus all but the last day's price movements are captured through variation margin payments.

Equity futures contracts follow the same cycle as all other futures: March, June, September and December. But unlike interest rate futures that offer several years of cover, only the nearest three contracts are available for trading, with most activity in the first one.

The market participants who use equity futures are typically portfolio managers, pension funds, fund managers and other equity holders. They may transact in futures to hedge their portfolio or to speculate on market moves. To calculate how many futures a hedge requires the following formula is used:

Calculation Summary	$$\text{Number of futures contracts} = \frac{\text{Portfolio value}}{\text{Equity index} \times \text{Index multiplier}}$$

The futures settlement price is calculated as:

$$\text{Settlement amount} = \text{Number of contracts} \times \text{Equity index movement} \times \text{Index multiplier}$$

The calculation of futures price follows the same logic as for any other futures contract:

Theoretical futures price = Cash price + Net cost of carry

where:

Cash price = Index level × Index multiplier

Net cost of carry = Funding cost − Dividend income

This can be summarised as:

Calculation Summary

$$\text{Futures price} = \text{Index level} \times \text{Index multiplier} \times \left(1 + i \times \frac{\text{days}}{\text{year}} - d \times \frac{\text{days}}{\text{year}}\right)$$

where:

i is the annual funding rate

d is the dividend yield on underlying equity.

Stock beta

Constructing a portfolio that would exactly replicate the index performance is not easy; thus a hedge using an equity index future will be imperfect, as the two values will move out of line. Stock beta gives a measure of individual stock volatility compared to the index. It is assigned by the exchange to each listed equity and the information is disseminated through the market information network. The portfolio beta is then derived as a capital-participation weighted average of individual share betas, i.e.:

Calculation Summary

$$\text{Portfolio beta} = \sum \frac{\beta_i \times V_i}{V_P}$$

where:

β_i is the individual equity beta

V_i is the individual equity share value

V_P is the total value of the portfolio.

Incorporating beta into the hedging strategy changes the amount of futures that need to be bought to:

$$\text{Beta-weighted number of futures contracts} = \frac{\text{Portfolio value} \times \beta}{\text{Equity index} \times \text{Index multiplier}}$$

An important point has to be made here. Betas are used to track the performance of a particular portfolio to an index. The index is a very close representative of the overall market performance, but at times it may move out of line with the market as a whole. This may cause problems to portfolio managers who are required to pay inflation-linked pensions or other instruments linked to the country's economy. They may deliberately choose not to track the index perfectly but to include some more volatile stocks, hoping that the potential increased profit will provide the sufficient tracking-error margin.

Stock index options

As the OTC market for equity index options is very limited, this section will concentrate on exchange-traded options.

The stock index option gives the holder the right but not the obligation to buy/sell a specified amount of the equity index (index level × index multiplier) at or before a specified future date. The premium is paid upfront and the contract is cash-settled, i.e. the equities underlying the index are not delivered. As with all option contracts, the option buyer chooses the option strike; in this case, the specific index level. This influences the required premium due, which is quoted as index points. Its monetary amount is based on the index multiplier, which is exchange-specific and may be different to the one used for futures contracts. The same principles underlying all exchange-traded products and the characteristics of option contracts discussed in previous chapters still apply.

Call option valuation is typically done using the Black–Scholes formula:

Calculation Summary

Black–Scholes for equity index options

$$C = Se^{-dt}N(d_1) - Ke^{-rt}N(d_2)$$

where the dividend yield d is assumed to be paid continuously.

The put price is then calculated using put–call parity:

> **Put–call parity for equity index options**
>
> $$C - P = Se^{-dt} - Ke^{-rt}$$

Single stock options

Single stock options are contracts that give the holder the right but not the obligation to buy/sell a specified amount of the underlying equity at a price agreed today on or before a specified future date. The premium is paid up-front and the contract is *physically settled*, i.e. the equity shares are delivered. They provide a useful tool for portfolio diversification, both for hedging and speculating purposes. The equities underlying exchange-traded options are specific to each exchange. The options positions can be closed out before expiry by reversing the transaction. This is the common practice of speculators, who trade for profit only and do not require the actual shares. The same principles underlying all exchange-traded products and the characteristics of option contracts discussed in previous chapters still apply.

Call option valuation is typically done using the Black–Scholes formula:

> **Black–Scholes for single stock options**
>
> $$C = SN(d_1) - Ke^{-rt}N(d_2)$$
>
> where dividend payments until expiry are captured by reducing the stock price by the present value of dividends. This is known as the 'known dividend model'.

The put price is then calculated using put–call parity:

> **Put–call parity for dividend-paying single stocks**
>
> $$C - P = S - D - Ke^{-rt}$$
>
> where D is the present value of expected dividend.

Different strategies, discussed in Appendix 1, can be used depending on the client's view of the stock market. For example, hedgers who believe that the prices of the stock they already hold will not fluctuate by much can take advantage of the 'covered call' strategy, i.e. they will sell calls on stocks they already have. The strike price is set above the current share price. If the stock value declines, the option will be abandoned and the premium income will provide a level of downward protection. If the price increases below the exercise level, the portfolio profits both from the market move and the full premium income. Only in the event of an unexpectedly large increase in the share price is the fund manager's strategy less profitable than the underlying position. This can be seen in Figure 10.2.

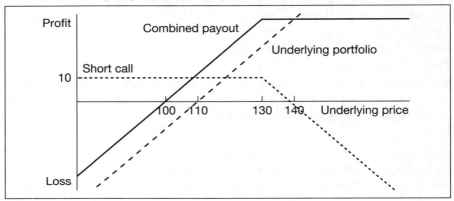

Figure 10.2

Payout profile of stock option covered call strategy

Equity index swaps

An equity index swap is an OTC contract between two counterparties to exchange cashflows at regular intervals for a time period where at least one leg is based on the percentage change in the value of a chosen equity index. The second leg, if not derived from stock index value, is typically related to a floating interest rate, such as Libor. The swap is based on a notional principal and is cash-settled (see Figure 10.3).

Figure 10.3

Graphical representation of equity index swap

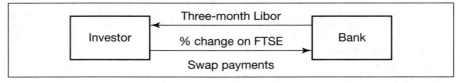

Equity index swaps are very useful investment tools for market participants that find it impractical or impossible to trade equities directly. Some of the main characteristics are discussed below:

Cash settlement reduces the counterparty risk, as no principals are exchanged.

Synthetic stock market investment is implicit in the swap; the exchange of interest rate cashflows for index tracking creates *stock market exposure* without actually having to buy stocks.

Cost of carry is eliminated; as stocks are not bought, there is no requirement to pay costs associated with holding shares (stamp duty, taxes etc.).

Income enhancement for fund managers who hold equities they believe will depreciate is provided by a swap of equity index into a floating interest rate or other type of cashflow.

Exposure to foreign index that otherwise may not be permissible is synthetically generated by a swap of domestic index movements for foreign index fluctuations.

Portfolio management burdens are eliminated by entering into a swap, as the responsibility is passed to the swap issuer. The portfolio manager can in this way stabilise portfolio returns without the need to change its underlying components.

Equity index swaps are priced using the same principles as other swap types, i.e. based on the concept that the NPV of both legs of the swap has to be equal at inception. More details were provided in Chapter 7.

Equity index swap valuation

PV(Swap) = PV(equity index leg) − PV(floating leg) = 0

Commodity and credit derivatives

BACKGROUND ON COMMODITY DERIVATIVES

Contracts for delivery of commodities at a future date were the pioneers of the derivatives market. The early agreements typically guaranteed the delivery of agricultural products (coffee, cocoa, grain, cotton etc.), nowadays known as 'soft' commodities. Present-day derivatives markets typically trade in contracts with energy (oil, gas and related products), bullion (precious metals) and base metals (copper, zinc, aluminium, nickel, lead and tin) as underlying securities. The major exchanges where derivatives are traded are the International Petroleum Exchange (IPE) in London, New York Mercantile Exchange (NYMEX) and Singapore International Monetary Exchange (SIMEX). Energy derivatives are the largest both by market capitalisation and trade volume; hence the sections below will be devoted to their uses and applications.

Exchange-traded commodity futures

Commodity futures are exchange-traded only. They are obligations between two counterparties to take or make delivery of a precisely defined *quantity and quality* of underlying commodity at the price agreed today at a specified future date. The counterparties may choose to settle the difference between the futures price and the prevailing market price at expiry in cash, rather than opt for physical delivery. The statement above has one major difference compared to the definitions of other futures contacts. The *quality* as well as quantity of security is precisely defined. As commodities are physical assets, unlike other previously discussed securities, it is vital that both parties understand what is actually being delivered. If an investor was paying for a brand-new BMW to be delivered in the future, he/she would not accept delivery of a run-down Ford Fiesta. Thus the contact specification cannot simply say 'a car', it has to be precisely defined. However, the quality of most exchange-traded commodities varies from one period to the next, due to natural variability. To try and minimise this variation, energy derivatives allow only a small range of deliverable assets. For example, oil derivatives are based on a small number of crudes, the most widely known being Brent Crude – a mixture from 19 oil fields.

The energy futures market is growing rapidly. At present the amount of futures traded in the market is more than 50 times larger than the level of physical production. This demonstrates how the trading practice changed over the years, from participants wishing to guarantee the price at delivery to those who simply trade for profit.

As with all other futures contracts, energy futures are legally binding agreements to take or make delivery of a specified quantity of a specific product cargo at a future date at a price agreed today on the recognised commodity exchange. The quantity of the product is a multiple of contract sizes specified by the exchange and they are typically cash-settled rather than delivered (if that weren't the case most of the contracts couldn't exist, as there simply isn't enough physical production to fulfil all outstanding obligations). Energy futures have different contract cycle and roll-over dates compared to other futures. There are 12 consecutive delivery months following the present month and the trading ceases at the end of the last business day before the 15th of the month.

At delivery/expiry date the futures contract is settled either by physically delivering the underlying, or the difference between the futures price and the prevailing spot market price is cash-settled. Due to the variation in margin payments, all but the last day's profits/losses are already incorporated into counterparty positions.

Pricing energy derivatives is extremely complex. Unlike interest rate and equity markets, energy markets respond to an excessive number of factors; from production and usage, extraction and refinement, transfer and storage, to market supply and demand, to name just a few. They are affected not just by economic cycles, but also by *seasonality*. For example, demand for heating fuel falls in spring and summer, whilst the use of electrical air-conditioners increases. Another important factor is *convenience yield*. The end users of energy are actually physically burning fuel; they cannot stop their plants and wait around for a better price. Thus energy prices often exhibit premiums in the cash market over the forward market, unobserved in other sectors. The energy derivative prices have to factor in all the characteristics of the underlying commodity as well as the 'usual' parameters influencing the standard derivative securities. None of the standard quantitative approaches can seamlessly capture the wide range of energy price drivers; hence their valuation is outside scope of this book.

Exchange-traded commodity options

An *energy option* gives the holder the right but not the obligation to buy/sell an agreed number of *energy futures contracts* at a price agreed today at or before a date in the future. These are in fact options with an underlying derivative, rather than an asset. A long option position will on exercise result in a long futures position and vice versa. The futures contract, however, will not be taken to expiry; it will be cash-settled immediately. As exchange-traded energy options are American style, most will be exercised or closed out before expiry. The exchange automatically closes out all the remaining open positions. All other properties of exchange-traded options still apply. Pricing energy options is very complex and is outside the scope of this book.

OTC energy swaps

Commodity swaps, or more specifically energy swaps, are the most recent addition to the range of swaps offered OTC. They are a very useful trading tool in commodities markets, as they overcome issues of specific delivery date, relatively short maturities, particular delivery points and quality grades associated with exchange-traded futures.

Energy swaps follow the same principles of other previously discussed swaps. They are contractual obligations between two counterparties to exchange a series of cashflows at regular intervals over a period of time until maturity. Maturities vary to suit clients' needs, but are typically in the range of one to five years. The cashflows in both legs of the swap are based on an agreed oil index price; one party pays a fixed index rate, whilst the other pays a floating index rate based on monthly average movement of the same index. The exchange of physical assets typically does not take place, but it is possible to construct the swap to allow for delivery. Thus the cashflows are calculated based on a notional quantity of cargo. As with all other swaps, the energy swap is priced so that the present value of both legs is equal at inception, i.e.:

Calculation Summary	Energy swap valuation
	PV(Swap) = PV(fixed oil index leg) − PV(floating oil index leg) = 0

In Chapter 7 on swaps, we saw that pricing interest rate swaps was based on the concept that a swap could be replaced by a strip of futures or FRAs, hence it implicitly had the same value, yielding the single swap rate that would cover the entire strip period. Pricing energy futures is not as straightforward as for their interest rate counterparts, as their underlying price factors are very complex. Thus energy (or other commodity) swap pricing is outside the scope of this book.

INTRODUCTION TO CREDIT DERIVATIVES

Credit derivatives are securities whose value is derived from the credit risk on an underlying asset, rather than the counterparties to the transaction itself. The underlying, also known as a *reference entity*, is a third party that has incurred debt. Credit derivatives are legally binding contracts between two counterparties whereby one party sells to another protection against the credit risk of the reference entity. The funds are payable following a credit event by one or more third parties.

The buyer and seller specify the credit events that apply to their transaction. Below are some examples:

- Bankruptcy (reference entity becomes insolvent).

- Failure to pay (the third party defaults on one of its obligations, such as a bond or a loan).

- Obligation acceleration (the third party obligation is moved forward in time, e.g. loan repayment is due immediately following the default).

The main users of credit derivatives are banks, hedge funds, insurance companies, pension funds and other corporations. Depending on the type of institution and their requirements, the contracts can be *funded* (entered into by financial institutions) or *unfunded* (used both by banks and corporations). Banks typically transact in funded credit derivatives by creating *special purpose vehicles* (SPVs) that are used to isolate the rest of the institution from financial risk. Payments due on credit derivative transactions are funded through *securitisation* (debt from various financial institutions is consolidated and resold in tranches as a separate security to other counterparties). Examples of these synthetic structures are collateralised debt obligations (CDOs), credit linked notes, single tranche CDOs, etc. Funded credit derivative transactions are typically rated by rating agencies, allowing the investors to select products depending on their risk-averseness. Under unfunded credit derivatives, both counterparties are responsible for meeting their obligations without resorting to other resources, i.e. each counterparty is exposed to the credit risk of the other. In contrast, under funded derivatives the seller of protection is required to make an initial payment that is used to settle any potential credit events, thus the protection buyer is not exposed to the credit risk of the protection seller.

Examples of unfunded credit derivative products include the following, some of which will be discussed in the subsequent sections:

- Credit default swap (CDS)

- Total rate of return swap (TROR)

- Constant maturity credit default swap (CMCDS)

- Contingent credit default swap

- Dynamic credit default swap

- First to default credit default swap

- Portfolio credit default swap

- Secured loan credit default swap

- Credit default swap on asset backed securities

- Credit default swaption

- Credit spread option (CSO).

Some examples of funded credit derivative products are:

- Credit linked note (CLN)
- Synthetic collateralised debt obligation (CDO)
- Constant proportion debt obligation (CPDO).

Credit default swap (CDS)

The credit default swap (CDS) is the most traded credit derivative instrument. It is a contract between a *protection buyer* and a *protection seller* to exchange cashflows in the case of a credit event associated with the debt obligations of a third party (usually a corporation). The protection buyer pays a fixed fee at regular intervals to the protection seller in return for a *contingent payment* by the seller upon a *credit event* affecting the obligations of the *third party* specified in the transaction. The credit events relevant to the transaction are precisely defined and are typically a failure to fulfil obligations or any other event from the list above. If any of these events occur and the protection buyer serves a credit event notice on the protection seller, the seller's payment is due. If the transaction is cash-settled, the difference between the full face value of the underlying obligation and its current value is paid. In the event of physical settlement, the underlying asset is actually delivered in exchange for its face value (even though its value is reduced). An important difference between CDSs and insurance products is that the protection buyer does not own the underlying obligation. Hence the protection seller has no legal means for recovering losses incurred by payments under the CDS. As the credit derivatives market is growing rapidly, new variations of the above concept are emerging, such as asset-backed securities, discussed in Chapter 12.

Total rate of return swap (TROR)

A total rate of return swap is a contract between two counterparties whereby they swap periodic payments for the period of the contract. Typically, one leg of the swap is based on the total return (interest payments plus any capital gains or losses for the payment period) from a specified reference asset, whilst the other pays/receives a specified fixed or floating cash flow (most commonly Libor + spread). Both legs are based upon the same notional amount.

Akin to equity swaps, the underlying motivation for entering into TRORs is the receiver's ability to derive financial risks and benefits of an asset without actually owning it. The seller's view is the opposite; if they believe that the underlying asset is temporarily going to depreciate in value, they use a TROR to stabilise their cashflows and lock in the spread over Libor.

The key difference between a *total rate of return swap* and a *credit default swap* is that the CDS provides protection against specific credit events; whilst TROR provides protection from potential losses irrespective of their cause, i.e. it mitigates both credit risk and market risk.

Credit spread swap

A credit spread swap provides protection from smaller downgrades in the credit rating of an underlying asset, rather than outright bankruptcy or default. It is a contract between two counterparties to exchange a series of regular payments, whereby one leg is based on a specific debt issued by a third party (e.g. bond), whilst the other is linked to a comparable government bond with added spread reflecting the difference in credit rating.

At inception, as in all other swaps, the value of the two legs is equal. If the underlying third party debt credit rating changes during the lifetime of the swap, the cashflows are exchanged between the two counterparties.

The motivation for trading credit spread swaps is similar to TRORs, as it allows the investor to lock in the spread over a benchmark yield, whilst providing the buyer with the opportunity for profit in the credit market without direct exposure.

Contingent credit default swap

Contingent credit default swaps are hybrid credit derivatives similar to classic credit default swaps. However, for the contingent payment to take place – in addition to the occurrence of a pre-specified credit event – they typically require a secondary source of credit exposure, i.e. a secondary trigger linked to another reference entity or a movement in interest rates, equity or commodity prices. As the payments are triggered by a joint occurrence of two events, they are less likely to take place compared to the standard credit default swap. Hence they offer less protection and are consequently cheaper. Their valuation is closely linked to the correlation between the two credit events, and the protection is deemed most optimal when the correlation is very low.

Dynamic credit default swap

Dynamic credit default swaps have been introduced to the OTC market to address the issue of uneven credit exposure the market participants are facing, affected by both the passage of time and the underlying market fluctuations. As swap counterparty exposure is a function of market volatility, forward interest rates and time – which in turn can affect the credit rating of the reference entity – having all the variables fixed at the inception of the contract is not ideal. Hence dynamic credit default swaps are tailored to have the notional linked to the mark-to-market value of a reference swap, or a basket of swaps. Thus, the contingent payment, incurred at the time of a credit event, is based on the market value (if positive) of the reference swap, whilst the protection buyer still pays the fixed fee throughout the contract, regardless of the fluctuations in protection provided. Even though the probability of losses to the protection buyer is small – only occurring in the event that both the protection seller and the reference entity default (a very unlikely event if the two are uncorrelated) – the level of protection is still unpredictable as it is contingent on market movements. Hence the protection buyer will typically pay lower fees as compensation.

Constant maturity credit default swap (CMCDS)

A constant maturity credit default swap (CMCDS) is similar to a standard credit default swap (CDS). Under a CMCDS contract, the protection buyer makes regular premium payments to the protection seller, and in return receives a payoff contingent on the credit event of an underlying financial instrument. In contrast to the standard CDS, the premium leg of a CMCDS is not fixed at the inception of the contract; instead it is a floating spread, using a traded CDS as a reference index. Specifically, given a pre-agreed time to maturity, each premium payment is equal to a spot CDS spread on the same reference credit (with the same time to maturity) traded in the market. The default or protection leg is typically structured in the same way as the standard CDS (i.e. the same contingent credit events apply). Comparison between the CDS and CMCDS is akin to the relationship between the fixed and the floating interest rates, whereby the former is known at the outset, but might hurt the borrower should the rates rise. Similarly, the purchaser of the CDS has obtained credit protection at a fixed cost, whilst the CMCDS buyer is exposed to market credit risk fluctuations. The choice between the two depends entirely on the type of investor and their view of the credit market.

First to default credit default swap

First to default swaps are typically used by investors aiming to increase yield on investment, rather than as credit protection vehicles. In this case the investor is the buyer of the risk, rather than risk protection. The risk buyer thus takes a position in each risk-bearing asset proportional to the notional sum invested. Throughout the swap the buyer receives coupon payments until occurrence of the first credit event. In the event of the first credit default (or other pre-specified contingent event), the investor no longer bears the risk of the credit entity. Depending on the specification, the contract is either immediately terminated, or carried forward until maturity. In either case, the losses incurred by the credit default (payable by the risk buyer) are equal to the difference between the par value and the final price of the reference entity. This is a very complex product, as credit assessment and probability of default are hard to predict, the timing of credit events even more so. However, these are attractive products that offer potential substantial yield enhancement. Their concept is further extended to capture second to default, third to default, or more generally n^{th} to default, hence the investor can specify which credit event their investment is linked to.

Credit spread option (CSO)

Even though all types of option contracts are available, the most popular credit spread option is the put option on an asset swap. The motivation behind such a contract is the option buyer's view that the credit spreads would widen. In such an event the bank would purchase a put option to deliver an asset (e.g. bond) at some future date. The strike is expressed as yield, rather than price (e.g. Libor + 50). The option will be exercised only if the bond yield is above Libor + 50, i.e. the bond price is lower than the original value. The bank will make a profit by selling the bond for more than it is worth.

Pricing credit derivatives

Credit derivatives valuation is a very complex issue, due to many unobservable price factors and the complexity of the traded products. Whilst interest rate derivatives have most of their price drivers directly observable in the market, predicting a bankruptcy of a particular corporation and translating it into a mathematical equation does not come easily.

A model used to price the risk of default at the minimum needs to incorporate (implicitly or explicitly): default probability, severity of loss given a credit event has occurred, timing of such a credit event and recovery rates (as the reference entity has defaulted, the amount recovered is contingent on many market and legal aspects). Another important issue is related to the model input parameters. In most other classes of derivative products, the liquidity and price transparency is such that it easily provides accurate and timely model parameter values. Due to the complexity of credit derivatives, market practitioners typically resort to making assumptions. This is due to the so-called 'dual observation issue', whereby the market-observed credit spreads can imply the severity of loss given default, but this data can only be used if an assumption is made about the likelihood of default. Hence the credit derivative pricing is a joint issue of market data validity and the sophistication of the pricing models.

There are two main approaches to pricing credit derivatives: numerical (probability model) and analytical (arbitrage-free) model. The parameters they have to incorporate are much more complex than those used by other markets. Hence the pricing of credit derivatives is outside the scope of this book.

OTC derivatives and hybrid securities

OTC derivatives

Hybrid securities

INTRODUCTION

This chapter offers a brief overview of the vast range of innovative OTC derivatives and hybrid securities. It provides an idea of the investment alternatives at clients' disposal. Some are traded in large volumes and are relatively simple to price using standard models, whilst others are extremely complex. Due to their number and nature, only a brief description is given.

OTC DERIVATIVES

Caps, floors and collars

Caps, floors and collars are OTC interest rate derivatives that offer a buyer a right, but not the obligation to secure the lending/borrowing rate. Unlike option contracts that have a single expiry date, they have periodic resets until maturity. Theoretically, the same protection could be achieved by purchasing a strip of options with different maturities that would cover the required period. But in practice the premium and margin requirements, as well as the management of a large number of transactions, would make this solution impractical.

Interest rate caps offer the buyer the right but not the obligation to fix the borrowing interest rate for a period of time, with regular reset periods against a benchmark (typically three-month Libor) in exchange for the premium payable up-front. They are in effect a strip of call options (*caplets*) as well as an OTC alternative to a strip of put options on interest rate futures. They can be priced using a slight modification of the standard Black–Scholes model. However, care must be taken over whether the caps are seen as puts on futures, or calls on interest rates, as the correct quotations and relevant volatilities must be used.

Interest rate floors offer the buyer the right but not the obligation to fix the lending interest rate for a period of time with regular reset periods against a benchmark (typically three-month Libor) in exchange for the premium payable up-front. Using the above analogy, they can be constructed using a strip of put options, or a strip of call options on interest rate futures. Depending on whether they are seen as calls or puts, either the Black–Scholes formula can be used directly, or their price can be derived from the put–call parity relationship.

Interest rate collars or *(cylinders)* are combinations of caps and floors, whereby the range of acceptable rates is fixed. They can be seen as either *borrower's collars* (buying a call for upward protection and selling a put and limiting benefits of downward interest rate movements), or as *lender's collars* (selling a call and buying a put). As the buyer is forgoing the benefits of a rate decrease below the floor level, the collars are much cheaper than caps and floors. The put and call strikes can be set in such a way as to provide a zero-cost collar.

Interest rate guarantees are one-period caps and floors, i.e. options on FRAs.

Captions and floorptions are options on caps and floors, and hence offer an investor an opportunity to abandon the cap or floor agreement if not needed. They are useful to investors who are uncertain if they will need floating rate financing in the future.

Swaptions are options on swaps (typically coupon swaps). The motivation for trades is the same as for caps, but unlike caps that have multiple exercise dates, the swaptions have only one and therefore have to exchange future payments even if that is no longer beneficial to the buyer. This makes them a cheaper alternative to caps.

Rate spread options offer an exposure to the basis between two benchmark rates (e.g. three-month Libor vs. six-month Libor).

Better performance bond options allow the buyer to receive the greater of two assets' returns over a specified period of time as long as they are both positive.

Structured finance products

Swap-linked notes exploit the difference in characteristics of long- and short-term bonds. Even though all bond prices rise with falls in yield, the impact is higher for bonds with greater duration (longer maturity and lower coupon). Long dated bonds also have less volatile yields compared to the short-term issues. Investors who do not wish to compromise between the two enter into swap-linked notes whereby the redemption value of a short-term note is linked to a long-term swap rate.

Delayed reset floaters or *Libor in arrears swaps* fix the floating leg of the swap only a few days before the payment is due, which is in contrast to standard swap arrangements where the rate is fixed at the beginning of the reset period and paid at the end. Clearly in a rising interest rate environment this is advantageous to the investor and this type of swap is more expensive than its 'vanilla' counterpart and vice versa.

Reverse floating rate notes (reverse FRNs) are short-term swap structures that offer an alternative to the classic FRNs which pay a fixed coupon in exchange for a floating rate in order to fix the cost of borrowing when rates are expected to rise. Reverse FRNs offer a potential gain is such a case, as their floating rates fall as the Libor increases (e.g. they pay 10 per cent – Libor). Hence under FRN, to protect against interest rate falls, the investor should receive the fixed rate, whilst to exploit increases in Libor, the floating rate should be received.

Capped/collared floaters are FRNs that set the limits on the floating coupon rate, either by limiting the potential profit (using caps only), or by fixing both the maximum and minimum level (using collars). In comparison to FRNs, capped FRNs are a cheaper alternative as their price incorporates a series of short call option premiums. Collars comprise both short calls and long puts, therefore depending on the strikes of the options bought and sold, collared FRNs can either be more expensive than capped versions, or they can incorporate OTM calls that offset a cheap purchase of a floor above prevailing market rates (thus making them a very cost-effective strategy).

Exotic options
Variation on standard option specification

Bermudan options are options with exercise specifications half-way between European (exercised at expiry only) and American options (exercised at any point until expiry). They offer several specific exercise dates during the option contract, which is an attractive prospect for an investor who may wish to have an option to cancel a swap at each coupon reset date.

Digital/Binary options pay a fixed amount on exercise, regardless of how much the option is in the money as long as it is ITM at expiry (all-or-nothing options) or if it has been ITM at any point until expiry (one-touch options). The payout from a short binary option can be approximated for hedging purposes by using a bull call spread strategy with narrowly spaced strikes (shown in Appendix 1).

Contingent options do not require up-front premium payment. It is only due if the option is exercised, but if the option is ITM, even by an amount smaller than the premium, it must be exercised. Their payoff profile is equivalent to a combination of long call/put and short digital call/put.

Chooser options are options that give the buyer the choice whether to exercise call or a put at a later date. These are single options that effectively incorporate call on a call and call on a put, each with zero strike. Their valuation is halfway between an ordinary call and a straddle (see Appendix 1).

Delayed options are options that give the buyer the right to receive at a future date another option with the strike set at the prevailing market value of the underlying on that date.

Path-dependent options

Average rate – Asian options do not pay the difference between the underlying and the option strike at exercise; the difference between the average price of the underlying and the strike is paid instead. The averaging can be done arithmetically or geometrically and can be applied to a period equal to the lifetime of the option, or just a part of it.

Average strike options, in contrast to Asian options, have the strike set to the average price of the underlying; the difference between the strike and the prevailing market price of underlying is paid on exercise.

Look-back options allow the buyer to set the strike at expiry to the most favourable value the underlying has achieved over the lifetime of the option. Obviously they are much more expensive than the standard options, as they have a much higher probability of expiring ITM, hence they are also known as 'no regret options'.

Barrier (knock-in or knock-out) or trigger options are activated or extinguished when the value of the underlying reaches a predetermined level. Regular barrier options start off as being activated (the barrier is set at a deeper OTM level than the strike) and are extinguished if the barrier is touched or crossed over. Reverse barriers start off as inactive (the barrier is set at a deeper ITM level than the strike) and are triggered once the barrier is touched or crossed over. Therefore this gives rise to four possible scenarios:

- Down and out calls (option extinguished at barrier, as it is OTM anyway)

- Up and in calls (option activated only when it is deeper ITM than the strike)

- Up and out puts (option extinguished at barrier)

- Down and in puts (option activated at barrier).

As the above options can be extinguished or may never even be activated, their premiums are much lower than for standard options. They are favoured by investors with a definite view of the market direction, providing them with a cheap investment strategy.

Cliquet or ratchet options are options with the strike reset at the prevailing underlying price at predetermined dates until option expiry, locking in their intrinsic value.

Ladder options are similar to cliquet options, but the strike is reset if and when the underlying price reaches predetermined levels during the lifetime of the option. They are harder to price, as there is an additional level of uncertainty. In the above scenario, the fixing dates were known but the underlying prices were not, whilst the ladder options are affected both by the uncertainty in the underlying value as well as the timing of resets.

Shout options give the investor the right to 'shout' when they wish to reset the strike value, regardless of the underlying value. The number of 'shouts' is typically limited.

Multi-factor options

Rainbow or outperformance options, if exercised, pay the buyer the difference between the best price and the strike (for call options) or the worst price and the strike (for put options) from a number of underlying securities. Obviously they are more expensive than standard option contracts.

Basket options pay to the investor the difference between the option strike and the average price of the basket of underlying assets. Pricing these derivatives is highly affected by the correlation of the underlying assets, type and the variance of their price distribution.

Spread options, if exercised, pay the difference between two asset prices. The strike can be set in relation to one of the assets, but if the option expires ITM the payout is based on the difference between the two assets.

Quanto options have their payout linked to one underlying value, but the amount is determined in reference to another asset. For example, the strike is set relative to the three-month Libor, but once the option is exercised the payoff is EUR denominated.

HYBRID SECURITIES

The term 'hybrid securities' refers to financial instruments that have properties of two or more unrelated securities, typically traded in their own specialised markets. In financial markets this term is adopted for the class of products that link *debt* and *equity* markets.

Even though hybrids have existed in various forms for a while, their popularity has grown in recent years since accounting regulations allowed them to be recorded largely as 'off-balance sheet' instruments. This enabled companies to trade in much larger volumes; typically issuing hybrids (to gain access to low-cost funds) and with their proceeds repurchasing equity shares for much higher returns. Below are some examples of various types of hybrid securities.

Convertible bonds

Convertible bonds are bonds with the call option attached that gives the holder the right but not the obligation to convert the bond into equity shares in the company that issued the bond. The option can be exercised at only one specified date (European style), or a series of predetermined dates (Bermudan). This optionality comes at a price, as the bond typically pays a lower coupon than a comparable issue without the conversion optionality attached. Valuation of convertibles is very complex, due to many underlying factors affecting their price. Typical approaches are: option pricing model (a variation of Black–Scholes), dividend valuation model or cross-over method. The Black–Scholes model is covered in Chapter 9, whilst the remaining two are outside the scope of this book.

Callable bonds

A callable bond gives the issuer the right but not the obligation to buy back at a future date the bond from the investors at the price agreed at inception. Clearly the coupon on this type of bond is higher than for a comparable bond without the optionality, as the investors receive the option premium as a compensation for the risk undertaken. From the investors' point of view the callable bond is the combination of straight bond and short call option, hence:

Value of callable bond = Value of straight bond − Call option

As the option value increases, the price of the callable bond decreases (bond yield increases). The amount of this change is determined by the interest rate environment.

In a *low interest rate* market, the price of the straight bond will increase, but the call option to buy it back at lower strike will also be high, leaving the value virtually unchanged.

In a *high interest rate* environment, the price of the straight bond will be low, but the option will be deeply OTM, hence worthless. Any further small changes in interest rates will have no effect on its value. Therefore, the callable bond follows the behaviour of the straight bond.

In a *highly volatile* interest rate environment, the value of a call option will significantly increase (as the probability of exercise increases), reducing the value of the callable bond.

Puttable bonds

A puttable bond gives the investor the right but not the obligation to sell the bond back to the issuer at a future date at the price agreed at inception. Using the earlier logic, the coupon on this type of bond is lower than for a comparable bond without the optionality, as the investors pay the put option premium to compensate the issuer for the risk undertaken. From the investors' point of view the puttable bond is the combination of straight bond and long put option, hence:

Value of puttable bond = Value of straight bond + Put option

In contrast to the callable bonds, as the option value increases, the price of the puttable bond also increases. The amount of this change is determined by the interest rate environment.

In a *low interest rate* market, the price of the straight bond will increase, but the put option will be worthless, leaving the value of puttable bonds comparable to the straight bond.

In a *high interest rate* environment, the price of the straight bond will be low, but the put option will be ITM, hence valuable. Thus, the value of the puttable bond will be virtually unchanged.

In a *highly volatile* interest rate environment, the value of the put option will significantly increase (as the probability of exercise increases), increasing the value of the puttable bond.

Both callable and puttable bonds can be priced numerically using the arbitrage-free binomial tree (discussed in Chapter 9).

Dual currency bonds

Dual currency bonds pay interest in one currency but are redeemed in another. This gives the investor the exposure to bond market as well as foreign exchange markets. Further complications arise with the option to fix the exchange rate at the issue date, the redemption date or an average of the two. The investor expects a higher coupon as a compensation for the risk of unfavourable exchange rate moves. From the issuers' point of view, this is an attractive security. As they operate in the redemption currency, they are not exposed to long-term exchange rate risk.

Mortgage derivatives

Mortgage derivatives are credit derivatives, but the following examples are covered here rather than in Chapter 11, as they are more exotic alternatives to those contracts covered in the previous chapter.

The property market as we know it today would not be possible without mortgages. As the mortgage market developed, so did the investors' interest in the property sector, resulting in numerous related derivative instruments. Mortgage derivatives refer to contracts whereby the investor receives cashflows based on an underlying pool of mortgages. Some more common variants are discussed below.

Collateralised mortgage obligations (CMOs)

The purpose of CMOs is the distribution of risks and returns from a pool of mortgages tailored to meet clients' needs. There are many variants of this basic concept, such as:

Sequential pay tranches are instruments where the CMO is split into several tranches ranked as A, B, C etc. The interest from the mortgage obligations is paid to each tranche proportionally to their investment, with tranche A receiving all the income until it is fully repaid. It is followed by tranche B and so on. These are risky investments as the pre-payment schedule, both in timing and the value of the cashflows, is unpredictable. However, property investors who would like a diversified portfolio, but find it impractical or impossible to achieve directly in the physical market, find the CMOs attractive. The upfront cash investment that might purchase only a few specific properties whose mortgage payments could be very volatile creates through the CMO a proportional exposure in a large number of unrelated properties whose overall returns are likely to be more stable. Hence CMOs are popular OTC products.

Stripped mortgage-backed securities are financial instruments based on a pool of mortgages, where the prepayment schedules are not known in advance. The main types are:

- *Principal only (PO) securities* receive payments based on principal loan amount only, i.e. there are no interest payments. Similar to zero-coupon bonds, they are priced at a discount. The faster the prepayment schedule, the higher the return of a PO.

- *Interest only (IO) securities* receive only the interest payments based on the loan amount, i.e. there is no principal payment. As the principal is repaid through the PO issue, the value of interest payments under IO decreases. Once the PO is repaid, no further cashflows are due to IO holder. It is a very unpredictable security, as it depends on prepayment schedules as well as interest rates.

Asset-backed securities

Asset-backed securities are in principle the same as mortgage-backed securities, but the underlying is a pool of assets, such as credit card debt or car loans. Different financial instruments are structured to incorporate asset-backed payments.

PRICING AND VALUATION TOOLS

Probability and statistics

INTRODUCTION

As we saw in Chapter 9, pricing derivatives, particularly securities with embedded optionality, requires assumptions on their future behaviour. Whether it is just the range of final values the security is likely to have, the paths it took to get there, or the future behaviour of several variables that impact on the value of derivative, they all require the use of probability and statistics. Hence this chapter is devoted to the main concepts of probability, together with probability distributions most relevant to financial modelling.

DEFINITION OF PROBABILITY

Very few things in life are certain. That is why we need some probability measure in order to estimate the likelihood of uncertain events. Probability theory aims to facilitate decision making where there are several possible outcomes. It was first developed for use in gambling, hence most examples use cards, coins, dice etc.

The financial world is very uncertain and decisions on investments have to be based on 'educated guesses'. Hence probability theory plays a big part in pricing and trading financial instruments.

THE MAIN CONCEPTS OF PROBABILITY

The probability of an event E occurring in a trial where there are several equally likely outcomes is:

Calculation Summary	P(E) = Number of ways E can occur / Total number of possible outcomes

| **Example** | When rolling a dice, what is a probability of getting six? |

As there are six equally likely numbers, the probability of throwing any one of them is 1/6.

This works well with cards, coins etc., i.e. whenever all the possible outcomes are known with certainty. But what happens when this is not the case?

The probability definition has to be extended to cater for such cases. The only approach that can be taken is to observe a sufficiently large number of trials and assume that the same frequency of a different event would continue into the future. In other words, probability can be defined as:

P(E) = Number of observed occurrences of E / Total number of observed occurances	**Calculation Summary**

If 100 people took a driving test and 54 passed, we can conclude that the probability of passing the test is:

P(pass) = 54/100 = 0.54 or 54%

Normally a much larger sample would be used, but the same logic would apply.

It is worth pointing out that the above discussion applies to 'countable' events (events where the number of instances can be observed exactly). In order to allow for events that are not discrete, the concept of distribution functions has to be introduced (discussed later).

Probability values

From the above examples it can be seen that probability ranges from 0 (0 per cent) to 1 (100 per cent). This means that event E that will certainly *not occur* has probability $P(E) = 0$ and the event that will certainly occur will have probability $P(E) = 1$. It follows from these definitions that the probabilities of all possible outcomes must add up to 1, as it is certain that one of them will occur. For example, when tossing a coin, the probability of both head and tail is 0.5, hence the probability of both events is 1, as it is certain that one will occur. The above definitions can be further extended to include the concept of NOT (probability of something not happening).

When rolling a dice, the probability of six is 1/6. The probability of NOT throwing six must then be the probability of all other events (1, 2, ..., 5), i.e. 5/6.

However, as we know that the probability of all events is 1, then the probability of all events but six must be

P(NOT 6) = 1 − P(6) = 1 − 1/6 = 5/6

In the above example either solution was equally easy, but the concept can come in really useful if not all the possible outcomes, or the probabilities of some of the outcomes, are known.

Joint probability

The probability of occurrence of two or more events often needs to be calculated, which requires the knowledge the relationship between those events. The tests in the experiments can be:

Independent, i.e. the outcome of one test has no impact on another

Dependent, the outcome of one test is affected by the preceding tests.

Furthermore, the outcomes from any one of the tests undertaken can be:

Mutually exclusive, i.e. they cannot occur simultaneously

Not mutually exclusive, i.e. they may occur together.

Example

A card randomly selected from a pack will affect all the future draws from the same pack unless it is replaced. Two random draws from the same pack are only independent if the card is returned to the pack.

Drawing a five and a spade are two non-exclusive events, as there is a card five of spades. However, drawing five of spades twice in a row (without returning the card into the pack) are two mutually exclusive events, as there is only one such a card, and can be drawn either on the first draw, on the second or not at all, but never twice.

These statements can be expressed by mathematical formulae as below.

Independent events

Summation rule

The probability of either of the two independent events occurring is equal to the sum of their individual probabilities:

Calculation Summary

Probability of occurrence of either independent event

$P(A \text{ or } B) = P(A) + P(B)$

Example

We are throwing two dice. What is the probability of getting number three on either of the two dice?

$P(3) = 1/6$

Since two throws are independent, the probability of the second draw is unaffected by the first outcome. Hence, $P(3 \text{ or } 3) = P(3) + P(3) = 1/3$
Mathematically, the summation rule corresponds to the operation OR.

Multiplication rule

The probability of two independent events occurring simultaneously is equal to the product of their individual probabilities:

Probability of simultaneous occurrence of independent events

$$P(A \text{ and } B) = P(A) \times P(B)$$

Calculation Summary

Using the same example as above (throwing two dice) what is the probability of getting number three on both?

$$P(3) = 1/6$$

Since two throws are independent, the probability $P(3 \text{ and } 3) = P(3) \times P(3) = 1/36$

Mathematically, the multiplication rule corresponds to the operation AND.

Dependent events

Summation rule

The probability of either one of the two dependent events occurring is equal to the sum of their individual probabilities minus their joint probability. This is because if both events can happen simultaneously, we will count their joint probability twice. Mathematically we can write this as:

Probability of occurrence of either dependent event

$$P(A \text{ or } B) = P(A) + P(B) - P(A \text{ and } B)$$

Calculation Summary

What is the probability of drawing a five or a diamond from a pack of cards?

There are 13 diamonds and 4 fives. Hence, it could be concluded that there are 17 ways of drawing either a five or a diamond. In fact, since one of these cards is a five of diamonds, it would be counted twice. Hence:

Probability of drawing a diamond is: $P(D) = 13/52$

Probability of drawing a five is: $P(5) = 4/52$

Probability of drawing a five and a diamond is: $P(5 \text{ of diamonds}) = 1/52$

$P(5 \text{ or diamond}) = P(D) + P(5) - P(5 \text{ D}) = 13/52 + 4/52 - 1/52 = 16/52 = 4/13$

Multiplication rule

Rules describing dependent events deal with *conditional probability*, as occurrence of one event influences the outcome of the other.

When two events are dependent, the probability of both occurring is:

Probability of simultaneous occurrence of dependent events

$P(A \text{ and } B) = P(A) \times P(B|A)$

where $P(B|A)$ is the probability of B occurring *given* A has occurred.

Example

Students had two maths tests. 25% of students passed both tests and 42% passed the second test. What percentage of students who passed the first test also passed the second test?

```
A – first test    B – second test
P(A and B) = 0.25
P(B) = 0.42
P(B|A) = P(A and B)/P(B) = 0.25/0.42 = 60%
```

Another example of a dependent event is drawing cards at random without replacing them:

In any pack of cards the probability of drawing a spade is $13/52 = 1/4$. However, the probability of drawing a spade after a spade has been drawn is:

```
1st draw: P(spade) = 13/52
2nd draw P(spade) = 12/51 (not 13/52 as it would be if we replaced the first card)
```

hence drawing two spades without replacing is:

```
P(2 spades) = 13/52 × 12/51 = 3/51 = 1/17
```

which is lower than the probability without replacing (1/16).

THE CONCEPT OF PROBABILITY DISTRIBUTION

When tossing a coin, based on its probability, the tail would be expected 50 per cent of the time. However, if 100 tosses were made, it is possible that only 46 would occur. If this experiment was repeated many times, most likely the results would range from as low as 10 to as high as 90. If the results were plotted on the graph, we would in fact be drawing a distribution, with the majority of the results concentrating around 50, but with a very wide spread.

Probability distributions are typically defined in terms of the probability density function. There are number of probability functions used in real-life applications.

For a *continuous function*, the *probability density function* (pdf) is the probability that the variable has the value x. Since for continuous distributions the probability is equivalent to the area under the curve, the probability at a single point is zero. For this reason probability is often expressed in terms of an integral between two points.

Probability that the *continuous* variable x has a value between a and b inclusive **Calculation Summary**

$$P[a \leq X \leq b] = \int_a^b f(x)\,dx$$

For a *discrete distribution*, the pdf is the probability that the variate takes the value x.

Probability that the *discrete* variable x has a value X or lies between a and b inclusive **Calculation Summary**

$$P[X = x] = f(x), \text{ or for the interval } P[a \leq X \leq b] = \sum_{x=a}^{b} f(x)$$

The *cumulative distribution* function (cdf) is the probability that the variable takes a value less than or equal to x. That is:

Probability that the *discrete* variable x has a value less than or equal to X **Calculation Summary**

$$F(x) = P[X \leq x] = \alpha \quad \text{or} \quad F(x) = \sum_{i=0}^{x} f(i)$$

For a continuous distribution, this can be expressed mathematically as:

Probability that the *continuous* variable x has a value less than or equal to X **Calculation Summary**

$$F(x) = \int_{-\infty}^{x} f(\mu)\,d\mu$$

TYPES OF PROBABILITY DISTRIBUTION

There are several types of probability distributions:

- Binomial
- Normal
- Log-normal
- Poisson
- Student's t
- χ^2 (chi-square)
- Exponential
- Gamma
- Cauchy.

Each distribution is characterised by several parameters:

- *Mean*: the arithmetic average of all possible outcomes.
- *Standard deviation*: measure of dispersion of all the outcomes around the mean (width of the distribution).
- *Mode*: most frequent of all the outcomes.
- *Median*: central value of all the outcomes. If all the outcomes were arranged in ascending order according to their frequency, then median in the middle value (in the case of an odd number of outcomes) or the average of the two middle values (in the case of an even number of outcomes).
- *Range*: range of values that the probability distribution can take.

The above list of distributions is certainly not exhaustive. All these distributions have their application as they describe particular types of behaviour. What is common to them all is that they are trying to quantify random and uncertain events. Given that in finance events are best described using binomial, normal or log-normal distributions, the following sections will concentrate on those. Poisson, student and chi-square distributions will be described only briefly, whilst others will not be covered.

BINOMIAL DISTRIBUTION

The binomial distribution is used when there are exactly two mutually exclusive outcomes of a trial. These outcomes are appropriately labelled 'success' and 'failure'. The binomial distribution is used to obtain the probability of observing x successes in N trials, with the probability of success in a single trial denoted by p. Following from the earlier observation that probabilities of all outcomes must add to 1, the probability of a failure is $1 - p$. The binomial distribution assumes that p is fixed for all trials.

If three cards are selected at random from a pack (each card being returned to the pack before the next one is drawn), what is the probability of drawing two spades? **Example**

Since there are four symbols in each pack (13 cards with each), the probability of any symbol (and therefore spades) is $P(S) = 0.25$. The probability of drawing any other symbol is $P(O) = 1 - P(S) = 0.75$. Since we are returning the cards to the pack, the draws are independent and the probabilities remain the same at each draw.

If we consider all possible outcomes:

SSS, SSO, SOS, OSS, SOO, OOS, OSO, OOO

We can see that their probabilities are:

All spades:	$0.25 \times 0.25 \times 0.25 = 0.015625$
Two spades:	$3 \times 0.25 \times 0.25 \times 0.75 = 0.140625$
Three spades:	$3 \times 0.25 \times 0.75 \times 0.75 = 0.421875$
No spades:	$0.75 \times 0.75 \times 0.75 = 0.421875$

However, instead of listing all possible outcomes (which can be very time-consuming), we can use the *binomial expression*. The formula for the binomial probability function is:

Binomial probability function **Calculation Summary**

$$P(x) = \frac{n!}{x!(n-x)!} \times p^x \times (1-p)^{n-x}$$

where the number of possible combinations of x successes in n trials is given by:

$$\frac{n!}{x!(n-x)!}$$

and the probability of x successes and $n - x$ failures in a trial is given by:

$$p^x \times (1-p)^{n-x}$$

Applying this expression to the above example, we have: **Example**

$$P(2) = \frac{3!}{2!(3-2)!} \times 0.25^2 \times 0.75^{3-2} = 3 \times 0.0625 \times 0.75 = 0.140625$$

which is much simpler than listing all the outcomes!

Properties of binomial distribution

Graphical representation of binomial distribution – a *histogram* – is a plot of all the outcomes along the x-axes with their corresponding frequency/ number of trials along the y-axes. Probability of observing a value between two points a and b is a sum of probabilities of all the points between a and b. If p = 0.5, the distribution is symmetric (the histogram is centred around p = 0.5), with p < 0.5 it is positively skewed (more items lie above the most frequent item), whilst for p > 0.5 it is negatively skewed.

Below are some statistics for the binomial distribution:

Mean	np
Mode	$p(n+1) - 1 \leq x \leq p(n+1)$
Range	0 to N
Standard dev.	$\sqrt{np(1-p)}$

Application in financial modelling

Binomial distribution is widely used in building binomial trees (for pricing options). Here it is assumed that the price can only go up or down and each move has a probability assigned to it. The advantage of a binomial model is that it is tractable and easy to understand, but building trees can be very time-consuming and inefficient. An example of building a binomial tree to price options was given in Chapter 9 and is further shown below.

NORMAL DISTRIBUTION

Binomial distribution deals with discrete data with only two possible outcomes. Normal distribution enables us to calculate probabilities of outcomes when the variable is continuous (data can take any value). There are many similarities between normal and the symmetrical binomial distribution, so that binomial distribution can be approximated by the normal distribution when there is a large data sample. However, whilst binomial distribution dealt with discrete values and its graphical representation was given by a histogram, normal distribution is represented by a continuous curve. The probability of observing a value between any two points is equal to the area under the curve between those points.

The main characteristics of normal distribution are:

- It is bell-shaped
- It is symmetrical
- The mean, median (central point) and mode (most frequent value) are equal

- It is asymptotic (tails never reach the x-axis)
- Total area under the curve = 1
- Area under the curve between any two points gives the probability of observing a value in that range
- Standard deviation measures the spread (width) of the distribution.

The general formula for the probability density function of the normal distribution is:

Normal distribution function　　　　　　　　　　　**Calculation Summary**

$$f(x) = \frac{e^{-(x-\mu)^2/2\sigma^2}}{\sigma\sqrt{2\pi}}$$

where μ is the location parameter (centre of the distribution) and σ is the scale parameter (determines total area under the curve). The case where $\mu = 0$ and $\sigma = 1$ is called the *standard normal distribution*.

The equation for the standard normal distribution is:

Standard normal distribution function　　　　　　　**Calculation Summary**

$$f(x) = \frac{e^{-x^2/2}}{\sqrt{2\pi}}$$

Some of the distribution statistics are:

Mean	location parameter μ
Median	location parameter μ
Mode	location parameter μ
Standard dev.	scale parameter σ

The location and scale parameters of the normal distribution can be estimated with the sample mean and sample standard deviation respectively.

The normal distribution is widely used. This is partly due to the fact that it is well behaved and mathematically tractable. However, the central limit theorem provides a theoretical basis for why it has wide applicability; it states that as the sample size (N) becomes large, the following occur:

- The sampling distribution of the mean becomes approximately normal regardless of the distribution of the original variable.
- The sampling distribution of the mean is centred at the population mean μ, of the original variable.

■ The standard deviation of the sampling distribution of the mean approaches $\sigma/\sqrt{N}$.

It may be interesting to note that the probability of observing a value in various intervals is as follows:

Interval	Probability
$\mu \pm 0.67\sigma$	0.5
$\mu \pm \sigma$	0.683
$\mu \pm 2\sigma$	0.955
$\mu \pm 2.33\sigma$	0.99
$\mu \pm 3\sigma$	0.997

Rather than using the distribution formula above, when the population is normally distributed the probability of observing a value in a particular range can be calculated using the z value:

$$z = \frac{x - \mu}{\sigma}$$

i.e. the distance of the observed value x from the mean μ expressed in standard deviation σ. This way all the values are standardised and probability can be looked up in normal distribution tables.

Normal distribution tables

There are several types of distribution tables, but the most common ones give the probability of observing a value beyond a point when moving away from the mean (in either a positive or a negative direction).

Example

If a stock price is 200 and the standard deviation is 40, what is the probability of:

1. A stock price falling below 150?

2. A stock price within one standard deviation?

3. A stock price rising to at least 220?

To answer these questions, the Z value for each case has to be calculated and the probability value found in the distribution table.

1. For x = 150 we have Z = (150–200)/40 = –1.25

The negative value corresponds to the point below the mean. In the distribution tables, the absolute value is found and interpreted according to the sign of the Z value.

In our case the probability corresponds to $Z = 1.25 = 0.10565$. This is the area of the curve beyond the point away from the mean. Hence for $Z = -1.25$ it corresponds to the stock values below 150.

2. Here $P(160 \leq x \leq 200) + P(200 \leq x \leq 240)$ is required, which is the same as taking the area $P(x \leq 200) - P(x \leq 160)$ twice, as the curve is symmetrical.

 Since $P(\leq 200) = 0.5$ and the probability $P(\leq 160)$ can be calculated as $Z = (160-200)/40 = -1$, with a corresponding probability of 0.15866, the probability of the stock price falling within one standard deviation of the mean is $P = 2 \times (0.5 - 0.15866) = 0.6827$

3. Finally, the probability of the stock price rising to at least 220 is calculated as $Z = (220-200)/40 = 0.5$, which corresponds to $P(\geq 220) = 0.30854$

Application in financial modelling

The most famous application of normal distribution is in the Black–Scholes formula. It is used for pricing stocks, interest rate derivatives etc. In principle, products that have some built-in optionality will have to assume a type of distribution that the underlying variable takes. Then the stochastic behaviour of the variable can be modelled and the product priced depending on the probabilities of all possible states. Good examples are:

- Caps, floors, collars
- Range accruals
- Limited price index (LPI) swaps etc.

Whether normal or log-normal (or shifted log-normal) distribution is used is mostly a matter of the practitioner's choice and the empirical evidence of variable behaviour.

LOG-NORMAL DISTRIBUTION

In the standard normal distribution the horizontal scale is linear, which means that for a mean $= 100$ the probability of 80 is the same as the probability of 120. In log-normal distribution the x-axis would be linear if logarithms of values were plotted. This implies that for a mean $= 100$, the probability of 200 is the same as the probability of 50.

More formally, a variable X is log-normally distributed if $Y = \ln(X)$ is normally distributed, with ln denoting the natural logarithm. The general formula for the probability density function of the log-normal distribution is:

Calculation Summary

Log-normal distribution function

$$f(x) = \frac{e^{-(\ln(x-\theta)/m)^2/(2\sigma^2))}}{(x-\theta)\sigma\sqrt{2\pi}} \quad x \geq \theta; \; m, \sigma > 0$$

where σ is the shape parameter (allowing for different shapes of distribution), θ is the location parameter (centre of the distribution) and m is the scale parameter (determining the area under the curve). The case where $\theta = 0$ and $m = 1$ is called the *standard log-normal distribution*. The case where only $\theta = 0$ is called the two-parameter log-normal distribution.

The equation for the standard log-normal distribution is:

Calculation Summary

Standard log-normal distribution function

$$f(x) = \frac{e^{-(\ln(x)^2/2\sigma^2)}}{x\sigma\sqrt{2\pi}} \quad x \geq 0; \; \sigma > 0$$

The most important distribution statistics for $\theta = 0$ and $m = 1$ are:

Mean	$e^{0.5\sigma^2}$	
Median	scale parameter m	(1 if m is not specified)
Mode	$1/e^{\sigma^2}$	
Range	0 to $+\infty$	
Standard Dev.	$\sqrt{e^{\sigma^2}(e^{\sigma^2}-1)}$	

Application in financial modelling

Many models (the interest derivative ones in particular) rely on log-normal distribution. In most cases interest rates are modelled as if they behave log-normally, hence this distribution is used directly in equations as well as in model calibration. Often in modelling shifted log-normal distribution is used (the larger the shift, the more it resembles normal distribution). There is ample empirical evidence to suggest that the stock prices also behave log-normally.

OTHER PROBABILITY DISTRIBUTIONS

Poisson distribution

The Poisson distribution is a discrete distribution that takes on the values x = 0, 1, 2, 3 etc. It is often used as a model for the number of events (such as the number of telephone calls at a business centre or the number of accidents at an intersection) in a specific time period. It is also useful in ecological studies, particle physics etc. The useful characteristic of the distribution is that it is not invalidated if one event replaces another, e.g. when counting photons hitting an x-ray target in a given time interval any missed photon can be replaced by a new incoming one.

The Poisson distribution is determined by one parameter, lambda. Lambda is a shape parameter specifying the average number of events in a given time interval. The probability density function for the Poisson distribution is given by the formula:

Poisson distribution function

Calculation Summary

$$f(x) = e^{-\lambda} \frac{\lambda^x}{x!}$$

Some of the Poisson distribution statistics are:

mean $= \lambda$

Range $= 0$ to $+\infty$

Standard deviation $= \sqrt{\lambda}$

Student's t-distribution

The t-distributions were discovered by statistician William Gosset who – being employed by the Guinness brewing company – could not publish under his own name, so he wrote under the pen name 'Student'.

T-distributions are normally used for hypothesis testing and parameter estimation, and very rarely for modelling. They arise in simple random samples of size n, drawn from a normal population with mean μ and standard deviation σ. Let x_1 denote the sample mean and s, the sample standard deviation. Then the quantity

$$t = \frac{x_1 - \mu}{s/\sqrt{n}}$$

has a t-distribution with n–1 degrees of freedom.

Note that there is a different t-distribution for each sample size, in other words, it is a class of distributions. For any specific t-distribution, the degrees of freedom have to be specified. They come from the sample standard deviation s in the denominator of the equation.

The t-density curves are symmetric and bell-shaped like the normal distribution and have their peak at 0. However, the spread is wider than in the standard normal distribution. This is due to the fact that, in the above formula, the denominator is s rather than σ. Since s is a random quantity varying with various samples, there is greater variability in t, resulting in a larger spread.

The larger the number of degrees of freedom, the closer the t-density is to the normal density. This reflects the fact that the standard deviation s approaches σ for large sample size n.

Chi-square (χ^2) distribution

The chi-square distribution results when ν independent variables with standard normal distributions are squared and summed. For simplicity the formula for probability density function is not included in this text. The chi-square distribution is typically used to develop hypothesis tests and confidence intervals and rarely for modelling applications.

Some of the χ^2 distribution statistics are:

mean = ν

Range = 0 to $+\infty$

Standard deviation = $\sqrt{2\nu}$.

BINOMIAL TREES

Binomial trees are used to model the behaviour of a variable that can take only discrete values, e.g. to estimate the probability of the fuel price reaching a certain level in the future. The price can ultimately either go up or down, i.e. change in only two possible ways, hence the name binominal. We can crudely break down the timeline to only now and the future date and take a guess at the possible up and down price movements. But a more practical approach would be to divide the timeline until the future date into a number of steps. The probability of up and down moves is assigned and at each move a certain price change is allowed. Those values can be constant for the entire tree, or change at every step. The size of the price movements reduces by increasing the number of time steps.

If the current price is 100, two months later it might be as high as 120, or as low as 90. If we divide this period into monthly intervals, we will have only two steps in our tree.

We assign:

p is the probability of an upward move

1 − p is the probability of a downward move

u is the amount by which the price moves up

d is the amount by which the price moves down.

The above variables can be estimated from the market conditions, but for illustration purposes we will assume that:

$p = 0.7$
$1 - p = 0.3$
$u = 10$
$d = 5$

Hence the probability tree will look like:

Period today	1 mth	2 mths
		D 0.49
	B 0.7	
A 1		E 0.21 (× 2)
	C 0.3	
		F 0.09
1	1	1

The probability of reaching D is the probability of moving up and then up again, i.e. $0.7 \times 0.7 = 0.49$. For E we can go up and down or down and up, hence $0.7 \times 0.3 = 0.21$ and so on.

The tree showing possible prices is as follows:

Period today	1 mth	2 mths
		D 120
	B 110	
A 100		E 105
	C 95	
		F 90

As we are only interested in the price at the end of one year, we can see that it can take (in our estimate) three possible values ranging from 90 to 120, but the least likely outcome (only 9% probability) is 90, whilst it is over 90% certain that it would increase from the original value.

The above was a very trivial example, but this principle can be extended to any real-life problem to assess the probability of different outcomes.

Yield curves

INTRODUCTION

In the previous chapters on money market and capital market instruments – futures, FRAs and swaps – we often used the term *implied interest rate* or *yield*. It is a measure of profitability of an investment. The client will base his investment decision on how much yield a particular security will bring compared to other products in the market. Yields for different tenors (time periods) are needed by investment banks and other security issuers to price their products and calculate PV of future cashflows. For this purpose, yield curves are constructed, using liquid market-traded financial instruments. Hence, *the yield curve is the relationship between the interest rate (or cost of borrowing) and the time to maturity of the debt for a given borrower in a given currency.*

Key Point Yield curve is the relationship between the interest rate (or cost of borrowing) and the time to maturity of the debt for a given borrower in a given currency.

By its definition, there is no single yield curve describing the cost of funds for all market participants. The most important factor in determining a yield curve is the currency in which the securities are denominated. Within the same currency, different institutions borrow money at different rates, depending on their credit rating. Banks with high creditworthiness borrow money from each other at the Libor rates. Thus they construct their yield curves (also known as 'swap curves') based on Libor-related instruments. Other market participants, such as corporations, typically have to borrow at higher rates (e.g. spread over Libor). Corporate yield curves ('basis curves') are often quoted in terms of a 'credit spread' or 'basis' over the relevant swap curve.

Securities of different tenors (from overnight borrowing to a 30-year swap) are used to calculate rates at their coupon payment (if any) and maturity points and the mathematical curve is drawn through them. This enables yield to be calculated at any point in the future. Even though the particulars of construction methodology are proprietary to each investment bank, there is a convention followed by all when it comes to choice of instruments and general construction principles. In this chapter several construction methodologies are described, but they are by no means exhaustive.

CHOICE OF FINANCIAL INSTRUMENTS FOR YIELD CURVE CONSTRUCTION

In investment banks the adopted yield curves aim to provide single source of rates for pricing products of all maturities. The instruments used in curve construction are: deposits, interest rate futures and interest rate swaps.

> **Key Point**
>
> The instruments used in curve construction are:
> Cash deposits
> Interest rate futures
> Interest rate swaps

The reason behind this choice is simple:

Cash deposits are liquid instruments and prices are readily available. There is no uncertainty, as the rates are known at the outset. The maturities are short and range from overnight borrowing up to one year.

Interest rate futures are exchange-traded securities and offer great liquidity and price transparency. The number of contracts available for trading is always the same (as one contract expires, another is introduced – a rollover process) and the expiry dates are fixed (third Wednesday in the delivery month, where the delivery months are March, June, September and December). This makes futures ideal for yield calculations. For currencies for which exchange-traded futures contracts are not available, FRAs have to be used. To make a suitable substitution, three-month FRAs that start on the IMM dates (futures contracts expiry dates) are chosen, taking into account *convexity adjustment* (described later).

Interest rate swaps are used for longer-dated periods for which futures contracts are not available. They take precedence over bonds, as their relationship to floating market rates is much easier to estimate. 'Vanilla swaps' are typically used, where fixed rate is exchanged for floating rate (Libor).

Futures take precedence over all other instruments. The point at which futures take over from deposits and the number of futures used in each curve depends on the currency and instruments being priced. A typical yield curve would consist of the grid points shown in Table 14.1.

Table 14.1	Standard yield curve grid points	
Instrument type	**Tenor (settlement date)**	**Rate % (example)**
Cash	Overnight (O/N)	5.61
Cash	Tomorrow/next date (T/N)	5.59
Cash	1 month (1M)	5.62
Cash	3 months (3M)	5.73
Futures	Jun 2010	5.76
Futures	Sep 2010	5.79
Futures	Dec 2010	5.84
Futures	Mar 2011	5.91
Futures	Jun 2011	6.07
Swaps	2 year (2Y)	6.01
Swaps	3 year (3Y)	6.13
Swaps	4 year (4Y)	6.18
Swaps	5 year (5Y)	6.24
Swaps	7 year (7Y)	6.37
Swaps	10 year (10Y)	6.44
Swaps	15 year (15Y)	6.57
Swaps	20 year (20Y)	6.55
Swaps	30 year (30Y)	6.56

Standard curves typically model three-month borrowing rates (three-month Libor in the UK), to be used for pricing instruments of all maturities. This choice is based on the fact that should the bank require funding to cover its position it would borrow at those rates. However, some market practitioners prefer pricing short-tenor instruments off a curve that models one-month interest rates (as they would typically only borrow funds in the market for a short period of time). To meet these requirements two curves are typically constructed for each currency:

■ Three-month curve
■ One-month curve.

The three-month curve construction methodology tends to use deposits, futures and swaps.

The one-month curve typically uses deposits and futures, as there is no need to include points at longer tenors, thus omitting swaps.

In addition to the above curves, a basis curve is often constructed and used to price cross-currency instruments. This curve models the market prices of such instruments more closely than the Libor curve as it captures the true cost of funding.

The methodology for all the above curves is described in subsequent paragraphs.

YIELD CURVE CONSTRUCTION METHODOLOGY

The three-month yield curve construction

As was stated earlier, the three-month curve is built using:

- Deposits
- Futures
- Swaps.

Deposits

Deposit (cash) rates are used until the first future or FRA contract becomes available. Discount factors are generated for the maturity date of each point in the curve using the equation for forward-forward rate and the relationship between the rate and the DF:

Yield curve discount factors derived from deposit rates — Calculation Summary

$$\left(1 + r_S \times \frac{days_S}{year}\right) \times \left(1 + r_{S,E} \times \frac{days_{S,E}}{year}\right) = 1 + r_E \times \frac{days_E}{year}$$

$$d = \frac{1}{1 + r \times \dfrac{days}{year}}$$

$$d_E = d_S \times d_{S,E} = d_S \times \frac{1}{\left(1 + r \times \dfrac{days_{S,E}}{year}\right)}$$

where:

$year$ is the number of days in the year

$days_S$, $days_E$ and $days_{S,E}$ are the relevant time periods

d_S and d_E are the discount factors for the period start and end date

$d_{S,E}$ is the discount factor for the period $days_{S,E}$

r_S and r_E are the spot rates for the period start and end dates

$r_{S,E}$ is the interest rate for the period $days_{S,E}$.

Futures

The relationship between the futures implied rate and the quoted price is $f = (100 - p)/100 + adj$, where f is the forward rate for the period starting at futures expiry date (expressed as a percentage) and adj is convexity adjustment (described below). As futures rate is given by:

Calculation Summary

Futures rate as a function of start and end period discount factors

$$f = \left[\frac{d_S}{d_E} - 1\right] \times \frac{year}{days_{S,E}}$$

where

$days_{S,E}$ is the time period covered

d_S and d_E are the discount factors for period start and end dates.

The DF for the end of the forward period can be calculated by rearranging the above equation:

Calculation Summary

Yield curve discount factors derived from futures prices

$$d_E = d_S \times \frac{1}{1 + f \times \frac{days_{S,E}}{year}}$$

Thus, the DFs at the end of each forward period can be calculated from the relevant futures price and the DF at the beginning of that period. Hence, the discount factor at the start date of the first future has to be known, i.e. the settlement date of the first futures contract should lie before the maturity date of the last deposit rate (thus it is necessary to include at least two cash rates into the curve).

A futures contract that settles at time t_1 (spanning the period from t_1 to t_2) that lies between two cash rates (e.g. 1M and 3M) gives two options for DF interpolation:

- Interpolating DF_1 for t_1 directly from DFs for 1M and 3M
- Interpolating rate at t_1 from 1M and 3M cash rates, and then deriving DF_1.

The decision on which method to use is simply a matter of choice.

Futures convexity adjustment

As discussed in Chapter 6, a FRA is sensitive to two rates:

■ The forward rate that determines the payment.

■ The spot rate that determines the DF used to calculate the present value of the cash flow.

In contrast, a future price is only sensitive to the forward rate as the variation margins are paid daily. Thus, the relationship between the future payoff and forward rate is linear, whereas it is convex for FRAs. Although this convexity effect is small at the short end of the yield curve, it becomes more significant as the maturity increases. As this is recognised by market practitioners, the implied futures rate is higher than the equivalent IMM FRA. This difference is often called convexity. As a market convention, convexity adjustment is defined as the difference between the futures rate and the FRA rate. Consequently, the curves using futures prices for construction incorporate this adjustment.

Swaps

As futures contract for longer tenors become less liquid they are substituted by swaps. The general equation for the DF of the last swap coupon payment will be deduced from an example of a two-year annual swap, where the present value (PV) of the future cashflows is calculated as the difference between the fixed and the floating legs:

$$PV(\text{swap}) = PV(\text{floating})$$

$$P \times C \times \left(d_1 \times \frac{\text{days}_1}{\text{year}} + d_2 \times \frac{\text{days}_2}{\text{year}} \right) = P \times \left(L_{0,1} \times d_1 \times \frac{\text{days}_1}{\text{year}} + L_{1,2} \times d_2 \times \frac{\text{days}_2}{\text{year}} \right)$$

where:

P is the notional principal

d_k is the discount factor for the end of period k, implying $d_0 = 1$

days_k is the number of days in the coupon period k

$L_{k-1,k}$ is Libor for that period

C is the fixed coupon rate for the duration of the swap.

As the interest rate r implied by the DFs for adjacent periods, calculated as:

$$r_{k-1,k} = \left[\frac{d_{k-1}}{d_k} - 1 \right] \times \frac{\text{year}}{\text{days}_k}$$

is equivalent to the Libor rate for that period; substituting $L_{k-1,k}$ for $r_{k-1,k}$ and d_0 with 1 reduces PV(floating) to:

$$PV(\text{floating}) = P \times (1 - d_2)$$

Hence:

$$C \times \left(d_1 \times \frac{days_1}{year} + d_2 \times \frac{days_2}{year} \right) = 1 - d_2$$

Thus d_2 can be calculated by rearranging the above equation:

$$d_2 = \frac{1 - C \times d_1 \times \dfrac{days_1}{year}}{1 + C \times \dfrac{days_2}{year}}$$

Hence, calculation of d_2 requires knowledge of d_1.

The above equation can be generalised to give the discount factors for all subsequent points:

Calculation Summary

Yield curve discount factors derived from swap rates

$$d_n = \frac{1 - C \times \displaystyle\sum_{k=1}^{n-1} d_k \times \frac{days_k}{year}}{1 + C \times \dfrac{days_n}{year}}$$

It is clear that in order to apply the above expression, all the swap rates and the DFs associated with all but the last payment date have to be known or otherwise interpolated. This process (known as 'bootstrapping') is performed in ascending order of maturity, commencing with the first point in the swap strip.

Bootstrapping the swap strip

If only the last discount factor (d_n) in the swap strip is unknown, it can be calculated directly from the last equation. However, if there are two or more DFs then all unknowns must be solved for simultaneously using iterative approximation.

The method of calculation of DFs for new swaps in the curve depends on the frequency of the two swap legs as well as the presence of the synthetic swap DFs (linearly interpolated from the market values). Synthetic DFs are typically introduced when the fixed leg has a higher frequency than the floating leg, so that the values at those intermediate points are readily available.

The following summarises all possible cases:

Fixed and floating leg frequency is the same: Each new swap introduces only one unknown (d_n) which is calculated directly from the last equation.

Different frequency, synthetic DFs available: The fixed leg payment rates can be derived from market data (used to calculate intermediate DFs, as described above), hence the case is directly solvable as above.

Different frequency, no synthetic DFs: The first market-quoted swap maturity is too far away from the last future contract and intermediate DFs are needed. This generates several unknown DFs that must be solved for simultaneously using iterative approximation. In this case, the first DF in the swap strip (beyond the futures strip) can be calculated by interpolating between the last future and the first market-quoted swap, repeating the process for all required points.

Two alternative interpolation methods that can be used for bootstrapping are described below.

Interpolation methods
Zero-rate linear interpolation

Zero-rate is the interest rate prevailing between two dates assuming that all the interest is paid at maturity. As zero-rate is a continuously compounded rate, it relates to DF and the spot rate as:

$$\exp\left(-z_k \times \frac{days_k}{year}\right) = d_k = \frac{1}{1 + r_k \times \dfrac{days_k}{year}}$$

which, when rearranged, gives:

$$z_k = -\frac{year}{days_k} \ln(d_k)$$

The unknown zero-rate z_x is interpolated by fitting a straight line between the two adjacent points z_1 and z_2:

$$z_x = z_1 + (z_2 - z_1) \times \frac{days_{1,x}}{days_{1,2}}$$

or

$$z = z_1 \times \frac{days_{x,2}}{days_{1,2}} + z_2 \times \frac{days_{1,x}}{days_{1,2}}$$

By substituting into the above equation, the DF for the unknown point can be calculated as:

Linear interpolation of yield curve discount factors   **Calculation Summary**

$$d_x = d_1 \wedge \left(\frac{days_x}{days_{1,2}} \times \frac{days_{x,2}}{days_1}\right) \times d_2 \wedge \left(\frac{days_x}{days_{1,2}} \times \frac{days_{1,x}}{days_2}\right)$$

where the symbol $\wedge$ denotes 'power of'.

Log-linear interpolation

Log-linear (geometric) interpolation assumes that the continuously compounded interest rate over any period within the given time interval t_1 to t_2 is the same as the continuously compounded rate over the entire period. Hence, using the same notation as above, the unknown DF can be calculated as:

Calculation Summary	**Log-linear interpolation of yield curve discount factors** $$d_x = d_1{}^{\wedge}\left(\frac{days_{x,2}}{days_{1,2}}\right) \times d_2{}^{\wedge}\left(\frac{days_{1,x}}{days_{1,2}}\right)$$ which can be rearranged into: $$d_x = d_1 \times \left(\frac{d_2}{d_1}\right){}^{\wedge}\left(\frac{days_{1,x}}{days_{1,2}}\right) = d_2 \times \left(\frac{d_1}{d_2}\right){}^{\wedge}\left(\frac{days_{x,2}}{days_{1,2}}\right)$$

THE ONE-MONTH YIELD CURVE CONSTRUCTION

Curve instruments

One-month curves are used by market practitioners to price short-term instruments (particularly those with one-month tenors). Since these instruments do not require long-term rates, the curve construction typically omits swaps and is based on:

- Deposits
- Futures/IMM FRAs

Curve construction

Constructing the one-month curve is much simpler than the process required by the three-month curve. As the curve only covers the short period, there is always sufficient market data for the calculation of DFs. Given that the periods covered by the interest rates are short, all the market rates r_k can be converted into continuously compounded rates z_k using:

$$z_k = \frac{year}{days_k} \times \ln\left(1 + r_k \times \frac{days_k}{year}\right)$$

Regardless of whether the deposit or future/FRA rate is used, the one-month rates can be calculated from the available market data using an expression akin to the futures or FRAs strip rate:

Derivation of one-month rates from available market rates

$$\left(1 + z_S \times \frac{days_S}{year}\right) \times \ldots \times \left(1 + z_E \times \frac{days_E}{year}\right) = 1 + z \times \frac{days}{year}$$

In other words, the effect of compounding the one-month rates has to be the same as the original continuously compounded rate. This is typically achieved by iteratively adjusting the rates until conversion criteria are reached.

The above procedure is repeated for all market rates used in the curve, thus obtaining a series of one-month rates for different tenors. They are used to calculate DFs as follows:

One-month curve discount factors derived from one-month rates

$$d_E = \exp\left(-z_{S,E} \times \frac{days_{S,E}}{year}\right)$$

where:

    year is the number of days in the year

    $days_{S,E}$ is the time period covered by one-month rates

    $z_{S,E}$ is the continuously compounded one-month rates for that period.

THE BASIS CURVE CONSTRUCTION

Introduction

The underlying assumption behind the three-month and the one-month curves described in the previous sections is that the funding rate prevailing in the market is Libor (or equivalent for a given currency). This is the rate used to represent floating rate funding as well as calculating DFs. However, not all market practitioners have access to Libor funding, particularly in cross-currency transactions.

Hence a curve – called a basis curve – that represents a true cost of funding is needed.

Basis curve methodology

The basis curve is typically constructed using deposits and swaps. The futures, as exchange-traded instruments, do not incur additional financing costs; hence they are replaced by swaps of shorter maturities in order to close the gap after the last deposit contract.

Thus the basis curve DFs are calculated as follows:

- Short-end DFs are calculated from the Libor rates increased by market-implied spread, to reflect the true cost of funding (basis).

- Medium-term DFs are calculated from swaps, by adding the predetermined spread to the Libor rates implied by futures.

- For long-term DFs, two unknown quantities (dn and Ln) are introduced for every new point and are calculated by simultaneously solving the basis and Libor curves.

The sections below describe this process in more detail.

Short-term rates (deposits)

The basis curve deposit discount factors are calculated using the following expression (slight modification of the Libor curve approach):

Calculation Summary

Basis curve discount factors derived from deposit rates

$$d_E = d_S \times d_{S,E} = d_S \times \cfrac{1}{\left(1 + (r + b) \times \cfrac{days_{S,E}}{year}\right)}$$

where:

r is the prevailing Libor rate

b is the estimated basis

$days_{S,E}$ is the time period covered

d_S and d_E are the discount factors for the period start and end dates

$d_{S,E}$ is the discount factor for the period $days_{S,E}$

r_S and r_E are the spot rates for the period start and end dates

$r_{S,E}$ is the interest rate the period $days_{S,E}$.

Medium-term rates (swaps)

To compensate for the lack of futures in the medium-term part of the curve, swaps of shorter maturities are used. However, they are not incorporated in the same way as for three-month Libor curve. As Libor rates are known at these maturities (as implied by the futures used in the Libor curve), d_n for every new swap point can simply be calculated from:

Basis curve discount factors derived from medium-term swap rates   **Calculation Summary**

$$\sum_{k=1}^{n}\left(L_{k-1,k} + b_n\right) \times d_k \times \frac{days_k}{year} = d_0 - d_n$$

using know Libor rates L_k and predetermined basis b_n.

Each basis curve can have one or more Libor curves, used for calculating floating swap legs, associated with it.

Long-term rates (swaps)

As the Libor curve is used for calculating floating leg cashflows, and the basis curve is used for discounting, each new swap point needs to satisfy both curves, i.e. the vanilla swap equation:

$$\sum_{j=1}^{n} L_{j-1,j} \times d_j \times \frac{days_j}{year} = C_m \times \sum_{i=1}^{m} d_i \times \frac{days_i}{year}$$

and the basis swap equation:

$$\sum_{k=1}^{n}\left(L_{k-1,k} + b_n\right) \times d_k \times \frac{days_k}{year} = d_0 - d_n$$

where:

    $days_k$ is the number of days in the coupon period k

    C is the fixed coupon rate for the vanilla swap

    $L_{k-1,k}$ is the Libor for the period k

    b_n is the basis over Libor for the particular swap.

The summation factors i, j and k are deliberately different to account for different leg frequencies of different swaps and their individual legs.

    Rearranging the second equation and substituting the first into it, gives:

Basis curve discount factors derived from long-term swap rates   **Calculation Summary**

$$C_m \times \sum_{i=1}^{m} d_i \times \frac{days_i}{year} + b_n \times \sum_{k=1}^{n} d_k \times \frac{days_k}{year} = d_0 - d_n$$

or for i = k (i.e. m = n):

$$\left(C_n + b_n\right) \times \sum_{k=1}^{n} d_k \times \frac{days_k}{year} = d_0 - d_n$$

The bootstrapping procedure is exactly the same as for the three-month curve, solving directly if only one d_n is unknown, or simultaneously for more than one DF.

SHAPE OF THE YIELD CURVE

There are several theories behind the yield curve shape:

1. *The pure expectations theory* states that the only determinant of the yield curve shape is investors' expectations of future short-term interest rates.

2. *The liquidity preference theory* is based on the assumption that the investors expect to be compensated for having their funds tied up for long periods, requiring ever increasing yields for longer maturities

3. *The preferred habitat theory* is similar to the above, implying that investors expect higher returns for longer maturities, as they are associated with more risk. However, the risk arises from liquidity of the longer-term securities (as most investors plan short and medium term), rather than purely from maturity.

Because the yield curve can reflect investors' expectations of interest rates, inflation, political and economic events as well as the impact of risk premiums for longer-term investments, interpreting the yield curve is complicated. Market practitioners put great effort into trying to understand exactly what factors are driving the yields.

Normal yield curve

A normal yield curve implies that yields rise with maturity (i.e., the slope of the yield curve is positive). This reflects market expectations of economic growth and increased inflation in the future. The typical response of central banks in such a scenario is raising short-term interest rates to encourage saving, rather than spending. There is also uncertainty associated with estimates of future interest rates and the funds put on long-term deposit. Investors price these risks by demanding higher yields for maturities further into the future.

Steep yield curve

Extending the logic from the above, the steep yield curve implies market expectations that the economy will grow at faster rate in the future than in the current period, such as at times of expansion.

Flat or humped yield curve

When all maturities have similar yields, a flat yield curve is observed. This implies uncertainty in the economy, whereby the market participants are holding off their investment decisions until the situation clarifies. Another possibility is a humped curve, created when medium-term yields are higher than those of the short term and long term. This typically implies market expectation of rapid economic growth in the short term with more uncertainty in the future.

Inverted yield curve

The inverted yield curve represents market expectation of worsening economy. In addition to economic decline, inverted yield curves also imply that the inflation is likely to remain low.

GRAPHICAL YIELD CURVE REPRESENTATION

The above curve construction methodologies are implemented as computer software which generates curves for each currency. Their output is typically a range of discount factors (DFs) for selected dates. If a DF is required for a non-grid point, interpolation is used to provide the rate or DF for that date. But the curves are often represented graphically to give some idea of market expectations, with the tenors on the x-axes and yields on the y-axes.

15

Quantitative analytics

ROLE OF QUANTITATIVE ANALYTICS

The quantitative analytics team (also known as 'quants') is the crucial part of the investment bank front office. They are highly educated individuals who typically hold PhDs in maths and physics, whose job is the creation of complex mathematical models used for pricing existing and innovative financial instruments. Their expertise is best utilised in derivatives markets, as they operate with many unknown variables. They tend to specialise in a particular class of products, so the teams are typically sub-divided into interest rate derivatives, equity and FX derivatives, commodity derivatives and credit derivatives. As the interest rate market is the biggest by volume and offers the widest range of derivatives products, the majority of quantitative analytics work is done in this field, which is reflected in the number of quants. Their work is usually complemented by the support of the quant IT team who 'translate' the mathematical models into computer software to be incorporated into a wide range of IT systems used by the bank.

CLASSIFICATION OF PRICING MODELS

There are numerous quantitative models used to price financial instruments. Whilst there is a market convention when it comes to the main concepts and techniques used to price different product classes, most investment banks use proprietary models or bespoke modifications to standard methods to price their products. This chapter offers a classification of the most popular, and publicly known, models used in derivatives pricing. For each model or technique only a brief description, with the pros and cons, is given. This was done deliberately, as these techniques are very complex, each requiring advanced knowledge of calculus and an entire book devoted to them. Hence this chapter aims just to give an overview of various pricing techniques, as a glimpse into the complexity involved in derivatives valuation.

The main division of existing pricing models is into:

- Numerical models
- Analytical models.

The numerical models can be further sub-divided by their use into:

- Models offering complete solutions by numerical methods
- Numerical solutions to complex analytical equations.

Whilst the analytical models can be:

- Equations used for pricing particular instruments
- Equations describing the behaviour of the underlying variables.

The main numerical methods currently in use in quantitative analysis are: Monte Carlo simulation, binomial and trinomial trees, finite difference methods and interest rate trees.

Summary of numerical quantitative methods — Key Point

Monte Carlo simulation

Trees (binomial, trinomial)

Finite difference methods

Interest rate trees

The main analytical quantitative methods currently in use are: simple pricing equations (money market products, bonds, swaps etc.); vanilla product models (Black–Scholes, Black models); models for exotic products (models of the entire yield curve) – further subdivided into equilibrium models and no-arbitrage models.

Summary of analytical quantitative methods — Key Point

Simple pricing equations (money market products, bonds, swaps etc.)

Vanilla product models (Black–Scholes, Black models)

Exotic products (models of the entire yield curve):

    Equilibrium models

    No-arbitrage models

NUMERICAL METHODS

Monte Carlo simulation

General principles

Monte Carlo simulation generates random samples of possible behaviours of a variable. Many samples are generated and an average is calculated as a most likely outcome. For example, Monte Carlo calculation of the constant π can be done by drawing a circle inside a square and randomly positioning dots inside the whole area of the square. Since the area of a square is well known ($A = a^2$) and the area of the circle inside it is $a^2 \pi/4$, π can be calculated from the ratio of dots that fall in and out of the circle. Similarly for the calculation of a payoff of a certain financial product that depends on the evolution of the entire yield curve, simulating different paths that the curve can take will provide an average (and most likely) payoff.

Pros and cons

The Monte Carlo technique is useful for pricing derivatives where the payoff is dependent on the history of the underlying variable or where there are several underlying variables. It can accommodate complex payoffs and complex stochastic processes. It is numerically very efficient, as the time taken for the simulation increases approximately linearly with the number of variables. Its drawback is that it can be used for European style derivatives only, i.e. no early exercise is allowed.

Binomial and trinomial trees

General principles

Binomial and trinomial trees are typically used to price options on an underlying variable (e.g. stock). They rely on the assumption that the stock price movements consist of very small binary steps in very short time intervals. The time to maturity is divided into small intervals and at each interval the stock price can only go up or down in by a predetermined amount. The probability of up and down movements is assumed. Since payoff at maturity is known, it can be calculated at each branch of the tree. Working backwards through the nodes enables the calculation of the option price today.

Pros and cons

Trees are useful for pricing products where decisions can be made at each step (e.g. American options) as well as for pricing dividend paying stocks. Options on indices, currencies and futures contracts can also be valued using this technique. Variables (interest rates, volatility) can be varied between the tree nodes. Binomial and trinomial trees can also be used in conjunction with *control variate* techniques. For example, the European option price can be calculated using the Black–Scholes formula and compared with the price obtained from the binomial tree. Assuming that this is the error that the tree introduces into pricing, the price of an American style option (obtained using the tree) can be adjusted by this amount. This approach can be easily extended to non-recombining trees, trees with more than up/down movements (e.g. trinomial trees that have a mid-path). However, tree building is time-consuming and computationally extensive. Furthermore, its main shortcoming is that it is not suitable for derivatives dependent on past history.

Finite difference methods

General characteristics

Finite difference methods are similar to trees, whereby the calculation works backwards from the terminal value to the start date. They are used to solve a differential equation that a variable satisfies when the equation does not have an analytical solution or is very difficult to solve. The equation is converted into a set of finite difference equations and those are solved iteratively. For example, a partial differential equation (containing derivatives of any order) in two variables can be represented by a two-dimensional mesh with one variable on the x-axis and another on the y-axis. Each (x, y) point represents one state of the world, with grid boundaries representing the final values. Akin to tree techniques, the value of the derivative is known at expiry (e.g. the value of a call option with strike 20 is 5 when the stock price at expiry is 25), hence it is used as boundary condition. First, second and higher order derivatives can also be represented by differences in grid positions. In this way a single differential equation is represented by a different equation at every grid point. The set of equations is solved to yield the price of a derivative at inception.

Pros and cons

Finite difference methods are used for the same types of derivative pricing problems as trees. Hence, they can price both American and European style options, but do not easily handle derivatives with a payoff dependent on historical values. Finite difference methods can also be combined with control variate techniques for improved accuracy. Furthermore, risk parameters (delta, gamma) can be calculated directly from the grid, making this approach very useful in risk evaluation and management. These techniques can be computationally extensive when used for problems involving several state variables.

Interest rate trees

General characteristics

The principle of interest rate tree construction is the same as for stock price trees (described earlier). Whereas in stock price trees the discounting rate is typically constant between the nodes, in interest rate trees the rate varies from node to node. It is often more convenient to use trinomial trees (rather than binomial ones) as they give more freedom. For example, trinomial trees can model mean reversion.

Pros and cons

As with all similar techniques, interest rate trees are used for pricing products where decisions can be made at each step (e.g. American options) as well as for pricing dividend-paying stocks, options on indices, currencies and futures contracts. Variables can be varied between the tree nodes. Binomial and trinomial trees can also be used in conjunction with *control variate* techniques. As with all tree-based techniques, this approach is computationally extensive. The main advantage is that it can be used to represent many yield curve models. Given the flexibility of the method, it can be used to fit any term structure.

Summary of the numerical methods

All of the above methods are reliable and tractable. Which one will be used depends mainly on the characteristics of the derivative being valued and the accuracy required. Monte Carlo simulation works forward from the beginning of the contract to maturity. It cannot be used for derivatives requiring knowledge of history. It is more efficient than tree and grid methods.

On the other hand, tree and finite difference methods work from the expiry backwards in order to evaluate the security in question. Computationally very demanding, these methods can accommodate early exercise. Interest rate trees are effectively just a sub-class of a standard tree, but give a flexibility that accommodates changes of discount rates between the nodes. As they can fit any yield curve term structure required, they can implement many of the analytical models.

ANALYTICAL METHODS

Simple pricing equations

This class of methods includes pricing products that have known payments, no optionality or other special features. Typically these products are:

- Simple money-market deposits
- Bonds
- Swaps.

These products all have known payment dates (simple deposits and zero coupon bonds typically have only one payment at maturity) and the payment values are either fixed or linked to the yield curve (floating rate). There is no uncertainty over whether the payments will take place, how much will be paid (we are not certain of the yield curve in the future, but current forward rates are the best estimate of the future cashflows). This is why there are no specific models to price these products. The equations are simple streams of future cashflows discounted to today using discount factors calculated from today's yield curve. They have all been extensively covered in previous chapters.

The above products have some features that require closer attention. For example:

- CMS/CMT (constant maturity swaps/constant maturity treasury) swaps have one or both legs linked to a long-term swap rate (rather than the Libor rate whose tenor matches payment frequency). In this case the model has to take into account convexity (non-linear relationship between the yield and the price) adjustment before it can continue pricing the swap in the same manner as its vanilla counterpart.

- RPI (retail price index – price index of common household goods, and thus a measure of inflation) swaps have one leg linked to the RPI index. This requires the knowledge of the forward inflation rates (in UK modelled using Gilts). LPI in particular has a feature that collars the movements of RPI index and as such has some features of caps and floors. This moves the product out of this 'simple' category, as we now have to assume that the inflation is stochastic and use Monte Carlo simulation (or other suitable method) to predict the most likely value out of the many paths inflation can take.

- Quanto swaps (where one or more legs are linked to an index in one currency, but payable in another) require calculation of the Quanto adjustment (correlation between the FX and the interest rate) before continuing with pricing using a 'vanilla' equation.

In summary, pricing the products with the known number, timing and often size of the cashflows reduces to calculating their present value in order to price the products at inception. At some future date the value of the position is calculated in the same way, taking into account all the outstanding payments. These products use yield curves (built from the most liquid products in the market) to project and discount the future cashflows. The discounting and projection index can be, but are not required to be, the same.

Vanilla product models

This class of models includes, for example, the Black–Scholes (used to price stock options) and Black models (used to price interest rate derivatives), both described in Chapter 9. These models are quick and robust but are not flexible enough to accommodate pricing more exotic products.

Black–Scholes model

Much quicker than any of the numerical methods, the B–S model uses a single equation to price call and put options on stocks. The model assumptions are:

1. No dividends or accrued interest on underlying.

2. No early exercise.

3. Constant risk free-interest rate.

4. Constant volatility.

5. Price of the underlying is normally distributed.

6. Continuous trading is assumed and no transaction costs/taxes.

7. Short selling of securities is allowed.

The B–S model has been extended (with minor modifications) to cover dividend-paying stocks (known dividend model), American style options (pseudo American model), options on indices, currency options

(Garman–Kohlhagen model), options on futures (Black model), American options with only one dividend (Roll–Geske–Whaley model) etc.

Black model

As mentioned above, the Black model is an extension of the B–S model, hence the same assumptions apply. In terms of implementation and the computational speed, it is the same as B–S. It uses the assumption of the B–S model that the security will be held until its maturity, thus the evolution of interest rates during the life of the security is irrelevant and all that matters is its value at maturity. Hence rates are treated as if they are tradable securities.

Pros and cons

- The model is simple to use, quick to implement and compute.
- One formula used for pricing a range of derivatives.
- It is widely used for valuing caps/floors, European bond options, swap options etc.
- Its drawback is that it does not model yield curve term structure.
- Due to the constant volatility assumption, it gives rise to volatility smile (the volatility of deep OTM and ITM options implied from the B–S and Black models is higher than for ATM options).
- Assumptions behind the model are not realistic.

Exotic products (models of the entire yield curve)

These models are attempting to accommodate different features of the products emerging in OTC markets. Their aim is to model the evolution of the entire yield curve (rather than working with the terminal values of interest rates). They can be broadly classified as: equilibrium models and no-arbitrage models.

Equilibrium models

Equilibrium models are also called *short rate models* as they describe behaviours of economic variables in terms of an instantaneous short-term rate r (the rate that prevails from one moment to the next). As this rate is not a tradable quantity it does not describe the real world. The models based on the short rate assume that derivative prices depend only on the process followed by r in a risk-neutral world (where the positions are perfectly hedged to create zero profit/loss regardless of market moves). Once the process for r is fully defined, it is assumed to implicitly define the initial term structure and its future evolution. The main disadvantage of the equilibrium model is that the initial yield curve term structure is the output of the model, rather than the input to it. Hence calibrating the model outputs to the available market data can be an issue.

One-factor models

In one-factor models the process for the instantaneous short-term rate r has only one source of uncertainty. The drift and the standard deviation are taken to be functions of r, but independent of time. One-factor models imply that, over any short time interval, all rates move in the same direction, albeit by potentially different amounts. This feature enables modelling of a very rich pattern of term structures, but does not allow for curve shape inversion (where long-term rates are lower than the short-term ones).

Examples of one-factor models are:

- Rendleman and Bartter model
- Vasicek model
- Cox, Ingersoll and Ross model.

Rendleman and Bartter model

- Assumes that the short-term rate exhibits properties of stock price.
- As a consequence, it can easily be represented by a binomial tree.
- Short-term rates have normal distribution (hence can be negative).
- Constant expected growth rate and volatility are implicitly assumed by the model.
- Due to only one factor in the model, mean reversion cannot be incorporated (no pull-back to some long-term average).

Vasicek model

- Akin to the above, constant expected growth rate and volatility are implicitly assumed.
- Short-term rates have normal distribution (hence can be negative).
- Unlike above, this model is extended to support mean reversion, albeit at a constant rate.
- Can be used to value options on zero-coupon and coupon-bearing bonds.

Cox, Ingersoll and Ross model

- The short-term rate is log-normally distributed (hence, it is non-negative).
- This approach also supports mean reversion at a constant rate.
- Standard deviation of the stochastic term is proportional to $r^{1/2}$, implying its increase or decrease with the instantaneous short-term rate.

Two-factor models

Here the process for the instantaneous short-term rate r is assumed to have two sources of uncertainty. The drift and the standard deviation are now taken to be functions of both r and time. This allows modelling term structures with an even richer pattern than in one-factor models. Given the two-factor approach, one factor can drive the curve level, whilst the second factor governs its 'tilt'. Thus the points along the curve can move in opposite directions, allowing for curve inversion. Examples of two-factor models are:

- Brennan and Schwartz model
- Longstaff and Schwartz model.

Brennan and Schwartz model

- The long-term rate is assumed to follow a stochastic process.
- A yield on a perpetual bond paying $1 annual coupon is used to model the long-term rate.
- The process governing the behaviour of the short rate reverts to a long-term rate.
- The analysis is simplified by the fact that the fictive bond used in modelling the long-term rate is a tradable security (i.e. in a risk-neutral world, the rate of increase in bond price must be equal to the risk-free interest rate reduced by the bond yield).

Longstaff and Schwartz model

- This model assumes stochastic volatility.
- It is quite tractable, hence favoured by market practitioners.

The disadvantage of all equilibrium models is that they do not automatically fit the market-driven yield curve term structure. However, careful parameter selection enables this class of models to approximately fit most of the term structures encountered in practice (albeit with significant errors). Thus traders and market practitioners are reluctant to rely on these models when pricing derivatives securities. This has led to the emergence of the no-arbitrage models described in the following section.

No-arbitrage models

No-arbitrage models implicitly fit today's term structure. They take today's term structure for granted and use it as an input to define the process of its evolution over time. Different no-arbitrage models use one of the three distinct (but equivalent) approaches:

- Modelling bond prices
- Modelling forward rates
- Modelling short rate.

Models of bond prices and forward rates (the first two approaches) are generally non-Markov[*] and have to be solved numerically using Monte Carlo simulation or a non-recombining tree. However, the choice of volatilities used in the model is left to the practitioner, with only one condition – the volatility has to approach zero at maturity.

Models of short rates are usually Markov and analytically tractable. However, unlike the approach above, in this case the practitioner does not have complete freedom of choice of volatility. The initial volatility is typically consistent with the modelled value, but the future model-implied volatility might be inconsistent with the market data.

Non-Markov models

An example of a non-Markov model based on forward rates is *Heath-Jarrow and Morton*. Its main characteristics are:

- It is a two-factor model of forward rates
- Rates are assumed to be log-normally distributed (thus non-negative)
- One factor drives the curve parallel shift, whist the other governs the twist (hence rates can move in opposite directions, allowing for inversion)
- Due to the model flexibility, a very realistic term structure can be achieved
- The future rate stochastic behaviour over a short period of time is defined by both the initial value of r as well as the path of its evolution
- As it is non-Markov, this model cannot be represented by a recombining tree; as an upward move followed by a downward move would not result in the same value as if an opposite route was taken
- Due to the above, it is typically implemented using Monte-Carlo simulation.

Markov models

Most Markov models are developed in terms of short rate r, assuming the drift to be a function of time (thus these models are typically consistent with the initial term structure). This makes them a logical extension of the equilibrium models described earlier. The Markov property also makes it possible to use recombining trees.

---

[*]*Markov process* is a particular type of stochastic process where only the present value of a variable is relevant for predicting the future. This implies that all the history is contained in the present state and is irrelevant for the future evolution of the process.

As these models are explicit functions of short rate r (not observable in practice), they tend to be consistent with only the short end, rather than the entire yield curve.

Some examples of Markov models are:

- Ho and Lee model
- Hull and White Model
- Black, Derman and Toy*
- Black–Karasinski*.

Ho and Lee model

- This is a one-factor model, with only one function of time.
- Interest rates are assumed to be normally distributed (hence can be negative).
- An exact fit to the current term structure is easily achieved.
- Volatility structure is governed by the model, rather than left to the practitioner's choice.
- Standard deviation of spot and forward rates is the identical.
- Due to only one factor, the model does not allow for mean reversion.
- The modelled interest rate average direction from one short period to the next is always the same and independent of the current rate level.
- The model is easy to apply and tractable, thus favoured by some market practitioners.

Hull and White model

- This is a two-factor model, with the same characteristics as the Vasicek model and the addition of time-dependent reversion level.
- Similarly, it is identical to the Ho and Lee model, with added mean reversion as a second parameter (hence Ho and Lee can be viewed as a special case of Hull and White with mean reversion parameter a = 0).
- Given their similarities, the analytical tractability of the Hull and White model is on a par with Ho and Lee, despite added complexity.
- The rate r is modelled so that on average it is consistent with the behaviour of the initial instantaneous rate. If it diverges, it reverts back at the rate a.
- Just as in Ho and Lee, the volatility is governed by the model, rather than by the user. However, its structure is determined by two factors – instantaneous standard deviation and mean reversion parameter – providing a wider range of structures than Ho and Lee.

---

* These are non-stationary models (several parameters are functions of time).

Black, Derman and Toy

- In this model the short rate r is assumed to be log-normally distributed (thus it is non-negative).

- It is easy to implement and quite tractable.

- It can be made to fit the initial term structure, as it can be easily calibrated to caplet market prices.

- However, as the mean reversion rate is governed by the model, rather than the user, it cannot be calibrated to both swaptions and caps simultaneously.

- Here, several parameters are a function of time, thus allowing for flexibility.

Black and Karasinski

- This model is very similar to Black, Derman and Toy in that the short rate r is assumed to be log-normally distributed (non-negative).

- Here, several parameters are a function of time, allowing for flexibility.

- Calibration to market prices of caplets is simple, hence it can fit the initial term structure.

- It is tractable and easy to implement.

- However, this model allows for adjustment of the mean reversion rate.

- Can be implemented using binomial trees, whereby varying time periods associated with different steps can lead to rich patterns.

In summary, short rate models are simple, easy to implement and fast to run. However, neither the short rate nor mean reversion and short rate volatility are directly observable in the market. Thus the models suffer from a general lack of transparency and a difficulty in incorporating market changes.

BGM model

The BGM (Brace–Gaterek–Musiela) model is an arbitrage-free model. It allows the arbitrage-free evolution of discrete points of a yield curve described either in terms of forward rates or swap rates. Unlike other models described earlier, it does not rely on the dynamics of unobservable or pseudo-observable quantities (e.g. instantaneous short rate, instantaneous forward rates, variance of the short rate etc.). Instead, it directly models market-observable variables, such as Libor forward and swap rates and their volatilities. Due to its direct link to market parameters, it is often called a 'market model'. It implicitly allows for straightforward calibration to market rates/prices, whilst the forward and swap rate volatilities can be directly derived from the model, as they are directly used for its creation.

For the derivation of no-arbitrage conditions, BGM approach requires the following:

■ The market completeness (all prices and parameters have to be observable)

■ The deterministic volatilities and correlations, or dependent on the same stochastic variables (forward or swap rates) incorporated in the yield curve.

Due to the above restrictions, BGM cannot be used when volatilities are stochastically independent or when there are very large random jumps.

The BGM model can be used to price:

■ Path-dependent securities (e.g. average rate options, average price options, outperformance options, trigger swaps etc.)

■ Single look derivatives with complex payoffs (captions, floorptions or swaptions).

Conclusion

The above was a brief summary of methods and models used by quantitative analytics to price a wide range of derivatives, with the emphasis on interest rate derivatives. Modelling interest rates is equally important for other classes of securities; as funding, cashflow projections and a host of other parameters are ultimately affected by the yield curve evolution. However, pricing credit and commodity derivatives is typically done using product-specific models. Due to the range and complexity of these derivatives, their pricing models are outside the scope of this book.

Summary of pricing formulae

NOTATION

i	annual interest rate
n	number of payments per year
days	number of days in the investment/coupon period
year	number of days in a year
N	number of years or coupon periods
P	price
APR	annual percentage rate, effective rate or equivalent annual rate
PV	present value
FV	future value
DF	discount factor

TIME VALUE OF MONEY

Effective and nominal rates

Relationship between the interest rate i with n payments per year and the APR:

$$APR = \left(1 + \frac{i}{n}\right)^n - 1 \qquad\qquad i = \left[(1 + APR)^{\frac{1}{n}} - 1\right] \times n$$

$$APR = \left(1 + i \times \frac{days}{year}\right)^{\frac{year}{days}} - 1 \qquad\qquad i = \left[(1 + APR)^{\frac{days}{year}} - 1\right] \times \frac{year}{days}$$

Continuously compounded rate

$$r = \frac{year}{days} \times \ln\left(1 + i \times \frac{days}{year}\right)$$

where i is the nominal interest rate.

For annual effective rate APR:

$$r = \ln(1 + APR)$$

Reinvestment rates

For unequal rates applying to different investment periods:

$$\text{Proceeds} = \text{Principal} \times (1 + i_1)(1 + i_2)(1 + i_3) \cdots (1 + i_N)$$

Short-term investments

$$FV = PV \times \left(1 + i \times \frac{\text{days}}{\text{year}}\right)$$

$$PV = \frac{FV}{1 + i \times \dfrac{\text{days}}{\text{year}}}$$

$$i = \left(\frac{FV}{PV} - 1\right) \times \frac{\text{year}}{\text{days}}$$

$$APR = \left(\frac{FV}{PV}\right)^{\frac{\text{year}}{\text{days}}} - 1$$

Long-term investments

$$FV = PV \times (1 + i)^N$$

$$PV = \frac{FV}{(1 + i)^N}$$

$$i = \left(\frac{FV}{PV}\right)^{\frac{1}{N}} - 1$$

Discount factors

$$\text{Simple interest DF} = \frac{1}{1 + i \times \dfrac{\text{days}}{\text{year}}}$$

$$\text{Compound interest DF} = \frac{1}{(1 + i)^N}$$

NPV and IRR

Internal rate of return (IRR) is the rate that discounts all the cashflows, including any cashflow now, to zero.

IRR discounts all the future cashflows to a given NPV.

MONEY MARKETS CALCULATIONS

Certificate of deposit (CD)

Proceeds at maturity:

$$P = \frac{F \times \left(1 + \text{Coupon} \times \frac{\text{days}}{\text{year}}\right)}{\left(1 + i \times \frac{d_{pm}}{\text{year}}\right)}$$

Secondary market yield:

$$\text{Yield} = \left(\frac{P_{\text{sale}}}{P_{\text{purchase}}} - 1\right) \times \frac{\text{year}}{d_{ps}}$$

Discount instruments

Proceeds at maturity:

Maturity proceeds P = F(face value)

Secondary market price:

$$P = \frac{F}{\left(1 + i \times \frac{d_{pm}}{\text{year}}\right)}$$

CAPITAL MARKETS INSTRUMENTS

Simple bond dirty price formula

$$P = \sum_{k=1}^{N} \frac{C_k}{\left(1 + \frac{i}{n}\right)^{\frac{d_k \times n}{\text{year}}}}$$

where:

C_k is the kth cashflow (including the final redemption amount)

i is the bond yield, based on the payment frequency

n is the number of coupons per year

d_k is the number of days until the kth cashflow.

Accrued coupon

$$\text{Accrued coupon} = 100 \times C \times \frac{d_{cs}}{\text{year}}$$

where d_{cs} is the time period between the last coupon date and the sale of the bond.

Clean bond price

$$P = \frac{100}{\left(1 + \frac{i}{n}\right)^f}\left[\frac{C}{n} \times \frac{1 - \dfrac{1}{\left(1 + \frac{i}{n}\right)^N}}{1 - \dfrac{1}{\left(1 + \frac{i}{n}\right)}} + \frac{1}{\left(1 + \frac{i}{n}\right)^{N-1}}\right]$$

where:

C is the annual coupon rate

N is the number of outstanding coupons

i is the annual bond yield, based on the payment frequency

n is the number of coupons per year

f is the ratio between the number of days until the next coupon and the full coupon period.

Ex-dividend

$$\text{Accrued coupon} = -100 \times C \times \frac{d_{pc}}{\text{year}}$$

where:

d_{pc} is the time period between the bond purchase and the next coupon.

Bond yield

Flat yield:

$$\text{Flat yield} = (\text{Coupon rate/Clean price}) \times 100$$

Simple yield to maturity:

$$\text{Simple yield to maturity (JGRY)} = \frac{\text{Coupon rate} + \left(\dfrac{\text{Redemption amount} - \text{Clean price}}{\text{Years to maturity}}\right)}{\text{Clean price} \Big/ 100}$$

Yield accounting for coupon payments and irregular first coupon period (derived from the pricing formula):

$$P = \frac{100}{\left(1+\frac{i}{n}\right)^f} \left[\frac{C}{n} \times \frac{1 - \dfrac{1}{\left(1+\frac{i}{n}\right)^N}}{1 - \dfrac{1}{\left(1+\frac{i}{n}\right)}} + \frac{1}{\left(1+\frac{i}{n}\right)^{N-1}} \right]$$

where:

C is the annual coupon rate

N is the number of outstanding coupons

i is the annual bond yield, based on the payment frequency

n is the number of coupons per year

f is the ratio between the number of days until the next coupon and the full coupon period.

Portfolio duration

Macaulay duration:

$$\text{Duration} = \frac{\sum\limits_{t=1}^{n} t \times PV_t}{\sum\limits_{t=1}^{n} PV_t}$$

Modified duration:

$$\Delta Y \times \text{Modified duration} = \frac{\Delta P}{P}$$

$$\text{Modified duration} = \frac{\text{Macaulay duration}}{1 + GRY}$$

FINANCIAL FUTURES

Futures price

$$\text{Price} = 100 - \text{Implied forward interest rate} \times 100$$

Futures settlement price

$$\text{Profit/Loss} = \text{Notional} \times \frac{\text{Sale price} - \text{Purchase price}}{100} \times \frac{1}{4}$$

Expressed in terms of 'ticks':

$$\text{Profit/Loss} = \text{Tick movement} \times \text{Tick size} \times \text{Number of contracts}$$

Futures strip rate

$$\left(1 + f_1 \times t_1\right)\left(1 + f_2 \times t_2\right) \cdots \left(1 + f_n \times t_n\right) = \left(1 + f_S \times t_S\right)$$

FORWARD RATE AGREEMENTS (FRAs)

FRA rate

$$\text{Forward–forward rate} = \left[\frac{1 + i_L \times \dfrac{d_L}{\text{year}}}{1 + i_S \times \dfrac{d_S}{\text{year}}} - 1\right] \times \frac{\text{year}}{d_L - d_S}$$

where:

i_L is the interest rate for the longer period

i_S is the interest rate for the shorter period

d_L is the number of days in the longer period

d_S is the number of days in the shorter period

year is the number of days in the year.

FRA settlement price

$$\text{FRA settlement price} = \text{Notional principal} \times \left[\frac{(f - \text{Libor}) \times \dfrac{d_f}{\text{year}}}{1 + \text{Libor} \times \dfrac{d_f}{\text{year}}}\right]$$

where:

f is the FRA interest rate

d_f is the number of days in the FRA period

year is the number of days in the year.

INTEREST RATE SWAPS

Short-term swap valuation at inception

$$1 = DF_N + \sum_{k=1}^{N} r_S \times \frac{days_k}{year} \times DF_k$$

where:

r_S is the swap rate

$days_k$ is the number of days covered by the kth FRA contract

DF_k is the discount factor derived from the kth FRA rate f using:

$$DF_k = \frac{1}{1 + f \times \dfrac{days_k}{year}}$$

Later valuation of short-term swap fixed leg

$$P = \left[DF_N + \sum_{k=1}^{N} r_S \times \frac{days_k}{year} \times DF_k \right] \times 100$$

where:

P is the value of the fixed leg at a later date

r_S is the swap rate, fixed at inception

$days_k$ is the number of days covered by the kth FRA contract

DF_k is the discount factor derived from the kth FRA rate f_k using:

$$DF_k = \frac{1}{1 + f_k \times \dfrac{days_k}{year}}$$

FOREIGN EXCHANGE

Spot rates

Given exchange rates X/Y and X/Z, the cross-rates are:

$$(Y/Z)_{bid} = (X/Z)_{bid} \div (X/Y)_{offer}$$
$$(Y/Z)_{offer} = (X/Z)_{offer} \div (X/Y)_{bid}$$

and

$$(Z/Y)_{bid} = 1/(Y/Z)_{offer}$$
$$(Z/Y)_{offer} = 1/(Y/Z)_{bid}$$

Given exchange rates Y/X and Z/X, the cross-rates are:

$(Y/Z)_{bid} = (Y/X)_{bid} \div (Z/X)_{offer}$
$(Y/Z)_{offer} = (Y/X)_{offer} \div (Z/X)_{bid}$

and

$(Z/Y)_{bid} = 1/(Y/Z)_{offer}$
$(Z/Y)_{offer} = 1/(Y/Z)_{bid}$

Given exchange rates Y/X and X/Z, the cross-rates are:

$(Y/Z)_{bid} = (Y/X)_{bid} \times (X/Z)_{bid}$
$(Y/Z)_{offer} = (Y/X)_{offer} \times (X/Z)_{offer}$

and

$(Z/Y)_{bid} = 1/(Y/Z)_{offer}$
$(Z/Y)_{offer} = 1/(Y/Z)_{bid}$

Forward outrights

$$FX_f = FX_s \times \frac{1 + r_v \times \frac{days}{year}}{1 + r_b \times \frac{days}{year}}$$

where:

FX$_f$ is the forward exchange rate

FX$_s$ is the spot exchange rate

r_v is the interest rate applicable to variable currency

r_b is the interest rate applicable to base currency.

Forward swaps

Forward swap = Forward outright – Spot

$$FS = FX_f - FX_s = FX_s \times \frac{r_v \times \frac{days}{year} - r_b \times \frac{days}{year}}{1 + r_b \times \frac{days}{year}}$$

where:

FS is the forward swap price

FX$_f$ is the forward exchange rate

FX$_s$ is the spot exchange rate

r_v is the interest rate applicable to variable currency

r_b is the interest rate applicable to base currency.

Cross-rate forwards

Given forward exchange rates X/Y and X/Z, the forward cross-rates are:

$$(Y/Z)_{bid} = (X/Z)_{bid} \div (X/Y)_{offer}$$
$$(Y/Z)_{offer} = (X/Z)_{offer} \div (X/Y)_{bid}$$

and

$$(Z/Y)_{bid} = 1/(Y/Z)_{offer}$$
$$(Z/Y)_{offer} = 1/(Y/Z)_{bid}$$

Given forward exchange rates Y/X and Z/X, the forward cross-rates are:

$$(Y/Z)_{bid} = (Y/X)_{bid} \div (Z/X)_{offer}$$
$$(Y/Z)_{offer} = (Y/X)_{offer} \div (Z/X)_{bid}$$

and

$$(Z/Y)_{bid} = 1/(Y/Z)_{offer}$$
$$(Z/Y)_{offer} = 1/(Y/Z)_{bid}$$

Given forward exchange rates Y/X and X/Z, the forward cross-rates are:

$$(Y/Z)_{bid} = (Y/X)_{bid} \times (X/Z)_{bid}$$
$$(Y/Z)_{offer} = (Y/X)_{offer} \times (X/Z)_{offer}$$

and

$$(Z/Y)_{bid} = 1/(Y/Z)_{offer}$$
$$(Z/Y)_{offer} = 1/(Y/Z)_{bid}$$

Cross-rate forward swaps

Given spot exchange rates X_s/Y_s and X_s/Z_s and forward exchange rates X_f/Y_f and X_f/Z_f, the forward cross-rate swap prices are:

$$(Y/Z)_{bid} = (X_f/Z_f)_{bid} \div (X_f/Y_f)_{offer} - (X_s/Z_s)_{bid} \div (X_s/Y_s)_{offer}$$
$$(Y/Z)_{offer} = (X_f/Z_f)_{offer} \div (X_f/Y_f)_{bid} - (X_s/Z_s)_{offer} \div (X_s/Y_s)_{bid}$$

Given exchange rates Y/X and Z/X, the forward cross-rates are:

$$(Y/Z)_{bid} = (Y_f/X_f)_{bid} \div (Z_f/X_f)_{offer} - (Y_s/X_s)_{bid} \div (Z_s/X_s)_{offer}$$
$$(Y/Z)_{offer} = (Y_f/X_f)_{offer} \div (Z_f/X_f)_{bid} - (Y_s/X_s)_{offer} \div (Z_s/X_s)_{bid}$$

Given exchange rates Y/X and X/Z, the forward cross-rates are:

$$(Y/Z)_{bid} = (Y_f/X_f)_{bid} \times (X_f/Z_f)_{bid} - (Y_s/X_s)_{bid} \times (X_s/Z_s)_{bid}$$
$$(Y/Z)_{offer} = (Y_f/X_f)_{offer} \times (X_f/Z_f)_{offer} - (Y_s/X_s)_{offer} \times (X_s/Z_s)_{offer}$$

OPTION CHARACTERISTICS

Put-call parity

$$C - P = S - K$$

where:

C is the call premium, P is the put premium

S is the futures price, K is the exercise price/option strike.

Physically settled options

$$C - P = S - Ke^{-rt}$$

where:

r is the continuously compounded interest rate

t is time to expiry expressed as $\frac{days}{year}$.

Options on dividend-paying stocks

$$C - P = S - Ke^{-rt} - D$$

where:

D is the present value of the expected dividend.

Options on stock index (dividend yield continuous)

$$C - P = Se^{-dt} - Ke^{-rt}$$

where:

d is the continuously compounded dividend yield.

Cross-currency options

$$C - P = Se^{-ft} - Ke^{-rt}$$

where:

f is the continuously compounded foreign currency interest rate

S is the spot exchange rate.

Options on futures with up-front premiums

$$C - P = S - K$$

Options on futures with margined premiums

$$C - P = Se^{-rt} - Ke^{-rt}$$

Option value sensitivities – 'option Greeks'

Options sensitivity to	Named as
Underlying	Delta
Changes in delta	Gamma
Volatility	Vega or kappa
Time decay	Theta
Interest rates	Rho

Position	Delta	Gamma	Vega	Theta
Long future	+	0	0	0
Short future	–	0	0	0
Long call	+	+	+	–
Short call	–	–	–	+
Long put	–	+	+	–
Short put	+	–	–	+

OPTION PRICING

Risk-neutral pricing using binomial trees

Call option premium boundaries:

$$C + PV(X) \geq S \quad \text{or} \quad C \geq S - PV(X)$$

Probability-weighted stock price

$$S \times u \times p + S \times d \times (1 - p) = fwd(S)$$

Pricing options using hedge ratio

$$(hS - C)e^{rt} = hS_u - C_u = hS_d - C_d$$

where:

$$h = \frac{C_u - C_d}{S_u - S_d}$$

Dividend paying stock options

$$p = \frac{e^{rt-yt} - d}{u - d}$$

$$(hS - C)\, e^{rt} = hS_u - C_u + hS_u\, (e^{yt} - 1) = hS_u\, e^{yt} - C_u$$

Cross-currency options

$$p = \frac{e^{r_d t - r_f t} - d}{u - d}$$

Option pricing using Black–Scholes

Black–Scholes model:

$$c = SN(d_1) - Xe^{-rt}N(d_2)$$

where:

$$d_1 = \frac{\ln(S/X) + (r + 0.5\sigma^2)t}{\sigma\sqrt{t}}$$

$$d_2 = d_1 - \sigma\sqrt{t}$$

and

S is the underlying stock/share price

X is the exercise price

r is the annual continuously compounded risk-free rate

t is the time (in years)

σ is the annual stock price volatility

N(d) is the cumulative probability that deviations less than d will occur in a normal distribution with a mean of 0 and a standard deviation of 1

$N(d_1)$ is the probability of the stock price rising to a certain level

$N(d_2)$ is the probability of the stock price rising above the strike (but it is irrelevant by how much).

Options on futures (premiums paid up front)

$$C = Fe^{-rt}N(d_1) - Xe^{-rt}N(d_2)$$

Options on futures (premiums margined)

$$C = FN(d_1) - XN(d_2)$$

Currency options

$$C = Se^{-r_f t}N(d_1) - Xe^{-r_d t}N(d_2)$$

Black model

Black model for interest rate derivatives:

$$c = FN(d_1) - R_x N(d_2)$$

where:

$$d_1 = \frac{\ln(F/R_x) + \sigma^2(t)/2}{\sigma\sqrt{t}}$$

$$d_2 = d_1 - \sigma\sqrt{t}$$

where F is the current market forward swap rate, and R_x is the underlying swap rate (option strike). All other variables have the same meaning as before.

BOND DERIVATIVES

Bond futures

Deliverable bond valuation:

Deliverable bond conversion factor = Deliverable bond clean unit price at which its yield equals the notional bond coupon

$$\text{Deliverable bond} = \text{Face value} \times \left(\frac{\text{EDSP}}{100} \times \text{Conversion factor} + \text{Accrued coupon}\right)$$

Bond futures price:

$$\text{Bond futures price} = \frac{(\text{Bond price} + \text{Accrued coupon now}) \times \left(1 + i \times \frac{\text{days}}{\text{year}}\right)}{\text{Conversion factor}}$$

$$- \frac{\left(\begin{array}{c}\text{Accrued coupon at delivery} + \\ \text{Intervening coupon reinvested}\end{array}\right)}{\text{Conversion factor}}$$

Forward bond price:

$$\text{Forward bond price} = (\text{Bond price} + \text{Accrued coupon now}) \times \left(1 + i \times \frac{\text{days}}{\text{year}}\right)$$

$$- \begin{array}{c}(\text{Accrued coupon at delivery} + \\ \text{Intervening coupon reinvested}).\end{array}$$

Bond repos

Initial repo price = Nominal bond amount × (Clean price + Accrued coupon)/100

$$\text{Repo price at maturity} = \text{Initial repo price} \times \left(1 + r \times \frac{\text{days}}{\text{year}}\right)$$

where r is the repo rate and days refers to number of days until maturity.

Bond options

Black model for bond options:

$$C = BN(d_1) - B_x N(d_2)$$

$$d_1 = \frac{\ln(B/B_x) + \sigma^2(t)/2}{\sigma\sqrt{t}}$$

$$d_2 = d_1 - \sigma\sqrt{t}$$

Put–call parity for bond options:

$$C - P = Fe^{-rt}N(d_1) - Ke^{-rt}N(d_2)$$

F is the futures price

K is the exercise price/option strike

r is the continuously compounded interest rate.

EQUITY DERIVATIVES

Equity index futures

Equity index futures contract size = Index level × Index multiplier

$$\text{Number of futures contracts} = \frac{\text{Portfolio value}}{\text{Equity index} \times \text{Index multiplier}}$$

The futures settlement price:

Settlement amount = Number of contracts × Equity index movement
× Index multiplier

Equity index futures price:

$$\text{Futures price} = \text{Index level} \times \text{Index multiplier} \times \left(1 + i \times \frac{\text{days}}{\text{year}} - d \times \frac{\text{days}}{\text{year}}\right)$$

where:

i is the annual funding rate

d is the dividend yield on underlying equity.

Stock beta

Portfolio beta:

$$\text{Portfolio beta} = \sum \frac{\beta_i \times V_i}{V_P}$$

where:

β_i is the individual equity beta

V_i is the individual equity share value

V_P is the total value of the portfolio.

$$\text{Beta-weighted number of futures contracts} = \frac{\text{Portfolio value} \times \beta}{\text{Equity Index} \times \text{Index multiplier}}$$

Equity index options

Black–Scholes for equity index options:

$$C = Se^{-dt}N(d_1) - Ke^{-rt}N(d_2)$$

where dividend yield d is assumed to be paid continuously.

Put-call parity for equity index options:

$$C - P = Se^{-dt} - Ke^{-rt}$$

Single stock options

Black–Scholes for single stock options:

$$C = SN(d_1) - Ke^{-rt}N(d_2)$$

where dividend payments until expiry are captured by reducing the stock price by the present value of dividends.

Put–call parity for dividend-paying single stocks:

$$C - P = S - D - Ke^{-rt}$$

where D is the present value of expected dividend.

Equity index swap valuation

PV(swap) = PV(equity index leg) − PV(floating leg) = 0

PROBABILITY AND STATISTICS

Main concepts of probability

Probability of an event E when there are several equally likely outcomes:

P(E) = Number of ways E can occur/Total number of possible outcomes

Sample-based probability:

P(E)
= Number of observed occurrences of E/Total number of observed occurrences

Joint probability

Independent events:

P(A or B) = P(A) + P(B)
P(A and B) = P(A) × P(B)

Dependent events:

P(A or B) = P(A) + P(B) − P(A and B)
P(A and B) = P(A) × P(B|A)

Probability distribution

Probability that the *continuous* variable x has a value between a and b inclusive:

$$P[a \leq X \leq b] = \int_a^b f(x)\,dx$$

Probability that the *discrete* variable x has a value X or lies between a and b inclusive:

$$P[X = x] = f(x), \text{ or for the interval } P[a \leq X \leq b] = \sum_{x=a}^{b} f(x)$$

Probability that the *continuous* variable x has a value less than or equal to X:

$$F(x) = \int_{-\infty}^{x} f(\mu)\,d\mu$$

Probability that the *discrete* variable x has a value less than or equal to X:

$$F(x) = P[X \le x] = \alpha \quad \text{or} \quad F(x) = \sum_{i=0}^{x} f(i)$$

Binomial distribution

Binomial probability function:

$$P(x) = \frac{n!}{x!(n-x)!} \times p^x \times (1-p)^{n-x}$$

where the number of possible combinations of x successes in n trials is given by:

$$\frac{n!}{x!(n-x)!}$$

and the probability of x successes and n − x failures in a trial is given by:

$$p^x \times (1-p)^{n-x}$$

Mean	np
Mode	$p(n+1) - 1 \le x \le p(n+1)$
Range	0 to N
Standard dev.	$\sqrt{np(1-p)}$

Normal distribution

Normal distribution function:

$$f(x) = \frac{e^{-(x-\mu)^2/2\sigma^2}}{\sigma\sqrt{2\pi}}$$

Standard normal distribution function:

$$f(x) = \frac{e^{-x^2/2}}{\sqrt{2\pi}}$$

Mean	location parameter μ
Median	location parameter μ
Mode	location parameter μ
Standard dev.	scale parameter σ

Log-normal distribution

Log-normal distribution function:

$$f(x) = \frac{e^{-(\ln(x-\theta)/m^2/2\sigma^2)}}{(x-\theta)\sqrt{2\pi}} \qquad x \geq \theta;\ m,\ \sigma > 0$$

Standard log-normal distribution function:

$$f(x) = \frac{e^{-(\ln(x)^2/2\sigma^2)}}{x\sigma\sqrt{2\pi}} \qquad x \geq 0;\ \sigma > 0$$

Mean	$e^{0.5\sigma^2}$	
Median	scale parameter m	(1 if m is not specified)
Mode	$1/e^{\sigma^2}$	
Range	0 to $+\infty$	
Standard dev.	$\sqrt{e^{\sigma^2}(e^{\sigma^2}-1)}$	

YIELD CURVES

Choice of instruments

1. Cash deposits.
2. Interest rate futures.
3. Interest rate swaps.

Deposit discount factors

The forward–forward rate is given by:

$$\left(1 + r_S \times \frac{days_S}{year}\right)\left(1 + r_{S,E} \times \frac{days_{S,E}}{year}\right) = 1 + r_E \times \frac{days_E}{year}$$

and the relationship between the rate and the DF is:

$$d = \frac{1}{1 + r \times \dfrac{days}{year}}$$

Hence it follows:

$$d_E = d_S \times d_{S,E} = d_S \times \frac{1}{\left(1 + r \times \dfrac{days_{S,E}}{year}\right)}$$

where:

year is the number of days in the year

$days_S$, $days_E$, and $days_{S,E}$ are the relevant time periods

d_S and d_E are the discount factors for the period start and end dates

$d_{S,E}$ is the discount factor for the period $days_{S,E}$

r_S and r_E are the spot rates for the period start and end dates

$r_{S,E}$ is the interest rate for the period $days_{S,E}$.

Futures discount factors

Given the futures rate:

$$f = \left[\frac{d_S}{d_E} - 1\right] \times \frac{year}{days_{S,E}}$$

the DF for the end of the forward period is given by:

$$d_E = d_S \times \frac{1}{1 + f \times \dfrac{days_{S,E}}{year}}$$

Swap discount factors

$$PV(fixed) = PV(floating)$$

$$P \times C \times \left(d_1 \times \frac{days_1}{year} + d_2 \times \frac{days_2}{year}\right) = P \times \left(L_{0,1} \times d_1 \times \frac{days_1}{year} + L_{1,2} \times d_2 \times \frac{days_2}{year}\right)$$

where:

P is the notional principal

d_k is the discount factor for the end of period k, implying $d_0 = 1$

$days_k$ is the number of days in the coupon period k

$L_{k-1,k}$ is the Libor for that period

C is the fixed coupon rate for the duration of the swap.

As the interest rate r implied by the DFs for adjacent periods can be calculated as:

$$r_{k-1,k} = \left[\frac{d_{k-1}}{d_k} - 1\right] \times \frac{year}{days_k}$$

It follows:

$$PV(floating) = P \times (1 - d_2)$$

$$C \times \left(d_1 \times \frac{days_1}{year} + d_2 \times \frac{days_2}{year}\right) = 1 - d_2$$

$$d_2 = \frac{1 - C \times d_1 \times \dfrac{days_1}{year}}{1 + C \times \dfrac{days_2}{year}}$$

In general:

$$d_n = \frac{1 - C \times \sum_{k=1}^{n-1} d_k \times \dfrac{days_k}{year}}{1 + C \times \dfrac{days_n}{year}}$$

Interpolation methods

Zero rate linear interpolation:

$$\exp\left(-z_k \times \frac{days_k}{year}\right) = d_k = \frac{1}{1 + r_k \times \dfrac{days_k}{year}}$$

which, when rearranged, gives:

$$z_k = -\frac{year}{days_k} \ln(d_k)$$

$$z_x = z_1 + (z_2 - z_1) \times \frac{days_{1,x}}{days_{1,2}}$$

or

$$z = z_1 \times \frac{days_{x,2}}{days_{1,2}} + z_2 \times \frac{days_{1,x}}{days_{1,2}}$$

DF for the unknown point can be calculated as:

$$d_x = d_1 \wedge \left(\frac{days_x}{days_{1,2}} \times \frac{days_{x,2}}{days_1} \right) \times d_2 \wedge \left(\frac{days_x}{days_{1,2}} \times \frac{days_{1,x}}{days_2} \right)$$

where the symbol $\wedge$ denotes 'power of'.

Log-linear interpolation

$$d_x = d_1 \wedge \left(\frac{days_{x,2}}{days_{1,2}} \right) \times d_2 \wedge \left(\frac{days_{1,x}}{days_{1,2}} \right)$$

$$d_x = d_1 \times \left(\frac{d_2}{d_1} \right) \wedge \left(\frac{days_{1,x}}{days_{1,2}} \right) = d_2 \times \left(\frac{d_1}{d_2} \right) \wedge \left(\frac{days_{x,2}}{days_{1,2}} \right)$$

RISK MANAGEMENT

Part
5

Credit risk on derivatives

INTRODUCTION

When an investment bank enters into a transaction with a client, it is exposed to the risk that the client may default on their obligation. Such risk is called *credit risk*. The bank may try to reduce the risk of default by only dealing with clients of high creditworthiness, but as history has shown, even large investment banks can go into bankruptcy. Therefore, it is a real and present danger in any transaction a bank undertakes. It is described in more detail in the following sections.

COUNTERPARTY RISK

In a nutshell, this is an estimate of the likelihood that the client would for some reason default and the bank will be exposed to a loss. The size of the loss would depend on whether it was a just a simple borrowing (incurring 100 per cent loss of the face value of a loan plus interest), or a derivative instrument where the loss is limited to the difference between the settlement price and the cost of replacing the security. Counterparty risk depends on a number of factors:

Customer risk: The risk that the counterparty will fail to fulfil their obligations.

Country risk: The risk that the client's domicile country will enter into financial or political problems that can indirectly affect the transaction between the counterparties.

Transfer risk: The risk that a foreign client will not be able to transfer funds to the bank due to issues with his domestic banking system.

PRODUCT RISK

Product risk determines the level of credit exposure, i.e. the amount of default. Depending on the transacted security, it can incorporate all or just some of the elements below:

Principal exposure applies only to transactions where principal is involved. Such instruments are also called 'balance sheet instruments', as they impact on the bank's balance sheet. It mainly applies to bank loans, but can also arise in swaps, or bank guarantees.

Interest rate exposure is implicit in all products, as all market transactions are subject to the interest rate effect. But it particularly applies to those instruments where interest payments are due at regular intervals (such as swaps) or at maturity (loans).

Replacement risk is associated with products which do not involve exchange of principal ('off-balance sheet' instruments). Hence virtually all derivative securities will be exposed to it. The bank may simply accept the loss, as it is only a fraction of the notional amount of the underlying security, or it may have to replace the contract at potentially significant cost.

Settlement risk can occur when the counterparty fails to repay the principal amount at maturity. This can potentially arise in transactions involving a foreign counterparty, as the market operation times may differ. Thus the bank can fulfil its side of the deal earlier than the customer is due, arising in significant exposure.

Collateral risk arises in transactions where the customer, wishing to reduce the cost of borrowing, deposits a security (collateral) with the bank as a guarantee. Should the security depreciate in value, the collateral would provide insufficient cover in case of client default. This situation is akin to a mortgage. If the borrower does not fulfil its obligations, the property is repossessed. However, if the housing market has declined since the purchase, the bank may not recoup the full mortgage value.

CREDIT RISK OF SPECIFIC FINANCIAL INSTRUMENTS

Exchange-traded products

Exchange-traded products are seen as virtually riskless, as they are guaranteed by the Clearing House. The system of margining is the buffer that gives Clearing House protection against default. Hence individual investors are only exposed to their individual risks of failing to make margin payments or deliver the underlying security. This applies to all exchange-traded products, regardless of their specification (contracts for delivery or settlement) and their underlying market.

OTC financial securities

Money market products

Money market products are used for short-term lending and borrowing. Lenders are exposed to the risk equal to the full contract amount in the event of counterparty default. As money market instruments are typically structured so that the interest is also repaid at maturity, the total loss is further amplified. In addition to the customer risks defined above, product risks relevant to money market instruments include: principal and interest rate exposure as well as settlement and replacement risk.

Capital market products

Capital market products are typically used for long-term lending and borrowing. Akin to the above, credit risk that lenders are exposed to in the event of counterparty default is equal to the full contract amount. However, instruments with maturities over one year typically pay interest at regular intervals, thus not increasing the amount of loss. All the risks defined in the previous section are applicable to this product class.

FRAs

The credit risk associated with FRAs contracts is relatively low, as the principal amount is not exchanged. Only the settlement amount (difference between the FRA rate and the prevailing market rate calculated on a notional amount) is at stake. Hence in addition to all customer risks potentially arising, the financial institution is exposed to the relatively low settlement risk (i.e. the probability of default might be substantial, but the amount at stake is low compared to the contract notional amount). However, if the FRA was a part of a structure or a hedging strategy its replacement might have to be done on potentially unfavourable terms, increasing the overall exposure.

Swaps

In most swap trades the investment bank acts as an intermediary between two counterparties, guaranteeing each side of the swap and earning the spread between the quoted rates. By doing so it accepts the credit risk of both counterparties, creating a huge exposure in case of default. This is particularly the case where exchange of principal takes place, different currencies are involved or there is a mismatch of payment dates. Hence, all of the risks defined in the previous section apply. This is particularly the case with more exotic swap structures, including legs with mismatched payment dates and/or frequencies, swaps with legs linked to different underlying markets (e.g. total return swap, equity index swap etc.) or where the interest is deferred until maturity.

Options

Exchange-traded options, just like futures, are margined and guaranteed by the Clearing House, hence virtually riskless. OTC contracts carry significant exposure to counterparty risk for the option buyer, in case the counterparty fails to deliver the security if the option is exercised. In the case of the option seller, as the premium is paid at the outset, default risk is removed. Some options, such as collars, carry a counterparty risk, whether bought or sold, as both sides can exercise depending on market conditions.

Foreign exchange instruments

Any type of financial instrument can be structured to involve foreign currency. Thus the credit risks inherent in the basic product (option, future, swap etc.) are further enhanced by the incorporation of more than one currency in the deal. Within the customer risk umbrella, the most significant exposure arises in country and transfer risks, whereas within the product range the interest rate exposure is the most significant, as the foreign exchange products not only incorporate the exchange rate between different currencies, but implicitly expose the counterparties to the interest rates in different countries. Replacement may also be an issue due to potentially limited access to the foreign currency market.

Bonds

Creditworthiness is implicit in bond pricing. Yield on any given bond is a reflection of the issuer's credit rating. Government bonds are seen as virtually riskless and consequently offer lower returns to investors compared to corporate bonds, not to mention junk bonds. Any change in the counterparty credit rating has a huge impact on the bond value. Thus credit risk associated with bonds is not limited to default scenarios only, it further extends to any downgrades in credit rating. Other features such as call or put options attached to bonds (as in callable and puttable bonds respectively) and options to convert all or part of a bond into equity (convertible bonds) further increase risk exposure, as the number of parameters affecting the potential loss increases. However, as bonds are typically issued directly in the market, i.e. without banks acting as intermediaries, the credit risk bearer is an investor. Bonds nevertheless feature in investment banks' portfolios, typically as part of asset-backed securities or other credit derivatives, where their credit risk is further complicated by the structure they are part of. All of the risks listed in the first two sections of this chapter potentially apply. Bond replacement, if required might be virtually impossible.

Equity derivatives

Equity derivatives offer exposure to equity markets without actual market participation. Their benefit to the investor can turn into significant credit risk in the event of counterparty default. As the investor often has no direct access to the equities market, or it is prohibitively expensive or impractical, replacement risk is a significant contributor to the overall credit exposure. Furthermore, inherent in the product structure is the exposure to a single company, industry sector or a market index, all of which carry their associated credit risks, thus exposing the investors to the multifold credit risks they have no means of mitigating. The range of applicable risk components described in the first two sections of this chapter depends on the derivative security type (e.g. option, future, swap etc. – all of which are covered in the previous sections).

Commodity derivatives

Commodity derivatives have over the years moved away from being solely means of guaranteeing the price and delivery, to being securities used mostly for hedging, arbitrage and speculation. Nevertheless, many products are still delivered, which is reflected in their pricing. Hence credit exposure in the event of default, in addition to all previously described risk components, involves the inconvenience (which may not be insignificant) of not acquiring a commodity. Furthermore, contract replacement at spot prices might incur significant losses, due to the pricing mechanisms that incorporate convenience yields (premiums payable for guaranteed access to the commodity), which price shorter-dated contracts higher than the longer-dated ones (an anomaly compared to other derivatives markets).

Credit derivatives

Credit derivatives have credit as their underlying security, thus credit exposure is inherent in all products. However, this exposure relates to the third party or asset default risk rather than the risk associated with the counterparty to the credit derivative contract. Nevertheless both the protection buyer and the protection seller accept a level of counterparty credit exposure, albeit to significantly different degrees. The protection seller receives regular premiums in exchange for accepting the third party credit risk, thus is exposed to a relatively small loss in the event of default. In contrast, the protection buyer's exposure is equal to the full amount of contingent payment.

CREDIT RATINGS

Credit ratings are introduced to the financial industry to establish a standard measure of creditworthiness of market participants. They are conducted by independent agencies to ensure impartiality. They carry out an evaluation of a borrower's overall credit history, current assets and liabilities, and based on that information assess their ability to repay a debt. Individuals, corporations and even countries are subject to credit rating. It impacts on their ability to borrow funds and execute financial transactions.

The best known credit agencies are *Standard & Poor's* and *Moody's.*

The Standard & Poor's rating scale is from excellent to poor: AAA, AA+, AA, AA−, A+, A, A−, BBB+, BBB, BBB−, BB+, BB, BB−, B+, B, B−, CCC+, CCC, CCC−, CC, C, D. Investment banks tend to transact only with AAA, AA+ and AA clients.

The Moody's rating system is similar: AAA, Aa1, Aa2, Aa3, A1, A2, A3, Baa1, Baa2, Baa3, Ba1, Ba2, Ba3, B1, B2, B3, Caa1, Caa2, Caa3, Ca, C. Only the top two are typically considered by investment banks.

CREDIT RISK MANAGEMENT

In order to successfully manage credit risk, the existing and potential risks inherent in any traded product or activity firstly have to be identified and estimated. Financial market participants tend to rely on the published credit ratings, as produced by the independent agencies, described above. Furthermore, additional resources and sophisticated models are typically employed to produce proprietary credit assessments that enhance the publicly available information.

Credit scoring models form a part of the framework used by investment banks to establish the level of credit lines extended to their customers. For corporate and commercial borrowers, these qualitative and quantitative models generally include, but are not limited to: independent credit rating, assessment of assets and liabilities, market performance, operating procedures, management expertise, historical credit quality, and leverage and liquidity ratios.

Once the credit risk is established or at least bounded, it is mitigated using several methods, depending on the product type or transaction the client is involved in.

Risk-based pricing

Risk-based pricing is the practice employed by lenders whereby a higher interest rate is charged to borrowers that are more likely to default. This is evident in the financial markets practice, whereby Libor and Libid are typically only applicable to the interbank transactions, whereas other market participants have access to funds at a much higher borrowing rate, or lower investment rate. Within risk-based pricing, the lenders typically consider credit rating, loan purpose and loan-to-value ratio, and credit spread (yield).

Credit limits

Further to employing the risk-based pricing, another significant measure in mitigating the credit risk is the establishment of credit exposure limits to single counterparties or groups of related counterparties. This is typically further extended to setting the credit limits applicable to particular products or product classes for each counterparty.

Covenants

Covenants are stipulations on the borrower's actions that lenders may require in order to extend the funds; they typically include (but are not limited to):

- Periodical reports of borrower's financial standing
- Limits to dividend payouts for the duration of the loan
- Further borrowing limits or other financial commitments that might impact on the timely repayment of the loan
- Acceleration of loan repayment upon pre-specified events, e.g. change in credit rating, change in interest coverage ratio or debt-to-equity ratio
- Being subject to regulatory investigation
- Being a target or originator or a merger or acquisition etc.

Diversification

Lenders to a narrow range of borrowers (from the same sector or requiring a similar type of funding with respect to product structure and maturity) are highly exposed to unsystematic credit risk, arising from a high concentration of correlated liabilities. Hence diversification is employed in order to mitigate this type of risk. However, as seen from the credit rating section, most investment banks tend to accept only the counterparties with the highest credit standing, thus only the range of products and their specifications is subject to diversification.

Credit insurance

Bond holders as well as lenders use credit insurance to hedge their credit exposure, thus transferring risk to the insurer in exchange for regular premium payments. Even the insurance issuers can seek further protection in a form of reinsurance, whereby the insurance contracts are pooled together by another counterparty acting as a backer to the insurance contracts.

Credit derivatives

Credit derivatives offer protection from default of an asset rather than an entity (counterparty). Nevertheless they are useful tools in mitigating credit risk exposure. Akin to insurance contracts, they transfer the third party or an asset risk to the protection seller in exchange for regular payments. Another parallel with credit insurance is that credit protection sellers can use securitisation (akin to reinsurance) to diversify their own credit risk exposure.

CREDIT RISK MANAGEMENT BEST PRACTICE GUIDELINES

All financial markets participants, including investment banks, should have a well-defined set of credit risk management principles. Whilst some are imposed by the regulatory structure, others should be followed as a part of prudent business operation. These include, but are not limited to:

- Establishing an appropriate credit risk environment
- Operating under a prudent and conservative credit limit policy
- Maintaining an appropriate credit risk recognition, assessment and management
- Ensuring adequate credit controls and revisions.

Appropriate credit risk environment

Financial institutions should identify, evaluate and manage credit risks inherent in all products and activities (including the counterparties to all transactions). Particular attention should be placed on new activities or counterparties, whereby suitable controls and management procedures need to be put in place, tested and approved. A credit risk management strategy and policy should be developed and periodically reviewed at the highest level of seniority. Furthermore, all staff involved in identifying, measuring, monitoring and controlling credit risks should be aware of and adherent to the policies.

Prudent and conservative credit limit policy

In addition to the use of externally established credit ratings, as provided by Standard & Poor's and Moody's (described above), investment banks should employ their proprietary credit evaluation methodology. This should be used when determining credit limits to individual counterparties and groups of related counterparties in conjunction with the assessment of credit purpose, structure and a planned repayment strategy. Particular care should be taken when extending existing credit limits or establishing new credit lines, both to the existing customers entering into new transaction types and to the new clients.

Appropriate credit risk recognition, assessment and management

A well-established, maintained and audited system for ongoing administration of all credit risk-bearing positions should be in place at all financial institutions, investment banks in particular. Furthermore, a system for monitoring the status of individual clients' credits should be established.

Internal reserving and capital provision policies should be regularly revised in line with market moves and credit downgrades. In addition, the information on the overall composition and quality of the credit portfolio must be readily reproducible. In order to achieve this, information systems, applications and analytical models should be developed enabling analysis of present and potential credit exposures by any classification (counterparty, sector, product, or in various hypothetical scenarios).

Ensuring adequate credit controls and revisions

In line with the requirement for the proprietary credit evaluation methodology, investment banks should establish a system of continual independent credit review of all counterparties. Furthermore, internal controls and other monitoring activities should be employed to ensure that internal and external policies, procedures and limits are adhered to and any exceptions reported and addressed in a timely manner. Controls over credit limit extension and establishment of new credit lines should take a key place within the control function. Finally, revision of all existing policies, procedures and the controls themselves should be done periodically to prevent problems and unforeseen losses due to unidentified or unmitigated credit exposure.

Market risk on derivatives

INTRODUCTION

Market risk is the potential loss on investment due to fluctuations in the market value of assets involved. Specifically, for derivatives products it is the negative impact that the fluctuations in the underlying security market value would have on the value of the derivative. The uncertainty is implicit in all derivative securities. It is the driving force behind their trading and development. However, some of the risk associated with it can be diversified away or hedged. The remaining factors that could potentially incur losses on investment are market risk. It arises from the characteristics of the instrument as well as unforeseen circumstances in the market as a whole. Whilst there is no way of knowing with certainty where the FTSE 100 level will be at expiry of the corresponding futures contract, this is implicit in the definition of the product itself. However, the impact that a tsunami or an earthquake would have on the option value is impossible to incorporate into trading strategy. Since 'playing safe' is not an option for an active investor, the potential for losses is always present. Another important concept that arises within this context is *non-traded market risk*. It is the risk associated with interest rate fluctuations that impact on the banks' balance sheet. All open positions are repriced daily for the purpose of P&L reporting, and thus are indirectly affected by the interest rate movement regardless of their underlying market. The impact is most evident in the wide mix of assets and liabilities resulting from the investment bank's role as an intermediary. Hence market risk management focuses on the calculation of probability of adverse circumstances and the financial impact they would have. Risk mitigation is a complex subject that could have an entire book devoted to it, but will be briefly discussed further in the chapter. Typical approaches are: active portfolio management enabling hedging risk exposure in different sectors and reserving policy. Reserving sufficient funds to cover potential losses, thus avoiding default, is the legal and regulatory requirement for all market participants.

BALANCE SHEET VS. OFF-BALANCE SHEET INSTRUMENTS

As discussed in previous chapters, financial instruments that involve the transfer or exchange of principal (deposits, loans, swaps etc.) impact on a bank's available assets, and thus appear on the company balance sheet. In contrast, derivative instruments that either do not require up-front payment, or where only a fraction of the underlying is involved (such as option margin), are off-balance sheet instruments. Even though their initial funding requirement is low, their market exposure is significant. Care must be taken to assess the exposure and reserve sufficient funds to cover potential losses due to unforeseen circumstances or market fluctuations that cannot otherwise be mitigated.

MARKET RISK ON SPECIFIC FINANCIAL INSTRUMENTS

Risks and benefits of various classes of products were already discussed in more detail in their corresponding chapters. They will be briefly revisited here for completeness and clarity. Furthermore, it should be stated that market risk exposure is in many instances desirable, as it is a source of profit in correctly anticipated market conditions. Hence banks and other financial institutions, as a management decision, in some instances intentionally leave open positions that are part of their business strategy and in line with their view of the financial markets and economic conditions.

Money market products

Money market products are used for short-term lending and borrowing. Their underlying price driver is the short-term interest rate. As banks tend to have access to funds at interbank rate (e.g. Libor), whilst transacting with clients at less favourable rates, hedging money market positions is relatively easy and thus they are perceived as virtually riskless. As maturities are short and markets very liquid, no concentrations, maturity gaps or other mismatches should remain, leaving a fully balanced portfolio.

Capital market products

Capital market instruments are used for long-term lending and borrowing, thus their price is affected by long-term interest rates. Akin to the above, as banks tend to have access to funds at the interbank rate (e.g. Libor), whilst transacting with clients at less favourable rates, hedging these positions is relatively easy and thus they are perceived as virtually riskless. As these products are very liquid, no concentrations, maturity gaps or other mismatches should occur. However, an important difference between long- and short-term funding is in the repayment structures, whereby the former includes periodic interest payments and the latter does not. Depending on the contractual specifications, repayment schedules in OTC products may include non-standard terms and features, making them potentially difficult to offset exactly. But overall the inherent market risk is very low for this class of instruments.

Financial futures

Financial futures are exchange-traded products and thus are subject to a margining system. Whilst the exposure to the underlying security market remains, all daily profits and losses are incorporated into the margin payments. Furthermore, an initial margin is placed as a collateral at the inception of the contract, as a buffer against large market fluctuations or counterparty default. Hence no large, sudden losses resulting from underlying market moves should arise from futures contracts. They are typically hedged using FRAs, accounting for convexity adjustments, as discussed in Chapter 6.

FRAs

FRAs are short- to medium-term interest rate derivatives, hence they are primarily affected by interest rate fluctuations. They can be hedged either by futures (accounting for convexity adjustments), or strips of FRAs can be hedged using swaps of corresponding maturity and payment frequency. As FRAs are the OTC equivalent to futures, they are bespoke instruments with varied notional amounts, start and end dates, hence offsetting them exactly might potentially be a problem. But overall their market risk management is deemed straightforward, as the product structure and pricing is simple and the market is liquid.

Swaps

In most swap trades the investment bank acts as an intermediary between two counterparties, guaranteeing each side of the swap and earning the spread between the quoted rates. In such a scenario, there is no market risk implicit in the transaction, as the spread is earned regardless of the rate fluctuations and the counterparties to the swap are bearers of the full extent of the market exposure. Interest rate swap positions can also be hedged using strips of futures or FRAs, making their risk management straightforward. Other swap structures expose the bank to market risk in the underlying instrument (equity, commodity, FX etc.) requiring hedging with suitable product classes.

As swap maturities sometimes extend up to 50 years, liquidity becomes an issue, hence finding willing counterparties for a hedging transaction might be an issue.

Options

Exchange-traded options, just like futures, are margined. Whilst exposure to the underlying security market remains, all daily profits and losses are incorporated into the margin payments. Furthermore, the initial margin is placed as a collateral at the inception of the contract, as a buffer against large market fluctuations or counterparty default. However, the market exposure of the option buyer and seller are markedly different. Whilst the potential loss incurred by the buyer is the option premium, the seller is exposed to the full value of the underlying security. Option sensitivities (Greeks, discussed in Chapter 9) are important factors in consideration of suitable hedges, as very volatile positions can render a previously suitable hedge worthless under changed market conditions.

Foreign exchange instruments

Any type of financial instrument can be structured to involve foreign currency. Thus the market risks inherent in the basic product (option, future, swap etc.) are further enhanced by the incorporation of more than one currency in the deal. Not only is the fluctuation of the FX rate crucial in determining the market risk, the interest rates in both currencies further compound the exposure. As this exposure arises in different markets, potential hedging issues may arise in accessing foreign markets and the rates thus achieved. This is particularly true for long-dated FX instruments, where the liquidity may render the appropriate hedging strategy impossible.

Bonds

Market risk on bonds is the risk that the bond market as a whole could decline, reducing the value of individual securities regardless of their individual characteristics. It is further compounded by the timing risk, i.e. that the bond would underperform after its purchase. There is also a liquidity risk, i.e. difficulty finding buyers for some bonds that may result in an unfavourable selling price. Further market risk arises in bonds with special features, such as callable, puttable and convertible bonds, as the timing and effect of exercising such options is hard to predict. Declining interest rates may accelerate the redemption of a callable bond, causing the principal to be repaid sooner than expected and thus reinvested at less favourable interest rates. As bonds are typically called at or close to par value, investors who paid a premium for their bond also risk a loss of principal. However, bonds are typically issued directly in the market, i.e. without banks acting as intermediaries. They nevertheless feature in investment banks' portfolios, typically as part of asset-backed securities or other credit derivatives, where their market risk is further complicated by the structure they are part of.

Equity derivatives

Equity derivatives offer exposure to equity markets without actual market participation. However, that does not insulate the investor from the equity market trends. On the contrary, the effect of gearing (whereby a relatively low capital investment results in large market exposure) associated with some products, makes the positions extremely risky. This is particularly the case when investing in single stocks or very specific equity sectors, whereby the price volatility can be significant without any means of diversification. Prudent hedging strategies employing diversified portfolios are mandatory market risk management practice.

Commodity derivatives

As commodities are physical goods traded for profit (arbitrage and speculation) as well as for hedging and delivery, pricing considerations as well as market risk associated with their derivative securities are different to other product classes. Prices of some commodity securities, energy derivatives in particular, are affected by a broad range of political and economic factors, government and regulatory policies and a host of issues difficult for market practitioners to foresee. Considerations of seasonality, convenience premiums and liquidity of more scarce products have to be weighed carefully in assessment of market risk. Hedging with equal and opposite transactions might not always be possible and finding a willing counterparty to accept a contract for delivery might prove difficult. Active market risk management by way of portfolio diversification and product, sector and maturity balancing is difficult to achieve, hence prudent reserving policy should be a cornerstone of commodity derivative market risk mitigation.

Credit derivatives

Credit derivatives are relative newcomers to the derivatives markets. As recent developments have shown, their impact on the world economy and the financial markets as a whole is far-reaching. In offering credit protection in the event of a third party or a reference asset default, credit derivatives affect several otherwise uncorrelated markets, extending the market risk across a wide range of factors. Examples of reference entities could be bonds, pools of commercial or residential mortgages, credit card or student loan debt, all with their associated risk of default (affected by a rise in interest rates, housing market decline, unemployment and a host of other issues). Their impact on the market value of the derivative security is difficult to estimate and hence mitigate. Again, prudent reserves should be put in place and careful monitoring of all open positions should be a standard practice.

MARKET RISK MANAGEMENT

As previously stated, market risk arises from trading activities as well as from indirect sources, such as interest rate fluctuation, that impact on the value of open positions and balance sheet. The first step in market risk management is its identification, followed by assessment. The simplest way of quantifying market risk exposure is marking to market. Marking to market is valuation of financial instruments compared to the prevailing market prices. It is used as a measure of current exposure to market fluctuations. In order to react to any unfavourable changes in the value of an investment portfolio, marking to market is done at regular intervals. In investment banks, this function is performed by the finance department. This process is called *independent pricing*, as it is done separately from valuation on the trading floor. If that were not the case, there would be the potential for misuse, as traders whose bonuses depend on the profit they are making could potentially underestimate losses.

Independent pricing involves valuation of all open positions. They are valued daily, weekly, monthly and annually. In order to have meaningful exposure assessment for any particular instrument, the price used for comparison has to be relevant. It is typically taken to be the cost of closing out the position. For example, if a company has purchased a cross-currency future that is making losses, the value of that open position is equal to the price it would achieve in the market by closing it out immediately.

For some product classes, such as money market instruments, performing the above calculation is an easy task, as there is sufficient liquidity and market prices are readily available. In contrast, exotic OTC securities, which are tailor-made to meet the clients' needs, will not have a comparable product in the market. Sometimes the structure is so specific that finding a counterparty to take the opposite side in a close-out deal is impossible. Hence marking to market cannot be done on a like-for-like basis.

In such circumstances the security valuation is done in stages. The factors that are used in pricing models are marked to market separately and then used to derive the 'market value' of the security. For example, if the exotic option model requires inputs for volatility, market-implied volatility for the closest matching instruments would be used with possible adjustment.

Another responsibility of the investment bank finance department is *reserve policy*. This is the mandate on the funds that have to be set aside for each class of products, or on individual trades. These funds are kept away from the trading books, to be used to cover potential losses on closing out unprofitable trades. Once the contract matures, or is terminated in a different way, the funds are released. The reserve calculation involves inputs from:

- *Quantitative analysts* – as they develop pricing models, they are aware of their limitations and the approximations used. Hence they can assess the impact the market fluctuations would have on validity of the prices derived from the models and the margins of error they would introduce.

- *Market risk department* – their responsibility is quantification of market risk for all open positions using standardised measures. They provide their expertise in assessment of potential losses on various types of trades.

Reserving policy is a passive form of market risk management, as it only allocates funds that can be used to cover potential losses. More active market risk mitigation is achieved by active portfolio management whereby analysis of risks by sector, product and maturity enables identification of concentrations or gaps in exposure. Balancing assets and liabilities, so that to a large degree they offset each other, was previously a norm in market risk management. With a rise in derivatives trading there is also a potential for cross-market hedging, where balance sheet instrument exposures are covered by suitable offsetting positions in derivative securities. Whatever the choice, active market risk management is the only way of ensuring prudent business practice and reliance on the reserves should be viewed only as a last resort.

MARKET RISK MANAGEMENT BEST PRACTICE GUIDELINES

Investment banks, as well as all other financial institutions and market participants should have a well-defined set of market risk management principles. Whilst some are imposed by the regulatory structure (such as the previously discussed reserving policy, and implementation of VAR, described later), others should be followed as a part of prudent business operation. These include, but are not limited to:

- Establishing an appropriate market risk management environment
- Maintaining an appropriate market risk recognition, assessment and management
- Operating under a prudent and conservative market risk exposure limit policy
- Ensuring adequate market risk exposure controls and revisions.

Appropriate market risk management environment

Financial institutions should identify, evaluate and mange market risks inherent in all products and activities, as well as those arising from non-trading sources. Particular attention should be placed on new securities or activities, whereby suitable controls and management procedures need to be put in place, tested and approved. This is particularly true in relation to derivative and hybrid securities, whereby novel pricing techniques and complicated product structures make it hard, if not impossible, to adequately assess the true extent of market exposure. A market risk management strategy and policy should be developed and periodically reviewed at the highest level of seniority. Furthermore, all involved in identifying, measuring, monitoring and controlling market risks should be aware of and adhere to the policies.

Appropriate market risk recognition, assessment and management

A well-established, maintained and audited system for ongoing administration of all open positions as well as banking books should be in place at all financial institutions, investment banks in particular. Furthermore, a system for monitoring the extent of individual and overall breaches of market risk exposure limits should be established. Internal reserving and capital provision policies should be regularly revised in line with market moves and fluctuations in interest rates. In addition, the information on the overall portfolio composition and quality must be readily reproducible. In order to achieve this, information systems, applications and analytical models should be developed enabling analysis of present and potential market exposures by any classification (maturity, sector, product, or in various hypothetical scenarios). Concentrations and gaps should be identified and hedged away wherever possible to ensure active and dynamic mitigation of market risk exposure. Care should be taken to assess the boundaries of hedge validity, i.e. the range of market conditions under which the market risk exposure is effectively mitigated. Rehedging (or position rebalancing) should be done as frequently as is warranted by product class, practicality and cost-effectiveness.

Prudent and conservative market risk exposure limit policy

In addition to the market risk management methodologies enforced by regulatory requirements (such as VAR, described later), investment banks should employ their proprietary market risk management policies and models. This should be used when determining trading limits in individual securities, product classes and maturities, as well as to individual counterparties and groups of related counterparties. Particular care should be taken when extending existing trading limits or introducing new OTC products, where full assessment of pricing methodology, independent valuation, reserving policy and hedging potential should be established and stress-tested before introducing any changes.

Ensuring adequate market risk exposure controls and revisions

In line with the requirement for the proprietary market risk management methodology, investment banks should establish a system of continual independent review of market risk capture, measurement, management and control. Furthermore, internal controls and other monitoring activities should be employed to ensure that internal and external policies, procedures and limits are adhered to and any exceptions reported and addressed in a timely manner. Controls over trading limit extension and establishment of new trading activities should have priority within the control function. Finally, revision of all existing policies, procedures and the controls themselves should be done periodically to prevent problems and unforeseen losses due to unidentified or unmitigated market risk (both traded and non-traded) exposure.

VALUE AT RISK (VAR)

A standard measure of market risk, adopted by all financial market participants, is value at risk (VAR). It is a regulatory requirement and its definition is precisely defined. VAR is the amount by which the investment value may fall over a specified period of time at a given level of probability. For example, VAR of £50,000 at 1 per cent probability for one day implies that there is a 1 per cent chance that the investment would lose £50,000 in value in one day.

Hence the main VAR inputs are:

- Unit of measurement (index points, currency etc.)
- Time interval
- Probability.

Approved VAR models

According to the Basle agreement, investment banks are approved to use two types of VAR models:

- Standardised models, used by the general public
- Internal models, developed internally by the investment banks.

Internal VAR models have to adhere to strict qualitative and quantitative standards and be approved by regulatory authority. Those are:

Quantitative standards:

- One per cent probability level
- Two-week holding period on all trades
- Calculated VAR should be multiplied by three, to allow for error margin introduced by potential weaknesses in the internal model.

Qualitative standards:

- Independent validation of the VAR model by a third party
- Integration of the VAR model into risk management
- Internal control over data inputs and changes in the model
- Separation of trading business from risk management (introduction of 'Chinese walls')
- Senior management involvement in risk management.

VAR calculated in this way tends to be excessively high, thus it is typically breached only once every four years.

VAR measurement

Investment banks tend to have their internal VAR models, particulars of which are proprietary. Nevertheless, the approaches they take can be classified as:

- Parametric
- Historical
- Historical simulation
- Stochastic simulation.

Parametric VAR measurement

Parametric VAR measurement is very popular due to its ease of use and readily available market inputs. It assumes that the investment returns are normally distributed and therefore can be described using variances and co-variances of the underlying investments. It uses historical data to estimate variance and correlations of relevant investments, from which the investment returns are derived. This information is used in conjunction with current security prices to derive VAR. For example:

- Current market price for a bond future is 110, based on £100,000 notional amount. Historical estimates give value daily mean of 0.002 for future returns, with the standard deviation of 0.3.

From Chapter 13, we saw that 99 per cent of all normally distributed variables lie within 2.33 standard deviations from the mean. Hence, the point below 1 per cent of returns is given by:

1% of daily returns $= 0.01 - 2.33 \times 0.3 = -0.689$

Hence the monetary value of VAR is:

VAR $= 0.689 \times 110/100 \times £100,000 = £758$

The main shortcomings of the parametric approach to VAR (also known as analytical or correlation method) are:

- Assumption of normal distribution of asset returns, which is in practice rarely observed
- Correlations between different variables impacting on investment returns are implicit in this model, even though the assets may be uncorrelated
- Volatility and correlation are assumed to be constant over a period of time.

Historical VAR measurement

Historical VAR measurement relies on taking a large sample of historical data and plotting the distribution. The bottom percentile can then be identified and VAR calculated using the same approach as above.

The pros and cons of this approach are:

- There is no implicit assumption about the distribution of investment returns
- No variance and co-variance estimates
- The shortcoming is that it is computationally extensive and requires complete recalculation on any change in VAR parameters.

Historical simulation (bootstrapping)

Historical simulation (bootstrapping) is used in the case of insufficient historical data on investments. Instead the historical data on parameters that impact on the value of investments is used. The investment performance through time is then simulated and VAR calculated as above.

The disadvantages of this approach are:

- Hard to identify the relevant price factors
- Needs extensive and reliable market data
- Extensive computational requirements, as the investments are evaluated using range of inputs many times in order to simulate their historical data.

Stochastic simulation

Stochastic simulation is similar to historical simulation, but instead of relying on historical market data for price factors, it constructs the distributions and parameters for each factor and then runs investment value simulations. It is popularly known as Monte Carlo simulation.

The main advantages of this approach are:

- No assumptions about the investment distribution
- No assumptions about asset returns
- Flexibility
- Ability to run a vast number of scenarios.

The disadvantages are:

- Excessive computational power is required
- Reliance on input parameters
- Reliance on sophisticated mathematical models.

Pros and cons of VAR

VAR is a market-standard measure of risk. However, it does have its disadvantages.

Its benefits are:

- Easy to understand
- Widely accepted
- A single measure of risk
- Easily applied.

Its shortcomings are:

- Does not account for risk in extreme circumstances
- Does not create reliable results for less frequently traded securities, as there isn't enough information
- Uses a uniform measure for all securities, even though in practice their exposure varies (e.g. a two-week holding period is excessive for short-term instruments).

APPENDICES

Option strategies

Introduction

This section covers a wide range of commonly used option strategies. They are categorised by the trade motivation into:

- Directional trades
- Volatility trades
- Arbitrage strategies.

Directional trades are entered into by investors with a definite view of the direction the market is likely to take. *Bullish* traders use strategies that exploit a rising market, whilst *bearish* traders expect the market to decline.

Volatility trades are utilised by investors with no view on market direction, but an expectation of fluctuations. Trading strategies are chosen depending on how large the fluctuations are anticipated to be.

Arbitrage trades exploit the price discrepancies between the options and the underlying asset price, or between different strategies.

Even though some of the trading strategies appear complex, all can be constructed using four basic option types (long call, short call, long put and short put), some in combination with the sale or purchase of the underlying asset.

Strategies using only one type of trade (a call or a put) are called *spreads*, whilst those involving both calls and puts are called *combinations*.

Spreads can be further divided into:

- *Horizontal spread*, whereby options of the same strike, but different expiry are used
- *Vertical spread*, using options of the same expiry, but different strike
- *Diagonal spread*, involving options of different strike and expiry.

A summary of all strategies presented in this section with their motivation is given in the following tables.

Note: The examples of the strategies presented are no reflection of the actual market prices and premiums that could be achieved. They are chosen for ease of graphical representation only.

Motivation	Trade type	
Directional	**Bullish**	**Bearish**
	Long call	Long put
	Short put	Short call
	Bull spread	Bear spread
	Synthetic long	Synthetic short
	Synthetic long call	Synthetic short call
	Synthetic short put	Synthetic long put
	Diagonal bull spread	Diagonal bear spread
	Cylinder	
Volatility	**More volatile**	**Less volatile**
	Long straddle	Short straddle
	Long strangle	Short strangle
	Short butterfly	Long butterfly
	Ratio back spread	Ratio spread
		Horizontal spread
Arbitrage	Conversion	
	Reversal	
	Box	

Directional very bullish	**LONG CALL**
Purchase of a call	Example: buy a 100 call at 5 premium
Loses value due to time decay	
Maximum risk: premium *Maximum reward*: unlimited *Breakeven*: strike + premium	Profit 100 /105 Underlying price 5 Loss
Directional neutral to bearish	**SHORT CALL**
Sale of a call	Example: sell a 100 call at 5 premium
Gains value due to time decay	
Maximum risk: unlimited *Maximum reward*: premium *Breakeven*: strike + premium	Profit 5 100 105 Underlying price Loss

Directional very bearish	**LONG PUT**
Purchase of a put	Example: buy a 100 put at 5 premium
Loses value due to time decay	
Maximum risk: premium *Maximum reward*: strike – premium *Breakeven*: strike – premium	
Directional neutral to bullish	**SHORT PUT**
Sale of a put	Example: sell a 100 put at 5 premium
Gains value due to time decay	
Maximum risk: strike – premium *Maximum reward*: premium *Breakeven*: strike – premium	

Directional bullish	**BULL SPREAD**
Buy a low strike call (put) and sell a high strike call (put)	Example: buy a 100 call at 5 premium, sell a 105 call at 3 premium
Loses value due to time decay	

Maximum risk: (c) net initial debit (p) strike difference – net credit *Maximum reward*: (c) strike difference – net debit (p) net initial credit *Breakeven*: (c) lower strike + net debit (p) higher strike – net credit	Profit 3 100 102 105 Underlying price 2 Loss

Directional bearish	**BEAR SPREAD**
Sell a low strike call (put) and buy a high strike call (put)	Example: sell a 100 call at 5 premium, buy a 105 call at 3 premium
Loses value due to time decay	

Maximum risk: (c) strike difference – net credit (p) net initial debit *Maximum reward*: (c) net initial credit (p) strike difference – net debit *Breakeven*: (c) lower strike + net credit (p) higher strike – net debit	Profit 2 100 102 105 Underlying price 3 Loss

Directional very bullish	**SYNTHETIC LONG**
Purchase of a call and sale of a put with same strike and expiry	Example: buy a 100 call at 3 premium and sell a 100 put at 5 premium
Replicates long futures position	
Maximum risk: strike +/– net premium (debit or credit) *Maximum reward*: unlimited *Breakeven*: strike +/– net premium	 Profit 98 100 Underlying price Loss
Directional very bearish	**SYNTHETIC SHORT**
Sale of a call and purchase of a put with same strike and expiry	Example: sell a 100 call at 3 premium and buy a 100 put at 5 premium
Replicates short futures position	
Maximum risk: unlimited *Maximum reward*: strike +/– net premium (debit or credit) *Breakeven*: strike +/– net premium	 Profit 98 100 Underlying price Loss

Directional very bullish	SYNTHETIC LONG CALL
Purchase of a stock or a future and purchase of a put	Example: buy a future at 100 and buy a put at 100 with 5 premium
Protects downside exposure whilst allowing for potential profit	
Maximum risk: stock/future purchase price – strike + premium *Maximum reward*: unlimited *Breakeven*: stock/future purchase price + premium	 Profit 100 /105 Underlying price 5 Loss
Directional neutral to bearish	SYNTHETIC SHORT CALL/COVERED PUT
Sale of a stock or future and sale of a put	Example: sell a future at 100 and sell a put at 100 with 5 premium
Gains value due to time decay	
Maximum risk: unlimited *Maximum reward*: stock/future purchase price –strike + premium *Breakeven*: stock/future purchase price + premium	Profit 5 100 105 Underlying price Loss

Directional very bearish	**SYNTHETIC LONG PUT**
Sale of a stock or future and purchase of a call	Example: sell a future at 100 and buy a call at 100 with 5 premium
Loses value due to time decay	
Maximum risk: strike – stock/future purchase price + premium *Maximum reward*: stock/future purchase price – premium *Breakeven*: stock/future purchase price – premium	
Directional neutral to bullish	**SYNTHETIC SHORT PUT/COVERED CALL**
Purchase of a stock or future and sale of a call	Example: buy a future at 100 and sell a call at 100 with 5 premium
Enhances returns in static markets, whilst providing limited protection against downturn	
Maximum risk: stock/future purchase price – premium *Maximum reward*: strike – stock/future purchase price + premium *Breakeven*: stock/future purchase price – premium	

Directional bullish	**DIAGONAL BULL SPREAD**
Sale of a short dated call and purchase of longer dated further OTM call	Example: sell a June call at 100 at 3 premium and buy a September call at 105 at 5 premium
Motivated by a very short-term view. Highest profit at short-term expiry, always at exercise price	
Maximum risk: dependent on relative premium movements *Maximum reward*: limited, at short dated expiry *Breakeven*: dependent on relative premium movements	

Directional, bearish	**DIAGONAL BEAR SPREAD**
Sale of a short dated put and purchase of longer dated further OTM put	Example: sell a June put at 105 at 5 premium and buy a September put at 100 at 3 premium
Motivated by a very short-term view. The biggest loss at short-term expiry, always at exercise price	
Maximum risk: limited, at short dated expiry *Maximum reward*: dependent on relative premium movements *Breakeven*: dependent on relative premium movements	

Directional bullish	**CYLINDER**
Buy a low strike put and sell a high strike call together with the purchase of underlying	Example: buy a 100 put at 5 premium, sell a 105 call at 3 premium with purchase of underlying at 100
Loses value due to time decay	
Maximum risk: capped by put *Maximum reward*: floored by call *Breakeven*: underlying price +/– net premium (debit or credit)	Profit 3 100 102 105 Underlying price 2 Loss
Volatility, exploits static market conditions	**HORIZONTAL SPREAD**
Sale of a short dated call/put and purchase of a longer dated call/put with the same strike	Example: sell a June call at 100 at 2 premium and buy a September call at 100 at 3 premium
Helped by quicker time decay of short dated option	
For American options only: *Maximum risk*: net initial debit *Maximum reward*: subject to relative changes in premiums *Breakeven*: subject to relative changes in premiums	Profit 4 98 100 102 Underlying price Loss

Volatility, exploits increasing fluctuations	**LONG STRADDLE**
Purchase of a call and a put with same strike and expiry	Example: buy a 100 call at 1 premium and a 100 put at 3 premium
Severe time decay as the options approach expiry	
Maximum risk: both premiums *Maximum reward*: unlimited *Breakeven*: lower: strike – both premiums higher: strike + both premiums	Profit 96 100 104 Underlying price 4 Loss
Volatility, exploits decreasing fluctuations	**SHORT STRADDLE**
Sale of a call and a put with same strike and expiry	Example: sell a 100 call at 1 premium and a 100 put at 3 premium
Unlimited risk, but helped by time decay, particularly close to option expiry	
Maximum risk: unlimited *Maximum reward*: both premiums *Breakeven*: lower: strike – both premiums higher: strike + both premiums	Profit 4 96 100 104 Underlying price Loss

Volatility, exploits increasing fluctuations	**LONG STRANGLE**
Purchase of a call and a put with different strike but same expiry	Example: buy a 102 call at 1 premium and a 98 put at 3 premium
Similar to long straddle, but at lower cost, as breakeven points are further apart	
If call strike is higher than the put: *Maximum risk*: both premiums *Maximum reward*: unlimited *Breakeven*: lower: lower strike – both premiums higher: higher strike + both premiums	Profit / Loss chart with axis points 94, 98, 100, 102, 106 and Underlying price; Loss value 4
Volatility, exploits decreasing fluctuations	**SHORT STRANGLE**
Sale of a call and a put with different strike but same expiry	Example: sell a 102 call at 3 premium and sell a 98 put at 1 premium
Similar to short straddle, but as breakeven points are further apart, takes longer to become unprofitable	
If call strike is lower than the put: *Maximum risk*: unlimited *Maximum reward*: both premiums – strike difference *Breakeven*: lower: higher strike – both premiums higher: lower strike + both premiums	Profit / Loss chart with axis points 94, 98, 100, 102, 106 and Underlying price; Profit value 4

Volatility, exploits decreasing fluctuations	**LONG BUTTERFLY**
Purchase of a low strike call/put, sale of two mid-strike calls/puts and purchase of high strike call/put	Example: buy 98 call at 3 premium, sell two 100 calls at 1.5 premium and buy a 102 call at 1 premium
Similar to long straddle, but at lower cost, as breakeven points are further apart	
Maximum risk: net initial debit

Maximum reward: (high–mid strike) or (mid–lower strike) minus initial debit

Breakeven: lower: lower strike + net debit higher: higher strike – net debit | |
Volatility, exploits increasing fluctuations	**SHORT BUTTERFLY**
Sale of a low strike call/put, purchase of two mid-strike calls/puts and sale of high strike call/put	Example: sell 98 put at 1 premium, buy two 100 puts at 1.5 premium and sell a 102 put at 3 premium
Alternative to long straddle or strangle	
Maximum risk: (high–mid strike) or (mid–lower strike) minus initial credit

Maximum reward: net initial credit

Breakeven: lower: lower strike + net credit higher: higher strike – net credit | |

Volatility, exploits decreasing fluctuations	**RATIO SPREAD**
Call: purchase of low strike call and sale of two or more high strike calls *Put*: purchase of high strike put and sale of two or more low strike puts	Example: buy a 100 call at 3 premium and sell two 102 calls at 2 premium
Unlimited downside exposure, limited profit	
When constructed with calls: *Maximum risk*: unlimited *Maximum reward*: strike difference + initial credit *Breakeven*: higher strike + maximum reward	
Volatility, exploits increasing fluctuations	**RATIO BACK SPREAD**
Call: sale of low strike call and purchase of two or more high strike calls *Put*: sale of high strike put and purchase of two or more low strike puts	Example: buy two 100 puts at 2 premium and sell a 102 put at 3 premium
Limited downside exposure	
When constructed with puts: *Maximum risk*: strike difference + initial debit *Maximum reward*: breakeven value *Breakeven*: lower strike – initial debit – strike difference	

Arbitrage	**CONVERSION/REVERSAL/BOX**
Motivation	*Conversion:* undertaken when synthetic short is expensive and underlying relatively cheap *Reversal:* used when synthetic long is cheap and underlying relatively expensive *Box:* exploits price discrepancies between a synthetic long at one strike and a synthetic short at another
Construction	*Conversion:* sell a call and buy a put with same strike and expiry (synthetic short) and purchase underlying stock/future *Reversal:* buy a call and sell a put with same strike and expiry (synthetic long) and sell underlying stock/future *Box:* buy a call and sell a put with same strike and expiry (synthetic long) and simultaneously sell a call and buy a put at different strike and same expiry (synthetic short)
Risks and rewards	Maximum risk: none Maximum reward: relative price difference
Sensitivity	Efficient markets would soon eliminate this prospect
Example	*Conversion:* sell a 100 call at 0.9, buy a 100 put at 1.8 and buy future at 99 *Reversal:* buy a 100 call at 0.9, sell a 100 put at 1.8 and sell future at 99.2 *Box:* buy a 100 call at 0.9, sell a 100 put at 1.9 sell a 99 call at 1.5, buy a 99 put at 1.4 Profit 0.1 99 100 Underlying price Loss

ISO (SWIFT) currency codes

AED	United Arab Emirates, Dirhams
AFN	Afghanistan, Afghanis
ALL	Albania, Leke
AMD	Armenia, Drams
ANG	Netherlands Antilles, Guilders (Florins)
AOA	Angola, Kwanza
ARS	Argentina, Pesos
AUD	Australia, Dollars
AWG	Aruba, Guilders (Florins)
AZN	Azerbaijan, New Manats
BAM	Bosnia and Herzegovina, Convertible Marka
BBD	Barbados, Dollars
BDT	Bangladesh, Taka
BGN	Bulgaria, Leva
BHD	Bahrain, Dinars
BIF	Burundi, Francs
BMD	Bermuda, Dollars
BND	Brunei Darussalam, Dollars
BOB	Bolivia, Bolivianos
BRL	Brazil, Brazil Real
BSD	Bahamas, Dollars
BTN	Bhutan, Ngultrum
BWP	Botswana, Pulas
BYR	Belarus, Rubles
BZD	Belize, Dollars
CAD	Canada, Dollars
CDF	Congo/Kinshasa, Congolese Francs
CHF	Switzerland, Francs
CLP	Chile, Pesos
CNY	China, Yuan Renminbi
COP	Colombia, Pesos

CRC	Costa Rica, Colones
CUP	Cuba, Pesos
CVE	Cape Verde, Escudos
CZK	Czech Republic, Koruny
DJF	Djibouti, Francs
DKK	Denmark, Kroner
DOP	Dominican Republic, Pesos
DZD	Algeria, Algeria Dinars
EEK	Estonia, Krooni
EGP	Egypt, Pounds
ERN	Eritrea, Nakfa
ETB	Ethiopia, Birr
EUR	Euro Member Countries, Euro
FJD	Fiji, Dollars
FKP	Falkland Islands (Malvinas), Pounds
GBP	United Kingdom, Pounds
GEL	Georgia, Lari
GGP	Guernsey, Pounds
GHS	Ghana, Cedis
GIP	Gibraltar, Pounds
GMD	Gambia, Dalasi
GNF	Guinea, Francs
GTQ	Guatemala, Quetzales
GYD	Guyana, Dollars
HKD	Hong Kong, Dollars
HNL	Honduras, Lempiras
HRK	Croatia, Kuna
HTG	Haiti, Gourdes
HUF	Hungary, Forint
IDR	Indonesia, Rupiahs
ILS	Israel, New Shekels
IMP	Isle of Man, Pounds
INR	India, Rupees
IQD	Iraq, Dinars
IRR	Iran, Rials
ISK	Iceland, Kronur
JEP	Jersey, Pounds
JMD	Jamaica, Dollars
JOD	Jordan, Dinars
JPY	Japan, Yen
KES	Kenya, Shillings
KGS	Kyrgyzstan, Soms

KHR	Cambodia, Riels
KMF	Comoros, Francs
KPW	Korea (North), Won
KRW	Korea (South), Won
KWD	Kuwait, Dinars
KYD	Cayman Islands, Dollars
KZT	Kazakhstan, Tenge
LAK	Laos, Kips
LBP	Lebanon, Pounds
LKR	Sri Lanka, Rupees
LRD	Liberia, Dollars
LSL	Lesotho, Maloti
LTL	Lithuania, Litai
LVL	Latvia, Lati
LYD	Libya, Dinars
MAD	Morocco, Dirhams
MDL	Moldova, Lei
MGA	Madagascar, Ariary
MKD	Macedonia, Denars
MMK	Myanmar (Burma), Kyats
MNT	Mongolia, Tugriks
MOP	Macau, Patacas
MRO	Mauritania, Ouguiyas
MUR	Mauritius, Rupees
MVR	Maldives (Maldive Islands), Rufiyaa
MWK	Malawi, Kwachas
MXN	Mexico, Pesos
MYR	Malaysia, Ringgits
MZN	Mozambique, Meticais
NAD	Namibia, Dollars
NGN	Nigeria, Nairas
NIO	Nicaragua, Cordobas
NOK	Norway, Krone
NPR	Nepal, Nepal Rupees
NZD	New Zealand, Dollars
OMR	Oman, Rials
PAB	Panama, Balboa
PEN	Peru, Nuevos Soles
PGK	Papua New Guinea, Kina
PHP	Philippines, Pesos
PKR	Pakistan, Rupees
PLN	Poland, Zloty

PYG	Paraguay, Guarani
QAR	Qatar, Rials
RON	Romania, New Lei
RSD	Serbia, Dinars
RUB	Russia, Rubles
RWF	Rwanda, Rwanda Francs
SAR	Saudi Arabia, Riyals
SBD	Solomon Islands, Dollars
SCR	Seychelles, Rupees
SDG	Sudan, Pounds
SEK	Sweden, Kronor
SGD	Singapore, Dollars
SHP	Saint Helena, Pounds
SLL	Sierra Leone, Leones
SOS	Somalia, Shillings
SPL	Seborga, Luigini
SRD	Suriname, Dollars
STD	São Tome and Principe, Dobras
SVC	El Salvador, Colones
SYP	Syria, Pounds
SZL	Swaziland, Emalangeni
THB	Thailand, Baht
TJS	Tajikistan, Somoni
TMM	Turkmenistan, Manats
TND	Tunisia, Dinars
TOP	Tonga, Pa'anga
TRY	Turkey, New Lira
TTD	Trinidad and Tobago, Dollars
TVD	Tuvalu, Tuvalu Dollars
TWD	Taiwan, New Dollars
TZS	Tanzania, Shillings
UAH	Ukraine, Hryvnia
UGX	Uganda, Shillings
USD	United States of America, Dollars
UYU	Uruguay, Pesos
UZS	Uzbekistan, Sums
VEF	Venezuela, Bolivares Fuertes
VND	Viet Nam, Dong
VUV	Vanuatu, Vatu
WST	Samoa, Tala
XAF	Communauté Financière Africaine, Francs
XAG	Silver, Ounces

XAU	Gold, Ounces
XCD	East Caribbean Dollars
XDR	International Monetary Fund (IMF) Special Drawing Rights
XOF	Communauté Financière Africaine, Francs
XPD	Palladium Ounces
XPF	Comptoirs Français du Pacifique Francs
XPT	Platinum, Ounces
YER	Yemen, Rials
ZAR	South Africa, Rand
ZMK	Zambia, Kwacha
ZWD	Zimbabwe, Zimbabwe Dollars

Glossary

Accrued interest Proportion of interest (**coupon**) earned on an investment between the last coupon payment until the **security value date**.

All-or-nothing option *See* **binary option**

American option An option that can be **exercised** at any date prior to expiry. (*See* **European option**)

Amortising A **principal** that is decreasing during the contract period, or is repaid in stages.

Amortising bond A **bond** that repays the **principal** in stages over the lifetime of the bond, hence the **coupons** are gradually reduced. (*See* **perpetual bond**)

Annual percentage rate (or **APR**) (*See* **effective rate, nominal rate**)

Appreciation Increase in market value of a security; in particular increase in the value of a currency compared to other currencies. (*See* **depreciation**)

APR (annual percentage rate) A rate paid at the end of the year that gives the same return on investment as a more frequently paid rate, where interest is **compounded**. (*See* **effective rate, nominal rate**)

Arbitrage Exploiting the price discrepancies between two products or two markets for riskless profit.

Asian option An option that pays at **maturity** the difference between the **strike** and the average price of the **underlying** during the option life. (*See* **European option, American option**)

Asking price Price at which traders sell securities. (*See* **offer, bid**)

Asset A valuable holding by a company, e.g. **security** or tangible commodity. (*See* **liability**)

Asset-backed security A security that is collateralised by a tangible asset, such as a property portfolio, and thus derives cashflows from that asset.

Asset swap A **swap** of cashflows whereby one leg is linked to payments from an asset, whilst the other is linked to the prevailing market rate. (*See* **interest rate swap, currency swap**)

At the money An option that has **strike** set to be equal to the prevailing market price of the **underlying** asset. (*See* **in the money, out of the money**)

ATM *See* **at the money**

Average rate option *See* **Asian option**

Average strike option In contrast to **Asian options**, the **strike** is set to the average price of the **underlying during the option contract**; the difference between the strike and the prevailing market price of underlying is paid on **exercise**.

Backwardation The market condition whereby the **forward** or **futures** price of a security is lower than the market **spot** price. (*See* **contango**)

Balance sheet security A financial instrument that appears on a company's accounts. (*See* **off-balance sheet security**)

Banker's acceptance *See* **bill of exchange**

Barrier option The **option** that is activated or extinguished when the **underlying** price touches or goes through a barrier. (*See* **knock-in, knock-out**)

Base currency In **exchange rates**, the currency against which the amount of another currency (**variable currency**) is calculated.

Basis In relation to **futures** contracts, it is the difference between the underlying **cash market** price and the futures price. In **swaps**, it refers to the difference between the tenors of underlying **floating** rates of two **swap legs**.

Basis points Used in interest rate quotations to imply 0.01 per cent.

Basis risk The risk of divergence between the two **security** prices. Also the exposure to two different floating rates, e.g. one-month **Libor** vs. three-month **Libor**. (*See* **basis**)

Basis swap A swap where both **legs** are based on a **floating** rate. (*See* **basis**)

Basket option An **option** that pays to the investor the difference between the option **strike** and the average price (at exercise) of the basket of **underlying assets**. (*See* **rainbow option**)

Bear market Market that anticipates falls in values of **securities**. (*See* **bull market**)

Bear spread An option-trading strategy involving a sale of a low strike **call** (put) and purchase of a high strike call (put). Undertaken with expectation of a fall in the value of the **underlying**. (*See* **bull spread**)

Bearer security An unregistered security that pays coupon to whoever is holding it, i.e. it provides anonymity.

Bermudan option An **option** that can be exercised at pre-agreed dates until expiry. (*See* **American option, European option**)

Better performance bond options Allows the buyer to receive the greater of two assets' returns over a specified period of time as long as they are both positive.

Bid A price at which the trader is willing to purchase the security. (*See* **asking price, offer**)

Bid/offer spread The difference between the price at which security can be sold and bought, created by traders to make a profit.

Bill of exchange A **money market** debt used by a company to finance commercial transactions. If endorsed by a bank, it becomes **Banker's acceptance**.

Binary option (or **Digital option**) An **option** that pays a fixed amount on **exercise**, regardless by how much the option is **in-the-money** as long as it is **ITM** at expiry (**all-or-nothing options**), or if it has been ITM at any point until expiry (**one-touch options**).

Binomial distribution A frequency distribution where only two mutually exclusive outcomes are possible. (*See* **trinomial distribution, normal distribution, log-normal distribution**)

Binomial tree A numerical approach to **option** valuation, whereby it is assumed that the **underlying** price can, in a very short time interval, move up or down with the probability of those moves assigned. The possible paths the option can take between inception and **expiry** result in a tree, which is used to value the option premium.

Black model A variation of **Black–Scholes model**, used to price interest rate **derivatives**.

Black–Scholes model A mathematical model used to analytically value **options**. It gives a value of a **call**, whilst the **put** value can be derived using **put-call parity**.

Bond A debt issued by a corporation or a government, usually paying a **fixed** or a **floating coupon** until **maturity**, when the **principal** is redeemed. (*See* **zero coupon bond**)

Bootstrapping A method of deriving **zero-coupon yields** from a combination of coupon-bearing **securities**. Used in **yield curve** construction to calculate **discount factors** for **swap** coupon dates.

Box An **option** trading strategy that exploits price discrepancies between a **synthetic long** at one **strike** and a **synthetic short** at another. It is constructed by buying a **call** and selling a **put** with the same **strike** and **expiry** (synthetic long) and simultaneously selling a call and buying a put at a different strike and same expiry. (*See* **conversion, reversal**)

Broker An individual who is paid a commission for executing customer orders. Also, a person who acts as an intermediary between a buyer and seller, for a fee. A **stock exchange** broker acts as an agent and must be registered with the exchange where the **securities** are traded. (*See* **trader**)

Bull market Market that anticipates rise in values of **securities**. (*See* **bear market**)

Bull spread An option trading strategy involving a purchase of a low strike call (put) and sale of a high strike call (put). Undertaken with expectation of rise in the value of the **underlying**. (*See* **bear spread**)

Butterfly An option strategy that exploits **underlying volatility**. Involves simultaneous sale/purchase of a low **strike call/put**, purchase/sale of two mid-strike calls/puts and sale/purchase of high strike call/put.

Calendar spread (or **diagonal spread**) A purchase/sale of a **security** with **maturity** at one date and simultaneous sale/purchase of the same or similar security that matures at a later date.

Callable bond A **bond** with in-built optionality that gives the issuer the right to redeem the bond at a date prior to **maturity**. (*See* **puttable bond**)

Call option A contract that gives the holder the right but not the obligation to buy an **underlying security** at a future date at the price agreed today. (*See* **put option**)

Cap A ceiling on the cost of borrowing, typically used when cashflows are due over a longer period of time, such as in **swaps**. (*See* **floor**).

Capital market A market for lending and borrowing funds for a period longer than one year. (*See* **money market**).

Capped/collared floater An **FRN** that sets the limits on a **floating coupon** rate, either by limiting the potential profit (using **caps** only), or by fixing both the maximum and minimum level (using **collars**).

Caption Option to enter into a **cap**. (*See* **cap, floor, floorption**)

Cash market Market for transactions on **underlying** undertaken now and settled on the full price of the asset.

CD *See* **certificate of deposit**

CDO *See* **credit default option**

CDS *See* **credit default swap**

Certificate of deposit A **security** issued by a bank to raise funds. Usually registered and **coupon** bearing.

Cheapest to deliver (or **CTD**) The bond that is most cost-effective to the seller to deliver under the **bond futures** contract. Futures are priced based on a **notional** bond, with several **deliverable** bonds, each with a **conversion factor** assigned.

Chooser option An **option** that gives the buyer the choice whether to exercise **call** or a **put** at a later date.

Clean price Price of a bond excluding **accrued coupon**. (*See* **dirty price**)

Clearing house In **exchange-trading**, an institution linked to the exchange that manages counterparty funds and **margin** payments.

Cliquet option (or ratchet option) An option with the strike reset at the prevailing underlying price at predetermined dates until option expiry, locking in their intrinsic value.

CMOs *See* collateralised mortgage obligations.

Collar An investment strategy that limits both the upside and downside exposure to the price of the underlying. It involves simultaneous sale of a call (put) and purchase of a put (call) at different strikes, usually both out of the money.

Collateral A tangible asset that is deposited with the counterparty as insurance against default. Often used to enhance the terms of the deal.

Collateralised mortgage obligations (or CMOs) Securities providing the distribution of risks and returns from a pool of mortgages, tailored to meet client's needs.

Commercial paper (or CP) A short-term security issued by a corporate or a bank to raise funds, usually zero-coupon.

Commodity A tangible asset, such as agricultural produce, precious metals, base metals or energy products.

Commodity derivative A derivative whose underlying asset is a deliverable commodity (typically settled as contract for differences).

Compound interest Interest that is paid before maturity and reinvested to boost earnings. Generally assumes that the reinvestment rate is the same as the original rate. (*See* simple interest)

Compounding frequency The frequency at which interest is paid, and hence can be reinvested.

Contango The market condition whereby the forward or futures price of a security is higher than the market spot price. (*See* backwardation)

Contingent option An option that does not require up-front premium payment. It is only due if the option is exercised; but if the option is ITM, even by an amount smaller than the premium, it must be exercised. The payoff profile is equivalent to a combination of long call/put and short digital call/put.

Continuous compounding A theoretical concept whereby the compounding period is infinitesimally small.

Conversion An option trading strategy that exploits price discrepancies when synthetic short is expensive and underlying relatively cheap. It is constructed by selling a call and buying a put with same strike and expiry (synthetic short) and purchase of the underlying stock/future. (*See* box, reversal)

[handwritten: Do they charge with massive volatility?]

Conversion factor In a **bond futures** contract, a factor assigned to each **deliverable bond** to make it comparable to **notional** bond underlying the futures price. Defined as the price of a single unit of a bond that makes its **yield** equal to the notional **coupon**.

Convertible bond A bond with the **call option** attached that gives the holder the right but not the obligation to convert the bond into **equity shares** in the company that has issued the bond.

Convexity In relation to **futures** and **FRAs**, it is the difference between the contracts' dependence on interest rates. In relation to **bonds**, it is the curvature of the relationship between the bond price and its **yield**.

Cost of carry A total cost of an open position.

Counterparty A party taking the opposite side of the deal.

Counterparty risk Exposure to the risk that the **counterparty** will not meet their obligations under the contract.

Country risk A component of the counterparty risk, associated with the **creditworthiness** of the counterparty domicile country. (*See* **customer risk, transfer risk**)

Coupon Interest paid at pre-determined intervals, based on the underlying principal.

Coupon-bearing security A type of **security** that pays regular **coupons** based on a **principal** amount (**nominal** amount or **face value**) as means of return on investment. (*See* **zero coupon**)

Coupon swap An **interest rate swap**, whereby one **swap leg** pays a **fixed** rate and another a **floating** rate. (*See* **asset swap, basis swap**)

Covered call/put A sale/purchase of a **call/put** where the **option writer** already holds (in case of a call) or has sold forward (in case of a put) the **underlying**. (*See* **naked option, synthetic transaction**)

CP *See* **commercial paper**

Credit default A failure to meet contractual obligations due to events associated with reduced **credit rating**.

Credit default option (or CDO) An option to enter into a **credit default swap** at a future date.

Credit default swap (or CDS) It is a **swap** where cashflows are exchanged in case of a **credit event** associated with debt obligations of a third party.

Credit derivative Security whose value is derived from the **credit risk** on a reference asset or a third party, rather than the **counterparty** to the transaction itself.

Credit event An event that affects the counterparty's ability to fulfil their obligations.

Credit exposure Exposure to the **creditworthiness** of a **counterparty** or a **security**.

Credit rating An assessment of **creditworthiness** of a legal entity or a security done by an independent agency.

Credit risk Risk associated with **creditworthiness** of a legal entity or a **security**.

Credit spread swap A **swap** that gives protection from smaller downgrades in **credit rating** of a third party or a reference asset, rather than outright bankruptcy or **default**.

Creditworthiness An assessment of past and present **assets** and **liabilities** of a legal entity as a measure of likelihood of **default**.

Cross-currency A security that involves two currencies.

Cross-rate An exchange rate between two currencies where neither is a major currency (USD, EUR, GBP). It involves rate calculations against the major currency.

Cross-rate forward A **cross-rate** applicable to a period commencing in the future.

Currency swap A **swap** where the **swap legs** are not paid in the same currency. It usually involves exchange of **principals**. (*See* **interest rate swap**)

Current yield Bond yield calculated as a ratio of **coupon** to the **clean price** per unit of 100. (*See* **yield to maturity** and **simple yield to maturity**)

Customer risk A **counterparty risk** component. The risk that the counterparty will fail to fulfil their obligations. (*See* **country risk, transfer risk**)

Cylinder A **directional** (bullish) **option** trading strategy, with desire for downside protection. Constructed by buying a low **strike put** and selling a high strike **call** together with the purchase of **underlying**.

Delayed option An **option** that gives the buyer the right to receive at a future date another option with the **strike** set at the prevailing market value of the **underlying** on that date.

Delayed reset floater (or **Libor in arrears swap**) An instrument that fixes the **floating leg** of the **swap** only a few days before the payment is due; which is in contrast to standard swap arrangements where the rate is fixed at the beginning of the reset period and paid at the end.

Deliverable bond A bond that is on the list of bonds that can be delivered under the **bond futures** contract. It is comparable to the **notional bond** by multiplication of its price by its **conversion factor**.

Delta The change of **option** value with the unit change of the **underlying** price.

Dependent events In probability, the events whose outcomes are related, i.e. the outcome of one is influenced by the outcome of the other. (*See* **independent events**)

Depreciation Decrease in market value of a security; in particular decrease in the value of a currency compared to other currencies. (*See* **appreciation**)

Derivative A **security** whose value is based on or derived from the value of another, referred to as **underlying**.

Diagonal spread An **option** strategy where two option contracts of the same type (**call** or a **put**) are bought/sold with the different **strike** and **expiry**. (*See* **spread, horizontal spread, vertical spread**)

Diagonal bear spread A directional **option** trading strategy, constructed with a sale of a short dated **put** and a purchase of longer dated further **OTM** put.

Diagonal bull spread A directional **option** trading strategy, constructed with a sale of a short dated **call** and purchase of longer dated further OTM call.

Digital option *See* **binary option**

Directional trade A trade entered into by investors with a definite view of the direction the market is likely to take. (*See* **bear market, bull market, volatility trade**)

Direct rate An exchange rate between two currencies where at least one is a major currency (USD, EUR, GBP). (*See* **cross-rate**)

Dirty price Bond price that includes **accrued coupon**. (*See* **clean price**)

Discount The reduction in value of an asset compared to its **nominal value** as a compensation for the lack of interest payments. Also, discounting is a way of comparison of future cashflows when brought back to the present day. In particular, in foreign exchange, the amount by which one currency is cheaper in terms of another. (*See* **premium**)

Discount factor A link between the **present value** and the **future value** of cashflows, calculated as a function of the interest rate reciprocal on the cashflow applied to the holding period.

Distribution A range of values a variable can take. (*See* **binomial distribution, normal distribution, log-normal distribution**)

Dividend Profit on **equity** holding, typically proportionate to the number of **shares** bought.

Dividend yield A proportion of **dividend** payments relative to the **equity** held.

Dual currency bond A **bond** that pays interest in one currency but is redeemed in another.

Duration (or **Macaulay duration**) A weighted average time until half of **bond** proceeds (**coupon** and **principal**) are repaid, using **present values** of the cashflows for weighting.

EDSP Exchange Delivery Settlement Price – an official **security** price against which all contracts are valued/settled.

Effective rate *See* **APR**

Equity (also **stock**) Ownership in a company. Also all the **assets** that belong to an individual or legal entity after all the debt is removed.

Equity derivative A financial instrument whose underlying is **equity** or **equity index**.

Equity index (also **stock index**) A measure of performance of **equity** (**stock**) market sector, or the market as a whole.

Equity index future A **futures** contract based on an **equity index**.

Equity index option An option with **equity index** or a single **stock** as an **underlying**.

Equity index swap An **OTC** swap where at least one **leg** is based on percentage change in the value of a chosen **equity index**.

Eurocurrency A currency other than the legal tender of the country where transaction takes place.

European option An option that gives the holder the right but not the obligation to transact at expiry date only. (*See* **American option**, **Bermudan option**)

Exchange-traded Contracts, such as **futures**, that are traded on recognised exchanges, rather than **OTC**. (*See* **stock exchange**)

Exchange rate A quotation for an amount of **variable currency** purchased/sold for one unit of **base currency**.

Ex-dividend The coupon on **security** (usually **bond**) is paid to the seller, rather than the buyer, even though the security has already been sold. It can also refer to a period immediately after the dividend has been paid.

Exercise Option transaction undertaken by the buyer whereby the seller has to fulfil his obligations.

Exercise price (or **strike**) A pre-agreed level of the value of **underlying** at which the **option** transaction can take place.

Expiry Termination of the **option** contract, i.e. the option cannot be **exercised** past the expiry date.

Exposure Impact of market movements on the value of security. Also an amount of liability related to a financial transaction.

Extrapolation Calculation of values outside the data range. (*See* **interpolation**)

Face value (or **nominal value**) An amount of **underlying** on which the contract is based (and **coupons**, if any, are paid).

Fixed rate Cost of funds that does not change with the market rates.

Floating rate A variable **interest rate** that is reset at regular intervals to the relevant prevailing market rate.

Floating rate note (or **FRN**) A long-term lending/borrowing capital market instrument where interest payable is reset at regular intervals to prevailing market rates.

Floor A minimum rate guaranteed on investment, typically used when cash-flows are due over a longer period of time, such as in **swaps**. (*See* **cap, collar**)

Floorption An **option** to enter into a **floor**. (*See* **floor, cap, caption**)

Forward General term for an instrument that is valued at a future date.

Forward cross-rate A exchange rate quotation (involving two currencies, neither of which is a major currency) for a period starting at a future date. (*See* **cross-rate, direct rate**)

Forward direct rate A exchange rate quotation (involving two currencies, at least one of which is a major currency) for a period starting at a future date. (*See* **cross-rate, direct rate**)

Forward exchange rate An exchange rate quotation applicable to a period starting at a future date.

Forward–forward An **interest rate** agreement starting on one future date and ending on another, typically involving exchange of **principals**.

Forward rate agreement (or FRA) A short-period interest rate **OTC** instrument for a period starting on a future date and ending on another, whereby the **present value** of the difference between the contract rate and the prevailing market rate is paid at the inception. (*See* **futures**)

Forward outright A sale or a purchase of foreign currency at a future date.

Forward-start swap A **swap** that starts at a pre-agreed date in the future.

FRA *See* forward date agreement

FRN *See* floating rate note

Futures An **exchange-traded** interest rate contract to buy/sell a specific quantity of **security** at a future date at a price agreed today. Typically only the difference between the contract price and prevailing market price on valuation date is settled. (*See* **FRA, OTC**)

Futures price (applicable to interest rate futures) A market quotation 100 − interest rate. Makes the behaviour of futures opposite to **FRAs**, as when rates rise futures prices fall, whilst FRAs rise and vice versa.

Future value A value of a cashflow at a future date achieved by investing the funds (principal and interest) at prevailing market rates. (*See* **present value, time value of money**)

Future volatility Volatility that will be present in the market in the future. Used in **Black–Scholes** and other pricing models, but as it is an unknown quantity it is replaced by estimates, such as **implied volatility** or **historic volatility**.

Gamma The change in **option delta** on unit change in value of **underlying**.

Greeks A collective term for **option** value sensitivities to changes in market variables: value of underlying – **delta**, delta – **gamma**, volatility – **vega**, interest rates – **rho**, time – **theta**.

Gross redemption yield (or **yield to maturity**) **Bond yield** that does not take transaction costs and taxes into account.

GRY *See* **gross redemption yield**

Hedge ratio A ratio between the size of a position in an instrument held as a protection against adverse value movements in another, and the size of the position in that instrument. In numerical **option** valuation it is used in **premium** valuation formulae.

Hedging Protecting against adverse movements in the market value of an instrument by taking an offsetting position in another instrument(s). (*See* **speculation, arbitrage**)

Historic volatility Fluctuations in value of security observed or derived from historical market data. (*See* **implied volatility, future volatility**)

Holder A purchaser of a security.

Horizontal spread (or **calendar spread**) An **option** strategy where two option contracts of the same type (**call** or a **put**) are bought/sold with the same **strike** but different **expiry**. (*See* **spread, vertical spread, diagonal spread**)

Hybrid security A financial instrument that has properties of two or more unrelated securities.

IMM date International Money Market date – the interest rate **futures** contracts **expiry** date (third Wednesday of March, June, September and December).

Implied volatility Volatility that is derived from the current market data, calculated as the volatility introduced into pricing models that would result in the current market price.

Independent events In probability, the events whose outcomes are not related, i.e. the outcome of one is not influenced by the other. (*See* **dependent events**)

Index (or **equity index** or **stock index**) A collective measure of market performance of a set of equities/stocks.

Index multiplier A monetary amount for each point of movement in a particular **equity index**.

Indirect rate An exchange rate quotation where the major currency is the **base currency** and the other currency is a **variable currency**.

Initial margin In **exchange-traded options**, funds deposited at the contract inception as a protection against adverse market movements. (*See* **clearing house, margin, variation margin**)

Initial public offering (or **IPO**) A company's first sale of **stock/equity shares** to the general public.

Interest rate A cost of funds expressed as a percentage.

Interest rate guarantee A one-period **cap** or **floor**, i.e. **option** on **FRA**.

Interest rate swap (or **IRS**) A **swap** of cashflows based on a **notional principal**, whereby both **swap legs** (**fixed** and **floating** or floating–floating) are denominated in the same currency. (*See* **swap, basis swap**)

Internal rate of return (or **IRR**) The **interest rate** applied to a series of present and future cashflows that results in **NPV** = 0. (*See* **net present value**)

Interpolation Calculation of an unknown data point from the set of available data where the unknown lies within the available range. (*See* **extrapolation**)

In the money (or **ITM**) An option that has strike set to be more favourable than the prevailing value of the **underlying** asset. Hence for **call options**, the **ITM** option has the strike lower than the market price, whilst for a **put option** it is higher. (*See* **at the money, out of the money**)

Intrinsic value Part of the **option premium** that reflects by how much the **option** is in or **out of money** compared to the prevailing price of the **underlying**. (*See* **premium, time value**)

IRR *See* **internal rate of return**

IRS *See* **interest rate swap**

Iteration A mathematical process whereby the calculation is repeated many times in order to estimate an unknown variable value, adjusting the criteria at each turn until preset conditions are met. It is a numerical approach used when the unknown cannot be calculated directly from the available data.

ITM *See* **in the money**.

Knock-in/-out A **barrier option** that is activated/extinguished when the preset level is reached or crossed over.

Ladder option An option similar to **cliquet option**, but the **strike** is reset if and when the **underlying** price reaches predetermined levels during the lifetime of the option.

Leg *See* **swap leg**.

Liability An outstanding obligation or debt to another party.

Libid A London interbank borrowing rate at which the London banks of high creditworthiness are prepared to borrow funds from one another. (*See* **Libor, Limean**)

Over the counter (or OTC) An off-exchange trading market, whereby the counterparties can transact privately or thorough investment banks.

Par A price of a **security** equal to its **face value**.

Path dependent option An **option** that has the payout linked to the path the **underlying** has taken during the lifetime of the option. (*See* **European, American, Bermudan, Asian, average strike, rainbow, cliquet, ladder option**)

Perpetual bond A **bond** that has no **redemption** date, i.e. pays **coupon** indefinitely. (*See* **amortising bond**)

Premium In **options** market, the price of the option contract payable at the outset. It comprises **intrinsic value** and **time value**. In foreign exchange, an amount by which one currency is more expensive in terms of another, for future delivery than in spot transaction. (*See* **option premium, discount**)

Present value (or PV) The value of future cashflows now, when **discounted** at a prevailing interest rate. (*See* **time value of money, future value**)

Primary market A market where a **security** is originally issued. (*See* **secondary market**)

Probability distribution A mathematical concept that refers to the likelihood of a variable being less or equal to a particular level. (*See* **binomial distribution, normal distribution, log-normal distribution**)

Put option An **option** that gives the holder the right, but not the obligation to deliver an **underlying security** at a future date at a price agreed today. (*See* **call option**)

Puttable bond A **bond** with in-built optionality that gives the investor the right to sell the bond back to the issuer at a date prior to **maturity**. (*See* **callable bond**)

Quanto option An **option** with the value related to one **underlying**, but the payout is linked to another.

Quanto swap A **swap** where one or both **legs** are based on an instrument in one currency, but payable in another.

Quantitative analytics A term describing mathematical modelling of traded securities, their underlying sensitivities to market variables and their pricing.

Rainbow option (or **outperformance option**) An **option** that, if exercised, pays the buyer the difference between the best price and the **strike** (for **call** options) or the worst price and the strike (for **put** options) from a number of **underlying securities**. (*See* **basket option**)

Ratchet option *See* **Cliquet option**

Rate spread option An option contract that offers exposure to the **basis** between two benchmark rates (e.g. three-month Libor vs. six-month Libor).

Ratio back spread An **option** trading strategy used to exploit **volatility**. It exploits increasing fluctuations. **Bullish** if constructed with **calls**, **bearish** if **puts** are used.

Ratio spread Option trading strategy used to exploit **volatility**. It exploits decreasing fluctuations. **Bullish** if constructed with **puts**, **bearish** if **calls** are used.

Redeem To repay the principal of the security. (*See* **redemption**)

Redemption Refers to the repayment of the principal. Redemption date is the contractual date at which the security is repaid.

Reinvestment rate The interest rate applicable to the interest received on the principal amount that typically cannot be invested at the rate agreed at contract inception.

Repo (or **repurchase agreement**) An agreement to buy/sell a security and repurchase it at a later date, equivalent to collateralised lending/borrowing. A purchaser of repo sells the security and receives cash, whilst the opposite transaction is referred to as a **reverse repo**.

Repurchase agreement *See* **repo**

Reversal Option trading strategy used for **arbitrage**. It exploits price discrepancies when **synthetic long** is cheap and **underlying** relatively expensive. Constructed by buying a **call** and selling a **put** with the same **strike** and **expiry** (synthetic long) and selling underlying **stock/future**. (*See* **box, conversion**)

Reverse floating rate note (reverse **FRN**) A short-term swap structure that offers an alternative to the classic FRN. Under reverse FRN floating rates fall as the **Libor** increases (e.g. they pay 10 percent – **Libor**).

Reverse repo *See* **repo**

Rho Measure of **option** sensitivity to **interest rate** movements.

Risk-neutral A position indifferent to the market moves. In **option** pricing it refers to the pricing strategy where a position is comprised of an option and a percentage of **underlying** in order to make zero profit/loss regardless of market moves.

Rollover Renewal of a loan. Specifically, in **futures** contracts, it refers to the removal of the expired (nearest) contract in the series and the addition of a new (longest-dated) one.

Rollover date Date of loan renewal. Specifically, in **futures** contracts, it refers to the date of the removal of the expired (nearest) contract in the series and the addition of a new (longest-dated) one. (*See* **rollover**)

Secondary market Market for trading **securities** after they have been issued. (*See* **primary market**)

Securitisation A process where debt from various financial institutions is consolidated and resold in tranches as a separate security to other counterparties.

Security A tradable financial product that has market value.

Settlement date *See* **value date**.

Share A share of ownership in a company. A company issues a number of shares with the value proportionate to their size compared to the total market value of **equity**. The share price at any other time reflects the increase/decrease in equity value. (*See* **equity, stock**)

Short position A position whereby the **counterparty** is a seller of a **security**. It also refers to surplus of lending over borrowing. (*See* **long position**)

Shout option An option that gives the investor the right to 'shout' when they wish to reset the strike value, regardless of the underlying value.

Simple interest Interest earned on investment that is paid at **maturity** only, i.e. no intermittent payments are made; thus there is no **reinvestment** opportunity.

Simple yield to maturity Bond yield calculated as the ratio of the sum of **coupon maturity** and **principal** gain/loss **amortised** over the time to **maturity**, and the **clean price**. Does not account for **time value of money**. (*See* **current yield, yield to maturity**)

Speculation A trading practice based on an expectation of certain market moves, as opposed to **arbitrage** or **hedging**.

Spot Refers to the immediate valuation. In most markets the price is taken now, but the settlement is two working days later, to allow for paperwork and bank transfers. (*See* **forward**)

Spread The difference between **bid** and offer **price**. Also refers to **option** trading strategy where one instrument is bought and a similar with different **strike**/date is sold. (*See* **calendar spread, horizontal spread, diagonal spread, diagonal bull spread, diagonal bear spread, horizontal spread, ratio back spread, vertical spread**)

Spread option An option that pays the difference between two **asset** prices.

Stack A set of **futures** (or **FRAs**) contracts all purchased on the same day with the intention to enter into consecutive rollovers into further contract with decreasing number of contracts. Designed to cover long-dated **exposure** where there is no sufficient liquidity in further-dated contracts. (*See* **strip**)

Standard deviation A measure of dispersion of all the outcomes around the mean (width of the **distribution**)

Standard log-normal distribution A **log-normal distribution** with $\theta = 0$ and m = 1.

Stochastic A process whose behaviour is non-deterministic, i.e. a present state does not fully determine its next state. Used in securities pricing.

Stock *See* equity.

Stock beta A measure of individual **stock volatility** compared to the **equity index**.

Stock exchange An organised marketplace where members trade securities. Members may act either as agents for customers, or as principals for their own accounts. (*See* **over the counter, OTC**)

Stock index *See* equity index.

Stock index future *See* equity index future.

Stock index option *See* equity index option.

Straddle An **option** trading strategy, exploiting market **volatility** by simultaneous purchase/sale of both **call** and the **put** with the same **strike** and the same **expiry**. (*See* **strangle**)

Strangle An **option** trading strategy, exploiting market **volatility** by simultaneous purchase/sale of both **call** and **put** with different **strikes** and the same **expiry**. (*See* **straddle**)

Strike *See* exercise price.

Strip In **derivatives** markets, a set of **futures** (or **FRAs**) contracts with consecutive delivery dates. Transacted with the intention to cover a longer interest rate period. (*See* **stack**) In **capital markets**, stripping refers to a process of separating **bond** cashflows (**coupon** and **principal**) and trading them as separate securities.

Swap An agreement to exchange payments at regular intervals over a period of time. Exchange of **principal** at inception and **maturity** is sometimes incorporated. (*See* **interest rate swap, currency swap**)

Swap leg (or **leg** for short) One side of the **swap** deal, i.e. a series of cashflows one swap **counterparty** is obliged to pay.

Swap-linked note A **swap** in which the redemption value of a short-term note is linked to a long-term swap rate.

Swaption An option on a **swap** (typically **interest rate swap** or **currency swap**).

Synthetic long Purchase of a **call** and sale of a **put** with the same **strike** and expiry. (*See* **synthetic short**)

Synthetic long call Purchase of a **stock** or **future** and purchase of a **put**.

Synthetic long put Sale of a **stock** or **future** and purchase of a **call**.

Synthetic short Sale of a **call** and purchase of a **put** with the same **strike** and expiry. (*See* **synthetic long**)

Synthetic short call (or **covered put**) Sale of a **stock** or **future** and sale of a **put**.

Synthetic short put (or **covered call**) Purchase of a **stock** or **future** and sale of a **call**.

Synthetic transaction A transaction (or a combination of transactions) equivalent to another transaction. For example, simultaneous purchase of a **call** and a **put** with the same **strike** is equivalent to a **long futures** position, hence the term **synthetic long**.

Theta **Option** sensitivity measure, expressed as the change in option value with a decreasing time to **expiry**.

Tick The minimum allowed **futures** price change.

Time deposit A **non-negotiable** deposit.

Time value of money The concept that links **the future value of money** with the **present value of money**, i.e. in a positive interest rate environment any cashflow is worth more today than in the future.

Total rate of return *See* **TROR**.

Trader Individual who takes positions in **securities** and their **derivatives** with the objective of making profits. Traders can be market makers with the objective to earn the **bid/ask spread**. They can also take **proprietary positions** in which they seek to profit from the directional movement of prices or **spread** positions.

Transfer risk A **counterparty** **risk** component. The risk that a foreign client will not be able to transfer funds to the bank due to issues with his domestic banking system. (*See* **customer risk, country risk**)

Treasury bill A government-issued short-term **security** with intention to raise funds. Usually **zero coupon**.

Trinomial distribution A frequency distribution where three exhaustive and mutually exclusive outcomes are possible. (*See* **binomial distribution, normal distribution, log-normal distribution**)

TROR (or **total rate of return**) A **swap** where one **leg** is based on the total return (interest payments plus any capital gains or losses for the payment period) from a specified reference **asset**; whilst the other pays/receives a specified **fixed** or **floating** interest rate (most commonly **Libor + spread**). Both legs are based upon the same **notional** amount.

Underlying A security upon which a contract depends. In **derivatives** the value of the derivative product is derived from or based on that security.

Value at risk (or VAR) An amount by which the investment value may fall over a specified period of time at a given level of probability.

Value date (also **settlement date** or **maturity date**) A date on which the contract expires and the proceeds are calculated. It may differ from the payment date, due to transaction time.

VAR *See* **value at risk**.

Variable currency In **exchange rates**, the quotation gives the number of units of variable currency needed for the sale/purchase of one unit of **base currency**.

Variance A measure of fluctuation in value of a variable around its mean. (*See* **standard deviation, probability distribution**)

Variation margin *See* **margin**.

Vega **Option sensitivity** measure, defined as the change in option value with respect to the change in the **volatility** of the **underlying**.

Vertical spread An **option** strategy where two option contracts of the same type (**call** or a **put**) are bought/sold with a different **strike** but the same **expiry**. (*See* **spread, horizontal spread, diagonal spread**)

Volatility A measure of fluctuation in the value of the variable. In financial markets it refers to the **standard deviation** of the **continuously compounded** return on the **underlying**. (*See* **historic volatility, implied volatility**)

Volatility trade A type of trading strategy utilised by investors with no view on market direction, but an expectation of fluctuations. (*See* **directional trade**)

Writer An **option** seller. (*See* **holder**)

Yield The **interest rate** that can be earned on investment based on the prevailing market rates, rather than **coupon**, which is based on contractual specifications.

Yield curve The relationship between the **interest rate** (or cost of borrowing) and the time to **maturity** of the debt for a given borrower in a given currency.

Yield to maturity (or YTM) The **internal rate of return** of a bond, i.e. the rate necessary to **discount** all future cashflows to make the **NPV** equal to the current price. (*See* **current yield, simple yield to maturity**)

YTM *See* **yield to maturity**.

Zero-cost collar A **collar** where the **premiums** paid and received are equal, netting to zero cost. (*See* **collar, cap, floor**)

Zero coupon A type of **security** that does not pay **coupon**. It is thus issued at **discount** to its **face value** to compensate for the loss of interest payments. (*See* **coupon-bearing security**)

Zero coupon bond A **bond** that does not pay **coupon**, thus its **yield** depends on the price **discount** compared to its **face value**, which compensates for the lack of interest payments. (*See* **bond**)

Bibliography

Books

Baxter, M. and Rennie, A. (1996) *Financial Calculus, An Introduction to Derivatives Pricing*, Cambridge University Press, Cambridge.

Black, F. and Scholes, M. (1973) 'The pricing of options and corporate liabilities', *Journal of Political Economy*, Vol. 81, No. 3, 637–654.

Cox, J. and Rubenstein, M. (1985) *Options Markets*, Prentice Hall, New Jersey.

Ford, D. (1996) *Mastering Exchange Traded Equity Derivatives*, Pearson Education, Harlow.

Hamming, R.W. (1973) *Numerical Methods for Scientists and Engineers* (2nd ed.), Dover Publications, New York.

Hull, J. (1997) *Options, Futures and other Derivative Securities* (3rd ed.), Prentice Hall, New Jersey.

Joshi, M.S. (2003) *The Concepts and Practice of Mathematical Finance (Mathematics, Finance and Risk)*, Cambridge University Press, Cambridge.

Kasapis, A. (2008) *Mastering Credit Derivatives* (2nd ed.), Pearson Education, Harlow.

McDougall, A. (1999) *Mastering Swaps Markets*, Pearson Education, Harlow.

Neftci, S.N. (2000) *An Introduction to the Mathematics of Financial Derivatives* (2nd ed.), Academic Press, San Diego.

Pilipovic, D. (1997) *Energy Risk*, McGraw-Hill, New York.

Price, J. and Henderson, S. (1988) *Currency and Interest Rate Swaps*, Butterworths, London.

Rebonato, R. (1996) *Interest Rate Option Models*, John Wiley & Sons, Chichester.

Steiner, R. (1999) *Mastering Financial Calculations*, Pearson Education, Harlow.

Stigum, M. and Robinson F.L. (1996) *Money Market & Bond Calculations*, Irwin Times Mirror Higher Education Group, New York

Taylor, J. (1996) *Mastering Derivatives Markets*, Pearson Education, Harlow.

Taylor, J. (2003) *Mastering Foreign Exchange and Currency Options* (2nd ed.), Pearson Education, Harlow.

Wilmot, P. Howison, S. and Dewyanne, J. (1995) *The Mathematics of Financial Derivatives*, Cambridge University Press, Cambridge.

Wilmott, P. (2007) *Paul Wilmott Introduces Quantitative Finance* (2nd ed.), John Wiley & Sons, Chichester.

Additional sources

Debt Management Office (2000), *The DMO's Yield Curve Model*, United Kingdom Debt Management Office, London.

Hyperion (1999) *Securities Institute Diploma – Financial Derivatives*, Hyperion Training, Cork.

Hyperion (2000) *Yields and the Yield Curve*, Hyperion Training, Cork.

Electronic sources

Corporate credit ratings, retrieved from:
  Standard and Poor's: http://www.standardandpoors.com/home/en/us
  Moody's: http://www.moodys.com/cust/default.asp

Equity indices, retrieved from: *Financial Times on-line*,
  http://markets.ft.com/ft/markets/worldEquities.asp

Fujii, M., Shimada, Y. and Takahashi, A. (2010) 'A note on construction of multiple swap curves with and without collateral', Financial Research and Training Center, retrieved from
  http://www.fsa.go.jp/frtc/seika/discussion/2009/20100203-1.pdf

International currency codes, retrieved from: *XE ISO 4217 Currency Code List*,
  http://www.xe.com/iso4217.php

International derivatives exchanges, retrieved from: *Futex*,
  http://www.site-by-site.com/futex_world.htm

Lesniewski, A. (2008) 'The forward curve', retrieved from
  http://www.math.nyu.edu/~alberts/spring07/Lecture1.pdf

LIFFE interest rate financial futures contract specifications, retrieved from:
  Euronext, http://www.euronext.com

Probability distributions, retrieved from: *NIST/SEMATECH e-Handbook of Statistical Methods*, http://www.itl.nist.gov/div898/handbook/

Ron, U. (2010) 'A practical guide to swap curve construction', Bank of Canada Working Paper, retrieved from
  http://www.bankofcanada.ca/en/res/wp/2000/wp00-17.pdf

Zero curve methodology, retrieved from
  http://www.powerfinance.com/help/Zero_Curve_Methodology.htm

Index

Page numbers in bold refer to entries in the Glossary